Scots in the
Mid-Atlantic Colonies
1635–1783

Scots

in the
Mid-Atlantic
Colonies

1635–1783

David Dobson

Introduction

Scottish settlement in the Middle Colonies of America dates from the early seventeenth century. Even before the establishment of English colonies in that region in the 1660s, there were a number of Scots pioneers living with the Dutch settlers of New Netherlands, and probably also in the Swedish settlements along the Delaware.

By the outbreak of the Revolution, several thousand Scots had settled in the Middle Colonies. Scottish immigration was small scale and sporadic to begin with, with the notable exception of the Quakers and the banished Covenanters who settled in East New Jersey during the 1680s. The immigration of Highlanders to New York began in 1738, and by the year 1742 over 400 people had arrived from the island of Islay led by Captain Lauchlan Campbell. The main phase of immigration from Scotland during the colonial period occurred in the aftermath of the French and Indian Wars and before the outbreak of the American Revolution. Soldiers brought over to fight in these wars often liked what they saw of the country and chose to be discharged there. Others who returned home encouraged their families to emigrate with them to the New World.

As would be expected, these new immigrants came from all over Scotland. Though the Lowland Scots integrated quickly with the existing population, the Gaelic speaking Highlanders tended to move as a group and settle in the frontier lands. In the Revolution of 1776 many of them took up arms in support of the Loyalist cause and later found it expedient to move north to Canada.

The ports of New York and Philadelphia attracted many Scots merchants, shipmasters, professionals, and craftsmen, some of whom formed St Andrew's societies. Two such members in Philadelphia were James Wilson from Ceres in Fife, and the Reverend John Witherspoon from Yester, East Lothian, both of whom later became signatories of the Declaration of Independence.

The following compilation is based largely on primary sources from both sides of the Atlantic.

David Dobson
St Andrews, Scotland, 2002

References

ARCHIVES

APB = Aberdeen Proprinquity Book, Aberdeen Archives
CLRO = City of London Record Office
DGA = Dumfries & Galloway Archives, Dumfries
DSA = Delaware State Archives
DU.lib = Dundee University Library
EUL = Edinburgh University Library
GA = Glasgow Archives
GRH = General Register House, Edinburgh
MBR = Montrose Burgess Register, Angus Archives
NAS = National Archives of Scotland, Edinburgh
NJSA = NJ State Archives, Trenton
NLS = National Library of Scotland, Edinburgh
PCC = Prerogative Court of Canterbury
PRO = Public Record Office, London
SCS = Scots Charitable Society papers, Boston

PUBLICATIONS

ACK = Alex. Cowan—His Kinsfolk and Connections [Perth, 1915]
ANY = Biographical Register of the St Andrews Society of New
      York
AO = Annandal Observer, series
AP = Historical Catalogue of the St Andrews Society of Philadel-
      phia
BFH = History of the Bethune Family
BLG = Burke's Landed Gentry [London, 1939]
CCMC = Colonial Clergy of the Middle Colonies
CD = Clan Donald [Inverness, 1904]
CEG = Catalogue of Edinburgh Graduates
CGS = Campbells and other Glengarry, Stormont and Harrington
      Pioneers
CM = Caledonian Mercury, series
CMA = Court Minutes of Albany, Colony of Rensselaerswyck and
      Schnectady [Albany, 1926–1932]
CTP = Calendar of Treasury Papers, series
DA = Dundee Advertiser, series
DCB = Dictionary of Canadian Biography, series
DGC = Dumfries & Galloway Courier, series
DGH = Dumfries & Galloway Herald, series

DNY = Documents Illustrative of the Colonial History of New
    York [C. B. O'Callaghan, NY, 1854]
DP = Darien Papers [J.H. Burton, Edinburgh, 1849]
DPCA = Dundee, Perth and Cupar Advertiser, series
DRC = Dutch Reformed Church, NY, registers
EA = Edinburgh Advertiser, series
EBR = Edinburgh Burgess Roll [C.B. Watson, Edinburgh, 1930]
EC = Edinburgh Courant, series
EEC = Edinburgh Evening Courant, series
EMA = List of Emigrant Ministers to America, 1690–1811
    [G. Fothergill, London, 1904]
EP = Emigrants to Pennsylvania 1641–1819 [M. Tepper, Baltimore,
    1979]
F = Fastii Ecclesiae Scoticanae [J. Scott, Edinburgh, 1915]
FAB = Fastii Aberdonensis 1494–1854 [C. Innes, Aberdeen, 1854]
FPA = Fulham Papers in the Lambeth Palace Library
    [W.W. Manross, Oxford, 1965]
GM = Glasgow Mercury, series
HA = House of Alexander [Edinburgh, 1877]
HBF = History of the Barclay Family [London, 1934]
HBRS = Hudson Bay Record Society, series
HOFL = History of the Frasers of Lovat
HSPC = History of Somonauk Presbyterian Church
Insh = Scottish Colonial Schemes 1620–1686 [G.P. Insh,
    Glasgow 1922]
KCA = Officers and Graduates of King's College, Aberdeen
    [P. Anderson, Aberdeen, 1893]
MB = The Macleans of Boreray [H. Mackenzie, Inverness, 1946]
MG = McClellans in Galloway [D.R. Torrance, Edinburgh, 1996]
NWI = New World Immigrants [M. Tepper, Baltimore, 1979]
NYGBR = New York Genealogical & Biographical Record, series
NYHM.Dutch = NY Historical Manuscripts, Dutch [Baltimore,
    1974]
NYMerc = New York Mercury, series
PaArch = Pennsylvania Archives, series
Pa.Chron = Pennsylvania Chronicle, series
PaGaz = Philadelphia Gazette, series
PCCol = Calendar of the Privy Council, Colonial, series
PCR = Records of the 1st and 2nd Presbyterian Churches of NY
PI = Passengers from Ireland [D.M. Schlegel, Baltimore, 1980]
PMHB = Pennsylvania Magazine of History & Biography, series
RPCS = Register of the Privy Council of Scotland, series
SA = Scotus Americanus [W. Brock, Edinburgh, 1982]
SCHR = Scottish Church History Records, series

Sgen = Scottish Genealogist, series
SM = Scots Magazine, series
SNQ = Scottish Notes and Queries, series
SP = Scots Peerage [Edinburgh, 1922]
SPAWI = Calendar of State Papers, America & West Indies, series
SPC = Calendar of State Papers, Colonial, series
SPG = Calendar of Letters of the Society for the Propagation of the
      Gospel 1721–1793 [London, 1972]
SSA = Scots and Scots Descendants in America [NY, 1917]
TGSI = Transactions of the Gaelic Society of Inverness, series
TV = Tay Valley Family Historian, series
UPC = History of the United Presbyterian Church
W = Witness, series
WMQ = William and Mary Quarterly, series

SCOTS IN THE MID-ATLANTIC COLONIES, 1635-1783

ABERCROMBIE, BOBBY, born1753, a servant from Dysart, Fife, via Leith to Philadelphia on the Friendship in May 1775. [PRO.T47/12]

ADAIR, JOHN, born 1730, a laborer in Beak, with wife Janet McNillie and children Janet, Jean, Agnes, and John, from Stranraer, to NY on the Jackie on 31 May 1775.[PRO.T47/12]

ADAIR, PATRICK, born 1724, a farmer in Glen Luce, with his children Agnes, Jean, and William, from Stranraer to NY on the Jackie of Glasgow, in May 1774. [PRO.T47/12]

ADAIR, WILLIAM, from Islay, Argyll, aboard the Happy Return in Nov. 1740 bound for NY and Wood Creek on the Hudson River, by 1763 he was dead and his cousin Duncan Reid claimed his right to a grant on the Argyle Patent, NY. [HSBC][NY.Col.MS#72/171]

ADAM, ALEXANDER, born ca.1655, an indentured servant, to East NJ on the Henry and Francis in 1685, settled in Pitscataway, in Freehold by 1694. [NJSA#EJD.A226]

ADAM, JEAN, born 1752, a spinner from Paisley, via Greenock to NY on the Commerce, in Feb. 1774. [PRO.T47/12]

ADAMS, JOHN, born 1721, a laborer, enlisted in Captain William Trent's Co. of the PA Regiment on 18 Aug. 1746. [PaArch#5/1/8]

ADAM, ROBERT, a Covenanter transported from Leith on the Henry and Francis to East NJ 25 Aug.1685. [RPCS.11.162/336]

ADAM, ROBERT, born 1759, from Stirling, via Greenock to New York on the Monimia, in May 1775. [PRO.T47/12]

ADAMS, WILLIAM, a cooper late in NY, settled in Halifax, Nova Scotia, by 1786. [NAS.CS17.1.5/303]

ADDISON, ALEXANDER, born 1759, educated at Aberdeen University, a minister, settled in western PA by 1785, a lawyer in Washington, PA, from 1787, judge 1790 to 1803, died in Pittsburgh, PA, on 27 Nov. 1807. [AP#99]

ADDISON, JOHN, from Glasgow, via Greenock to NY on the George, in May 1774, arrived 12 July 1774. [PRO.T47/12][SM#36/446]

AGGIE, CATHERINE, born 1759, a spinner from Paisley, via Greenock to NY on the Commerce, in Feb. 1774. [PRO.T47/12]

AGGIE, JANET, born 1739, a spinner from Paisley, via Greenock to NY on the Commerce, in Feb. 1774. [PRO.T47/12]

AGGIE, MARGARET, born 1738, spinner from Paisley,via Greenock to NY on the Commerce, in Feb. 1774. [PRO.T47/12]

AGNEW, AGNES, born 1755, a spinner from Paisley, via Greenock to NY on the Commerce, in Feb. 1774. [PRO.T47/12]

AGNEW, ALEXANDER, born 1734, husbandman from Galloway, with his wife Janet and children Forbes and William, from Stranraer to NY on the Galein May 1774. [PRO.T47/12]

AIKEN, JAMES, born 1733, millwright, via Whitehaven to NY on the Golden Rule, in June 1774. [PRO.T47/9-11]

AIKEN, JOHN, to America 1773 and settled in Pincader, Mulinghouse, Newcastle, Del. [NAS.CS.Dal.ICS/136]

AIKEN, ROBERT, born Dalkeith, Midlothian, during 1734, a publisher in PA, died 1802. [SSA#86]

AITKEN, ALEXANDER, born in 1757, a weaver from Paisley, via Greenock to NY on the Commerce, in Feb. 1774. [PRO.T47/12]

AITKEN, ROBERT, born in Dalkeith, Midlothian, 1734, merchant from Paisley, to Philadelphia in 1769, a bookseller and publisher there, died in Philadelphia during July 1802. [AP#101][Hugh Simm papers, Princeton University]

AITKEN, SAMUEL, born 1750, farmer from Inverness, via Greenock to NY on the George in May 1774. [PRO.T47/12]

AITKEN, WILLIAM, born 1744, farmer from Perth, via Greenock to NY on the Commerce, in Feb. 1774. [PRO.T47/12]

ALCORN, ALEXANDER, a petitioner in NY 1701. [DNY.IV.954]

ALEXANDER, ANDREW, to East NJ in 1684, settled in Perth Amboy. [Insh#273][NJSA.EJD.Liber B/325]

ALEXANDER, COSMO, a portrait painter from Edinburgh, to Rhode Island, by 1766 in Philadelphia, died in Edinburgh. [AP#102]

ALEXANDER, DAVID, an indentured servant, to East NJ in 1685. [NJSA.EJD.A225]

ALEXANDER, GEORGE, settled Essex Co., East N.J., 1688. [NJSA.EJD.Liber B/426]

ALEXANDER, HUGH, born 1729, carpenter in Galloway, with wife Agnes and children John, Ann, Hugh, Alexander, James and Robert, via Stranraer to NY on the Gale, in May 1774. [PRO.T47/12]

ALEXANDER, JAMES, born in 1690s, a Jacobite in 1715, to America, husband of Mary Sprott; Surveyor General of NY and founder of the American Philosophical Society, died 1756. [HA]

ALEXANDER, JOHN, settled Essex Co., East N.J., 1688. [NJSA.EJD.Liber B426]

ALEXANDER, JOHN, born 1753, tailor/indentured servant who absconded from Hartshorne Fitzrandolph, Morris County, NJ, 1775. [NYGaz-Merc.22.5.1775]

ALEXANDER, PATRICK, indentured servant, to East NJ in 1684. [NJSA.EJD.Liber A]

ALEXANDER, ROBERT, born 1749, a house-carpenter in Dailly, from Stranraer to NY on the Gale, in May 1774. [PRO.T47/12]

ALEXANDER, WILLIAM, born 1750, shoemaker in Dunfermline, via Greenock to NY or GA on the Christy, May 1775. [PRO.T47/12]

ALISON, COLIN, transported from Leith to East NJ on the Henry and Frances, in Aug. 1685.[RPCS#11/154]

ALLAN, DAVID, born 1751, wright from Breadalbane, Perthshire, via Greenock to NY on the Commerce, in June 1775. [PRO.T47/12]

ALLAN, ELIZABETH, born ca.1681, indentured for 5 years in Chester County, PA, on 5 Aug. 1697. [Sgen.29.1.13]

ALLEN, JAMES, born 1709, an indentured servant from Glasgow, who emigrated via London to PA in July 1728. [CLRO/AIA]

ALLAN, JAMES, born 1747, laborer in Greenock, from Greenock to Philadelphia on the Magdalene, in Aug. 1774.[PRO.T47/12]

ALLEN, MARGARET, born by 1682, stepdaughter of James Carlisle and Margaret Allen in Leith, settled in Elizabethtown, NJ, married Eliphet Frazie. [NAS.EQR.15/336]

ALLAN, MARGARET, born Strathspey 1745, via Greenock to NY on the George in May 1774, arrived 18 July 1774. [PRO.T47/12][SM#36/446]

ALLISON, JAMES, born 1758, weaver from Paisley, via Greenock to NY on the Commerce, Feb.1774, arr. 16 Apr. 1774. [PRO.T47/12]

ALLISON, ROBERT, a petitioner in NY 1701. [DNY.IV.934]

ANDERSON, CHARLES, born 1752, gentleman, via London to NY on the Earl Dunmore in Feb.1774. [PRO.T47/9-11]

ANDERSON, JAMES, born 17 Nov. 1678, a minister educated at Glasgow University around 1703, from Glasgow to Philadelphia 1710, settled in Newcastle, Del., NY and Virginia, married Suit Garland on 5 Feb. 1712, died on 16 July 1740. [AP#164][F#7/662][SA#102][NAS.CH1.2.49.44]

ANDERSON, JAMES, gentleman lately from Madeira, drowned near Staten Island 17 Aug.1763, buried in Richmond Church. [NY Mercury, 29.8.1763]

ANDERSON, JAMES, born 1748, a wright from Alloa, Clackmannanshire, via Greenock to NY or GA on the Christy, in May 1775. [PRO.T47/12]

ANDERSON, JAMES, born 1753, wright from Glasgow, via Greenock to Philadelphia on the Magdalene, in Aug. 1774. [PRO.T47/12]

ANDERSON, JANET, born 1757, from Alloa, Clackmannanshire, via Greenock to NY or GA on the Christy, in May 1775. [PRO.T47/12]

ANDERSON, JOHN, deceased by 1692. [NY, Wills, liber 3/4, fo.368]

ANDERSON, JOHN, Captain of the Unicorn on the Darien Expedition 1698-1699, settled in NJ 1699, Judge and Governor of N.J., died 28 March 1736. [MNJ][OMO#112]

ANDERSON, JOHN, born 1750, wright from Alloa, Clackmannanshire, via Greenock to NY or GA on the Christy, during May 1774. [PRO.T47/12]

ANDERSON, MARGARET, indentured servant, to East NJ 1684. [NJSA.EJD.A266/B325]

ANDERSON, MARGARET, born 1754, from Alloa, Clackmannan, via Greenock to NY or GA on the Christy, in May 1775. [PRO.T47/12]

ANDERSON, MARY, a widow, with her children Duncan Leech and Mary Leech, from Islay, Argyll, aboard the Happy Return in Nov. 1740 bound for NY and Wood Creek on the Hudson River, in 1763 she and her two daughters were granted 200 acres on the Argyle Patent, NY. [HSBC][NY.Col.MS#72/170]

ANDERSON, PATRICK, with Catherine McLean his wife, from Islay, Argyll, aboard the Happy Return in June 1739 bound for NY and Wood Creek on the Hudson River, in 1763 his widow and two daughters were granted 200 acres on the Argyle Patent, NY. [HSBC][NY.Col.MS#72/170]

ANDERSON, ROBERT, indentured servant, to East NJ 1683. [NJSA.EJD.E330]

ANDERSON, ROBERT, a petitioner in NY 1701.[DNY.IV.934]

ANDERSON, ROBERT, born 1727, died 28 July 1745.[NY Wky Postboy:29.7.45]

ANDERSON, ROBERT, born 1749, farmer from Stirling, via Greenock to NY on the Matty in May 1774. [PRO.T47/12]

ANDERSON, WALTER, born 1746, laborer from Kippen, Stirlingshire, via Greenock to NY on the Lilly, in May 1775. [PRO.T47/12]

ANDERSON, WILLIAM, a petitioner in NY 1701, [DNY.IV.934]; sheriff of NY in 1708. [Bodleian MS, Clarendon#102/164]

ANDERSON, WILLIAM, born 1752, servant from Anass, Isle of Lewis, via Stornaway to Philadelphia on the Clementina in July 1775. [PRO.T47/12]

ANDREW, WILLIAM, indentured servant, to Philadelphia on the Anne galley, 1745. [EP#79]

ANDREWS, WILLIAM, a minister in 1700, settled at Mohawk Castle, NY, as a missionary of the Society for the Propagation of the Gospel to the Six Nations in 1712, died 1728. [SCHR#14/143]

ANGUS, ANNE, from Dunbartonshire, wife of James Finlay, settled in Princeton, NJ before 1775. [NAS.RS-7/172]

ANGUS, JOHN, born 1744, farmer from Forfar, Angus, via Greenock to NY on the Lilly, in Apr. 1775. [PRO.T47/12]

ANGUS, WILLIAM, born 1750, laborer from Galloway, via Stranraer to NY on the Gale of Whitehaven, in May 1774. [PRO.T47/12]

ANNAN, ROBERT, minister from Ceres, Fife, to America 1761, settled in Philadelphia. [AP#338][UPC#654]

ANNAND, WALTER, transported from Leith to East NJ on the Henry and Francis, in Aug. 1685.[RPCS#11.137]

ARBUCKLE, JOHN, from Leith to East NJ on the Henry and Francis 1685. [NWI.1.422]

ARBUTHNOTT, ALEXANDER, a merchant from Inverbervie, Kincardineshire, before 1720, settled in Philadelphia. [NAS.B51.12.1]

ARMOR, JAMES, a merchant, from Leith to East NJ on the Henry and Francis, in Sep. 1685. [NAS.E72.15.32]

ARNOT, ANDREW, a minister, to PA in 1753. [AP#278]

ARTHUR, HELEN, born 1753, servant from Edinburgh, from Leith to Philadelphia on the Friendship, in May 1775. [PRO.T47/12]

ARTHUR, ISABEL, born 1748, servant from Edinburgh, via Leith to Philadelphia on the Friendship, in May 1775. [PRO.T47/12]

ASTINE, ISOBEL, born 1757, servant from Nairn, via Stornaway to Philadelphia on the Clementina, in July 1775. [PRO.T47/12]

ATCHESON, WILLIAM, born 1746, laborer from Dunbarton, via Greenock to NY on the Lilly, in Apr. 1775.[PRO.T47/12]

AUSTIN, WILLIAM, a surgeon's mate, son of Joseph Austin in Kilspindie, Perthshire, died in Albany, NY, during 1764. Probate 1764 PCC

BABIE, KENNETH, born 1761, servant from Stornaway, Isle of Lewis, via Stornaway to Philadelphia on the Friendship in May 1774.[PRO.T47/12]

BAILLIE, ANNE, born 1750, servant from Inverness, via Stornaway, Isle of Lewis, to Philadelphia on the <u>Clementina</u> in July 1775.[PRO.T47/12]

BAILLIE, GILBERT, a gypsy, transported from Greenock to NY on 21 Oct. 1682. [NAS.HH11]

BAILLIE, HUGH, a gypsy, transported from Greenock to NY on 21 Oct. 1682. [NAS.HH11]

BAILLIE, JAMES, a gypsy, transported from Greenock to NY on21 Oct. 1682. [NAS.HH11]

BAILLIE, JOHN, a gypsy, transported from Greenock to NY on 21 Oct. 1682. [NAS.HH11]

BAILLIE, MARGARET, a gypsy, transported from Greenock to NY on 21 Oct. 1682. [NAS.HH11]

BAIN, ANDREW, born 1751, farmer from Strathspey, via Greenock to NY on the <u>George</u> in May 1774. [PRO.T47/12]

BAINE, HELEN, indentured servant, to East NJ in 1684. [NJSA.EJD.A255]

BAIN, ISABEL, born 1757, from Strathspey, via Greenock to NY on the <u>George</u> in May 1774. [PRO.T47/12]

BAIN, JAMES, born 1742, farmer from Strathspey, with his wife Christian and children Ann, William, Alexander and Isobel, from Greenock to NY on the <u>George</u> in May 1774. [PRO.T47/12]

BAIN, JOHN, a typefounder in St Andrews, Fife, in 1742, later in Camlachie, Glasgow, settled in Philadelphia. [SA#86]

BAIN, MARGARET, born 1738, servant from Stornaway, Isle of Lewis, via Stornaway to NY on the <u>Peace and Plenty,</u> in Nov. 1774. [PRO.T47/12]

BAIN, MATTHEW, born 1749, wright from Glasgow, via Greenock to NY on the <u>Matty</u> in May 1774. [PRO.T47/12]

BAIN, ROBERT, born 1745, wright from Stirling, via Greenock to NY on the <u>Monimia,</u> in May 1775. [PRO.T47/12]

BAIRD, ALEXANDER, born Edinburgh 1672, son of Robert Baird and Elizabeth Fleming, married Magdalena Van Vleck in NY 1700. [NYGBR]

BAIRD, ANDREW, from Scotland, married Magdalena Van Vleck, a widow, in the Dutch Reformed Church in NY on 24 Apr. 1700. [DRC]

BAIRD, ELIZA, born 1754, a spinner from Paisley, via Greenock to NY on the <u>Commerce,</u> in Feb. 1774. [PRO.T47/12]

BAIRD, JAMES, born Aberdeen ca1655, indentured servant, to East NJ 1683. [NJSA.EJD.A]

BAIRD, JOHN, born Aberdeen ca.1655, to East NJ as an indentured servant in 1683, settled in Monmouth. [NJSA.EJD.A/B403]

BAIRD, PATRICK, in Philadelphia, was admitted as a burgess of St Andrews, Fife, on 2 Oct. 1759. [St Andrews Burgess Roll]

BAIRD, WILLIAM, born 1753, a laborer from Linlithgow, West Lothian, from Greenock to NY on the <u>Lilly</u> in Apr. 1775. [PRO.T47/12]

BALD, WILLIAM, born in 1745, a wright from Glasgow, from Greenock to NY on the <u>Monimia</u> in May 1775.[PRO.T47/12]

BALDRIDGE, DANIEL, born around 1712, absconded from John King, Society Hill, Philadelphia, 3 Oct.1762. [NYMerc.1.11.1762]

BALFOUR, HENRY, a soldier who settled in NY by 1765. [PCCol#4/818]

BALFOUR, JANET, born in 1757, a servant from Edinburgh, from Leith to Philadelphia on the Friendship of Philadelphia, in May 1775. [PRO.T47/12]

BALLANTINE, THOMAS, born in 1758, a weaver from Dundee, from Leith to Philadelphia on the Friendship of Philadelphia, in May 1775. [PRO.T47/12]

BANKS, JAMES, born 1731, 5'6", reddish complexion, red hair, a jobber and a   soldier of Captain John Singleton's Co. of the PA Regiment in May 1759. [Pa.Archives#5/1/276]

BARCLAY, ALEXANDER, a Customs Controller, died in Philadelphia during Jan.1770. [SM#33/109]

BARCLAY, ANDREW, arrived via Curacao, a merchant in NY, died on 19 June 1775, probate 25 May 1775 NY

BARCLAY, DAVID, a merchant, from Leith to East NJ on the Exchange of Stockton on 6 Aug. 1683. [NAS.E72.15.26]

BARCLAY, DAVID, son of David Barclay of Urie, Kincardineshire, and Katherine Gordon, from Aberdeen to East NJ on the America in Aug. 1685, died at sea. [NAS.E72.15.26][HBF.III.97]

BARCLAY, JAMES, born 1750, farmer from Stewarton, Ayrshire, from Greenock to NY on the Christy, in May 1775.   [PRO.T47/12]

BARCLAY, JOHN, born in 1659, son of David Barclay of Urie and Katherine Gordon, Stonehaven, Kincardineshire, with wife Catherine and son John, in 1684, settled in Plainfields, Perth Amboy, NJ, died in 1731. [NJSA.EJD.Liber A/234; B/169] [Insh#264][HBF.III.97][NAS.RD4.83.421]

BARCLAY, JOHN, a mariner in NY, probate 13 Aug. 1775 NY

BARCLAY, ROBERT, born 1751, farmer from Stirling, from Greenock to NY on the Matty in May 1774. [PRO.T47/12]

BARCLAY, THOMAS, born 1664 at Collairnie Castle, Fife, educated at St Andrews University in 1688, in 1707, settled in St Peter's, Albany, NY, married Anne Dorothea Drauyer, father of Thomas, Henry, Andrew, and John, died in Albany during 1734.[EMA#12][BLG#2547][SCHR#14/144]

BARCLAY, THOMAS, born 1746, a farmer from Stewarton, Ayrshire, from Greenock to NY on the Christy, in May 1775. [PRO.T47/12]

BARLAS, WILLIAM, from Fowlis Wester in Perthshire, a minister in Whitehill, Aberdeenshire, from 1779 to 1799, later a teacher and bookseller in NY. [UPC.I.136]

BARR, AGNES, born 1752, a spinner from Paisley, from Greenock to NY on the Commerce, in Feb. 1774. [PRO.T47/12]

BARR, ANDREW, born 1755, a gardener from Dalkeith, Midlothian, via Leith to Philadelphia on the Friendship of Philadelphia, in May 1775. [PRO.T47/12]

BARTRAM, ALEXANDER, son of George Bartram in Biggar, Lanarkshire, emigrated before 1777, a merchant in Philadelphia. [NAS.RS42.20.426]; Loyalist in 1776. [PRO.AO1.40.105]

BAXTER, ALEXANDER, born 1741, a butcher from Glasgow, via Greenock to NY on the <u>Commerce,</u> in Feb. 1774. [PRO.T47/12]

BAXTER, WILLIAM, born in Aberdeen around 1756, a sailor who deserted the transport <u>Pacific</u> in NY(?) June 1777. [NYGaz-Merc.30.6.1777]

BEAN, ANN, born in 1681, indented in Chester County, PA, on 5 Aug. 1697. [Sgen.29.1.13]

BEATON, ALLAN, born 1756, butcher from Dundee, Angus, via Greenock to NY on the <u>George</u> in May 1774. [PRO.T47/12]

BEATON, MARY, from Islay, Argyll, to NY in July 1738 to have settled at Wood Creek on the Hudson River, by 1763 she was a widow with a married son, granted 200 acres on the Argyle Patent, NY. [HSPC] [NY.Col.MS#72/170]

BEATTY, ADAM, born 1684, indented for 8 years in Chester Co., PA, 14 July 1697. [Sgen.29.1.12]

BEATTY, WILLIAM, born 1734, laborer from Galloway, with his wife Agnes and daughter Mary, via Stranraer to NY on the <u>Gale,</u> in May 1774.[PRO.T47/12]

BELL, ALISON, transported from Greenock to NY on 21 Oct. 1682. [NAS.HH11]

BELL, DUNCAN, settled in Argyle township, Charlotte County, NY, before 1776, a Loyalist and a Sergeant of the King's Regiment who moved to 3rd township, Isle au Naix, Canada. [PRO.AO13.11.132]

BELL, JOHN, born 1749, a farmer from Paisley, via Greenock to NY on the <u>Matty</u> in May 1774.[PRO.T47/12]

BELL, MARY, born 1751, a spinner from Paisley, via Greenock to NY on the <u>Commerce,</u> in Feb. 1774. [PRO.T47/12]

BELL, WILLIAM, born 1745, farmer from Glasgow, from Greenock to NY on the <u>Matty</u> in May 1774. [PRO.T47/12]

BELL, WILLIAM, born 1749, a farmer from Paisley, via Greenock to NY on the <u>Matty</u> in May 1774. [PRO.T47/12]

BELL, WILLIAM, settled in Argyle township, Charlotte County, NY, a Loyalist in 1776, a Sergeant Major of the King's Regiment, moved to Canada by 1783. [PRO.AO13.11.132]

BELL, Mrs ...., born in 1744, from Paisley, via Greenock to NY on the <u>Matty</u> in May 1774. [PRO.T47/12]

BENNY, AGNES, indentured servant, to East NJ 1684. [NJSA.EJD.A187]

BERRY, JAMES, born in 1757, a clockmaker from Queensferry, West Lothian, from Leith to Philadelphia on the <u>Friendship</u> in May 1775. [PRO.T47/12]

BERTRAM, ALEXANDER, a merchant in Philadelphia, eldest son of George Bertram a blacksmith in Biggar, Lanarkshire, 1772. [NAS.CS16.1.179]

BETHUNE, ANGUS, settled in NY before 1776, a Loyalist who moved to Quebec. [PRO.AO13.11.82]

BEVERIDGE, JOHN, a Covenanter from Islay, Argyll, transported from Leith to East NJ on the <u>Henry and Francis</u> in Aug. 1685. [RPCS#11/330]

BEVERIDGE, JOHN, born 1703, teacher from Edinburgh, settled in New England and later in Philadelphia, teacher in the College of Philadelphia and by 1759 master of the Grammar School, died in June 1767.[AP#112]

BIGGAM, THOMAS, born 1734, weaver from Galloway, via Stranraer to NY on the Gale with his wife Mary and children Andrew and Jean, in May 1774. [PRO.T47/12]

BIGGAM, WILLIAM, born 1734, a farmer from Galloway, via Stranraer to NY on the Gale in May 1774. [PRO.T47/12]

BIGGAR, JOHN, born 1754, tailor from Paisley, from Greenock to NY on the Commerce in Feb. 1774. [PRO.T47/12]

BISSETT, ANDREW, married Jannetje de Vou, in the Dutch Reformed Church in NY on 5 Oct. 1712. [DRC]

BLACK, HUGH, born 1733, farmer in Perthshire, from Greenock to NY, with his wife Janet, on the Monimia, in May 1775. [PRO.T47/12]

BLACK, JAMES, son of Robert Black of Easter Portsburgh [died on 16 Mar. 1790] and Rachel Ray [died on 8 Mar. 1798], settled in Philadelphia.[St Cuthbert's g/s, Edinburgh]

BLACK, JOHN, a Covenanter from the Water of Orr, Dumfries-shire, transported via Leith to East NJ on the Henry and Francis, in Aug. 1685.[RPCS#11.154]

BLACK, JOHN, born 1750, a farmer from Kilsyth, Stirlingshire, via Greenock to NY on the Christy, in May 1775. [PRO.T47/12]

BLACK, WILLIAM, born 1723, weaver, enlisted in Captain William Trent's Company of the PA Regiment on 21 July 1746. [PaArch#5/1/8]

BLACKBURN, GEORGE, born 1743, a mason from Perthshire, via Greenock to NY on the Monimia, in May 1775. [PRO.T47/12]

BLACKHALL, AGNES, born 1748, spinner from Paisley, via Greenock to NY on the Commerce, in Feb. 1775.[PRO.T47/12]

BLACKIE, HELEN, born 1750, servant from Gifford, East Lothian, via Leith to Philadelphia on the Friendship of Philadelphia, May 1775. [PRO.T47/12]

BLACKIE, JAMES, born 1729, farmer from Stirling, with his wife Margaret Davie from Greenock to NY on the Monimia, in May 1774.[PRO.T47/12]

BLACKTON, HANNAH, born 1754, servant from Edinburgh, via Leith to Philadelphia on the Friendship of Philadelphia, in May 1775. [PRO.T47/12]

BLAIN, WILLIAM, settled in NJ 1774 as a planter, a Loyalist in 1776, moved to England in 1783. [PRO.AO12.13.153; AO.13.108.106]

BLAIN, PATRICK, born 1740, a farmer from Galloway, with wife Eliza and children Jean and Jenny, from Stranraer to NY on the Gale in May 1774. [PRO.T47/12]

BLAIN, WILLIAM, settled Woodbridge, NJ, 1774, Loyalist. [PRO.AO12.13.153]

BLAIR, JOHN, in Philadelphia 1784. [NAS.CS17.1.2/53]

BLAIR, THOMAS, a merchant from Dundee, probate 27 Feb. 1767 NY

BLAIR, WILLIAM, son of William Scott Blair in Dalry, Ayrshire, died at Oswego in 1756. [HAF#1.417]

BLAKE, DONALD, soldier of the 42nd Regiment, married Jennet McDonald, a widow, in NY on 16 Dec. 1758. [PCR]

BLAKE, JOHN, a Presbyterian in NY, 1723. [NAS.CH1.2.49.55]

BLANE, THOMAS, late a merchant in NY, now in London, 1787. [NAS.CS17.1.6,271]

BOATH, ELIZABETH, born 1753, a spinner from Paisley, via Greenock to NY on the Commerce, in Feb. 1774. [PRO.T47/12]

BOGLE, ROBERT, merchant, late of NY, died in Wilmington, NC, in Dec. 1785. [GM#IX.427.80]

BOOG, JOHN, born 1749, weaver from Paisley, via Greenock to NY on the Commerce, in Feb.1774. [PRO.T47/12]

BOYCE, JANET, born1758, spinner from Paisley, via Greenock to NY on the Commerce, in Feb.1774. [PRO.T47/12]

BOYD, JAMES, born in Kirkcowan, Wigtownshire, a merchant in Galloway, married Jean McMaster, from Stranraer to NY on the Gale of Whitehaven, in May 1774, settled in Albany, NY, father of David and James. [PRO.T47/12][ANY#2.39]

BOYD, JOHN, indentured servant, to East NJ 1685. [NJSA.EJD.A225]

BOYD, JOHN, son of George Boyd in Borland, educated at Glasgow University around   1701, a minister, to America before 1706, settled in Tennant, NJ, died there on 30 Aug. 1708, cnf Edinburgh 10 Apr. 1710. [NAS.CC8.8.84]

BRACKENRIDGE, HUGH HENRY, born in Campbeltown, Argyll, during 1748, with his parents to York County, PA, educated at Nassau Hall and Princeton College, graduated in 1771, chaplain, lawyer and legislator, died Carlisle, PA, 25 June 1816. [AP#124]

BRADNER, JOHN, minister educated at Edinburgh University, by 1715, settled at Cape May and in Orange County, NY, father of Benoni, died 1733. [F#7/662]

BRADY, JOHN, from Islay, Argyll, on the Happy Return to NY in 1740, he had five children and in 1763 his son Hugh, then living in Amboy, New Jersey, claimed his father's right to a grant on the Argyle Patent, NY. [NY.Col.MS#72/171]

BRANDER, LAURENCE, probate 7 July 1768 NY

BREMNER, GEORGE, late of the 42nd Regiment, granted 200 acres east of the Hudson River, Albany County, NY, on 13 Feb. 1767. [NY.Col.MS#7/905]; a Loyalist in Willsborough, Charlotte County, New York, in 1776, settled in St John's, Canada, 1783. [PRO.AO13.11.83]

BREMNER, JAMES, a musician from Edinburgh, to Philadelphia in 1763. ['Scotland and America in the Age of Enlightenment, p.259, R. Scher, Edinburgh, 1990]

BREYMER, THOMAS, born 1760, groomboy from Dundee, via Leith to Philadelphia on the Friendship of Philadelphia, in May 1775. [PRO.T47/12]

BRISBANE, WILLIAM, a petitioner in NY, 1701. [DNY.IV.934]

BROA, MARGARET, born 1750, spinner from Paisley, via Greenock to
NY on the <u>Commerce,</u> in Feb. 1774. [PRO.T47/12]

BROCK, WALTER, born 1746, a merchant from Glasgow, via Greenock
to NY on the <u>Lilly</u> in Apr. 1775. [PRO.T47/12]

BRODIE, JAMES, in NY 19 June 1698. [SPAWI.1698.593/xiii]

BRODIE, ROBERT, born 1738, wright from Perthshire with wife
Katherine Black, from Greenock to NY on the <u>Monimia,</u> in May
1775.[PRO.T47/12]

BRODIE, WILLIAM, indentured servant, to East NJ 1684.
[NJSA.EJD.A196]

BRODIE, WILLIAM, born in 1721, enlisted in Captain John Deimer's
Company of the PA Regiment in 1746. [Pa.Arch#5/1/6]

BROWESTER, JOHN, born in 1753, a weaver from Paisley, via
Greenock to NY on the <u>Commerce</u> in Feb.1774. [PRO.T47/12]

BROWN, ALEXANDER, transported from Greenock to NY on 21 Oct.
1682. [NAS.HH11]

BROWN, ALEXANDER, born in 1763, a servant from Wester Leys, Isle of
Lewis, from Stornaway to Philadelphia on the <u>Clementina of</u>
<u>Philadelphia</u> in July 1775.[PRO.T47/12]

BROWN, ANDREW, born in 1729, a gentleman from Dumfries, from
Greenock to Philadelphia on the <u>Magdalene,</u> in Aug. 1774.
[PRO.T47/12]

BROWN, CHRISTIAN, from Islay, Argyll, aboard the <u>Happy Return</u> in
Nov. 1740 bound for NY and Wood Creek on the Hudson River.
[HSBC]

BROWN, DAVID, born in Glasgow during 1695, a minister educated at
Glasgow University around 1719, settled in Belhelvie,
Aberdeenshire, by 1748, settled in Philadelphia, died in Scotland on
10 Mar. 1751. [F#7/662]

BROWN, DUNCAN, from Islay, Argyllshire, a mariner in NY, husband
of Hannah, probate 19 Feb. 1772 NY.

BROWN, DUNCAN, Wallkill Precinct, Ulster County, NY, father of John,
Gilbert, Archibald and Christian wife of Peter McLauchlan,
probate 4 June 1772 NY

BROWN, GEORGE, a Covenanter who was transported from Leith to East
NJ in Aug. 1685. [RPCS#11/154]

BROWN, HUGH, born in 1737, a farmer from Inverness, from Stornaway
to Philadelphia on the <u>Clementina of Philadelphia</u> in July 1775.
[PRO.T47/12]

BROWN, JEAN, daughter of John Brown and Jean Westland in Midmar,
Aberdeenshire, to Philadelphia in 1743, later to Barbados, in 1749
settled in St Croix, married Daniel Aspinall a carpenter, died in 1758.
[Aberdeen Proprinquity Book, 3/202]

BROWN, JOHN, a servant in Perth Amboy, East NJ, 1686.
[NJSA.EJD.A260]

BROWN, JOHN, took the Oath of Association in NY on 26 May 1696.
[PRO.C213:OR470]

BROWN, JOHN, a stonecutter in Woodbury, Gloucester County, NJ,
probate 23 Dec.1788 NJ [NJA.Liber 31/37]

BROWN, NEIL, an indentured servant, from Scotland to Philadelphia on the Anne galley, assigned to George Houston for six years from 24 Sep. 1745. [EP#75]

BROWN, PETER, born in 1752, a barber from Glasgow, from Greenock to NY on the Monimia in May 1775. [PRO.T47/12]

BROWN, WILLIAM, born in Nunton, Dumfries-shire, around 1737, son of John Brown and Mary Clerk, to America by 1751, a student at the College of William and Mary from 1751 to 1753, a journalist and printer in Philadelphia, NY, Barbados and Quebec, died in Quebec on 22 Mar. 1789. [DCB]

BROWNLIE, ROBERT, born in 1739, a laborer from Perthshire, from Greenock to NY on the Monimia, in May 1775.   [PRO.T47/12]

BRUCE, ANNE, born in 1759, a servant from Edinburgh, from Leith to Philadelphia on the Friendship of Philadelphia in May 1775. [PRO.T47/12]

BRUCE, DAVID, born in Edinburgh, a Moravian missionary in PA, NY, and NJ, from 1740 to 1749, died in Sharon, Connecticut, on 9 July 1749. [CCMC]

BRUCE, GEORGE, indentured servant from Montrose, Angus, to East NJ on the Thomas and Benjamin, in Nov. 1684. [NJSA:EJDeeds]

BRUCE, GEORGE, born 1686, indented for 10 years in Chester Co., PA, 14 July 1697. [Sgen.29.1.12]

BRUCE, JAMES, born in 1727, a farmer, with his wife Janet Black, from Greenock to NY on the Monimia,in May 1775.   [PRO.T47/12]

BRUCE, JANET, born in 1757, a servant from Edinburgh, from Leith to Philadelphia on the Friendship of Philadelphia, in May 1775. [PRO.T47/12]

BRUCE, ROBERT, born in 1752, a gardener from Galloway, from Stranraer to NY on the Gale of Whitehaven, in May 1774. [PRO.T47/12]

BRUCE, WALTER, from Scotland, married Helena Bidset, in the Dutch Reformed Church in NY on 22 Apr. 1698. [DRC]

BRUCE, WILLIAM, born 1683, indented for 8 years in Chester Co., PA, 1696. [Sgen.29.1.14]

BRUCE, WILLIAM, in NY, surgeon to the Royal Artillery in North America, probate 24 May 1780 NY

BRUNTOUN, JANET, transported from Greenock to NY on 21 Oct. 1682. [NAS.HH11]

BRYCE, ALEXANDER, born in 1728, a husbandman from Kirkbride, Anwoth, Kirkcudbrightshire, with his wife Mary and daughter Jane, to NewYork on the Gale of Whitehaven, in May 1774. [PRO.T47/12]

BRYSON, JAMES, born in 1756, a farmer from Glasgow, from Greenock to NY on the Matty in May 1774. [PRO.T47/12]

BUCHAN, ALEXANDER, indentured servant, to East NJ 1684. [NJSA.EJD.A266/B167]

BUCHAN, JAMES, born in 1764, from Paisley, from Greenock to NY on the Commerce, in Feb. 1774. [PRO.T47/12]

BUCHAN, THOMAS, born in 1745, a farmer from Stirling, from Greenock to NY on the Monimia, in May 1775. [PRO.T47/12]

BUCHANAN, ARCHIBALD, born during 1740, a pewterer from
    Edinburgh, from Greenock to NY or GA on the Christy, in May
    1775.[PRO.T47/12]
BUCHANAN, JAMES, baptised on 6 Nov. 1769, son of David Buchanan
    and Margaret Grubb in Montrose, Angus, later a merchant in NY,
    died there during 1786. [ANY#1.219]
BUCHANAN, JOHN, born in 1716, a farmer from Galloway, from
    Stranraer to NY on the Gale of Whitehaven, in May 1774.
    [PRO.T47/12]
BUCHANAN, MARION, prisoner in Edinburgh Tolbooth, transported from
    Greenock to NY 21 Oct.1682. [NAS.HH11]
BUCHANAN, MARGARET, born during 1740, from Glasgow, via
    Greenock to NY on the Lilly in May 1775. [PRO.T47/12]
BUCHANAN, MATTHEW, an Episcopal minister, to NY 1704, later in
    Carolina. [EMA#17]
BUCHANAN, THOMAS, born on 24 Dec. 1744 in Glasgow son of George
    Buchanan,a maltman in Glasgow, and Jean Lowden, educated at
    Glasgow University, to NY in 1763, a merchant there, died on 10
    Sep. 1815. [ANY][NAS.RS54.PR36/308] [NAS.CS17.1.23/124]
BUCHANAN, WILLIAM, born in 1750, a weaver from Paisley, from
    Greenock to NY on the Lilly in May 1775.   [PRO.T47/12]
BUCHANAN, WILLIAM, probate 10 July 1775, Ulster County, NY.
BURD, JAMES, born on 10 Mar. 1726, only son of Edward Burd of
    Ormiston, East Lothian, and Jean Haliburton, before 1755, militia
    officer and engineer, settled in Lancaster, PA, died on 5 Oct. 1793,
    buried in Middletown Cemetery, Dauphin County, PA. [AP#133]
    [NAS.CS16.1.165; CS17.1.13,422]
    [NAS.RD2.212.867][NAS.RS27.173.177]
BURNETT, ANDREW, an indentured servant, emigrated to East
    New Jersey in 1684. [NJSA.EJD/A]
BURNETT, JAMES, born in 1718, a laborer who enlisted in Captain
    Samuel Perry's Company of the PA Regiment on 11 July
    1746.[PaArch#5/1/14]
BURNET, WILLIAM, to East NJ in 1684. [Insh#242][NJSA.EJD.A197]
BURNS, JOHN, born in 1739, a weaver from Paisley, fr.Greenock to NY on
    the Commerce in Feb. 1774, settled in New Paisley, 24 miles west of
    Albany. [PRO.T47/12][Hugh Simm papers, Princeton University]
BURNSIDE, HARRY, born in 1735, a laborer from Perthshire, from
    Greenock to NY on the Monimia in May 1775 [PRO.T47/12]
BURT, CHARLES, born in 1748, a wright from Glasgow, from Greenock
    to NY on the Matty in May 1774. [PRO.T47/12]
BUTTER, WILLIAM, born in 1745, a coppersmith from Perth, from
    Leith to Philadelphia on the Friendship of Philadelphia, in Mar. 1774.
    [PRO.T47/12]
CADDELL, JOHN, born in 1749, a mason from Perth, from Greenock to
    NY on the George in May 1774. [PRO.T47/12]
CADDIE, JAMES, born in 1742, a farmer from Montrose, Angus, from
    Greenock to NY on the George in May 1774. [PRO.T47/12]

CAIRNS, JOHN, born in 1751, a wright from Fife, from Leith to
Philadelphia on the Friendship of Philadelphia in May 1775.
[PRO.T47/12]

CALDER, JAMES, born in 1756, a farmer from Strathspey, from Greenock
to NY on the George in May 1774. [PRO.T47/12]

CALDER, JANET, settled in Albany County, NY, before 1776, a Loyalist
who moved to Quebec. [PRO.AO13.11.C1]

CALDER, MARGARET, born in 1750, from Strathspey, from Greenock
to NY on the George in May 1774. [PRO.T47/12]

CALDER, NINIAN, born in 1756, a weaver from Paisley, from Greenock
to NY on the Commerce in Feb.1774. [PRO.T47/12]

CALDER, WILLIAM, born in 1739, a weaver from Paisley, with Anne
Roddan his wife, and children James, Agnes, Margaret, Elizabeth,
and Robert, from Greenock to NY on the Commerce, in Feb. 1774.
[PRO.T47/12]

CALDERHEAD, Reverend **ALEXANDER**, born around 1751, from
Cambuslang, Lanarkshire, a minister in Berwickshire from 1787 to
1802, settled in West Middleton, PA and later in Ohio, died 31 Jan.
1812. [UPC.I.419]

CALDWELL, FRANCIS, soldier of the 27th Regiment, married Catherine
Haley, in NY on 6 Feb. 1759. [PCR]

CALDWELL, JOHN, with his wife Mary Nutt, and sons Alexander and
James, from Islay, Argyll, in June 1739 aboard the Happy Return
bound for NY and Wood Creek on the Hudson River, by 1763 he and
two sons had moved to PA and a married daughter was in NY.
[HSBC]

CALDWELL, JOHN, settled in Happy Valley, Tryon County, NY, before
1776, a Loyalist who moved to Quebec.[PRO.AO13.11.C1]

CALDWELL, ROBERT, settled in White Creek, Albany County, NY,
before 1776, a Loyalist who moved to the Bay of Chaleur, Canada.
[PRO.AO13.11.C1]

CAMERON, ALEXANDER, born in Glenmoriston, Inverness-shire, during
1727, to NY in 1773, settled on the Kingsborough Patent, a Loyalist
in 1776, a soldier of the Royal Regiment of NY from 1780 to 1783,
to Cornwall, Ontario, died in Jan. 1823. [DFpp]

CAMERON, ALEXANDER, born in 1742, a farmer from Strathspey, with
his wife Jean, and children Janet, Elspa and Jean, from Greenock to
NY on the George in May 1774. [PRO.T47/12]

CAMERON, ALEXANDER, born in 1744, a servant from Auchall, Isle of
Lewis?, from Stornaway to NY on the Peace and Plenty in Nov.
1774. [PRO.T47/12]

CAMERON, ALEXANDER, born in 1761, a servant from Garboost, Isle of
Lewis, from Stornaway to Philadelphia on the Friendship in May
1774. [PRO.T47/12]

CAMERON, ALEXANDER, sr., settled in Tryon County, NY, before
1776, a Loyalist who settled in Montreal. [PRO.AO13.11.C1]

CAMERON, ALEXANDER, jr., settled in Johnstown, Tryon County, NY,
before 1776, a Loyalist and a private soldier of the 1st Battalion of the

King's Royal Regiment of NY who settled in Montreal.
[PRO.AO13.11.C1]

CAMERON, ALEXANDER, settled in Johnstown, Tryon County, NY, by
1776, a Loyalist who settled in St John's, Canada. [PRO.AO13.12.2]

CAMERON, ALEXANDER, settled in Tryon County, NY, before 1776, a
Loyalist who moved to Shelbourne, Nova Scotia. [PRO.AO13.11.C1]

CAMERON, ALLEN, settled in NY before 1776, a Loyalist and soldier of
The King's Royal Regiment of NY. [PRO.AO13.12.43]

CAMERON, ANGUS, settled in Tryon County, NY, before 1776, a
Loyalist who moved to Montreal. [PRO.AO13.11.C1]

CAMERON, ANGUS, born in 1728, a farmer from Breadalbane, Perthshire,
with Katherine McDonald his wife, and children Mary, John and
Alexander, from Greenock to NY on the Commerce in June
1775.[PRO.T47/12]

CAMERON, CATHERINE, born in 1775, from Beauly, Inverness-shire,
from Stornaway to Philadelphia on the Clementina in July 1775.
[PRO.T47/12]

CAMERON, CHARLES, born in 1770, from Beauly, Inverness-shire,
from Stornaway to Philadelphia on the Clementina in July 1775.
[PRO.T47/12]

CAMERON, DANIEL, born ca1685, an indentured servant sold by James
Trent in Burlington, NJ, on 21 July 1697. [Sgen.29.1.14]

CAMERON, DANIEL, born in 1736, a clerk from Inverness, who enlisted
in the PA Regiment on 2 May 1759. [Pa.Archive#5/1/287]

CAMERON, DONALD, son of John Cameron, settled on the Kingsborough
Patent, NY, a Loyalist in 1776, moved to Cornwall, Ontario. [DFpp]

CAMERON, DONALD, born in 1710, from Beauly, Inverness-shire, from
Stornaway to Philadelphia on the Clementina in July 1775.
[PRO.T47/12]

CAMERON, DONALD, born in 1751, a servant from Beauly, Inverness-
shire, from Stornaway to Philadelphia on the Clementina in
July1775.[PRO.T47/12]

CAMERON, DONALD, settled on the Mohawk River, NY, by 1776, a
Loyalist and soldier of the 84th [Royal Highland Emigrant] Regiment.
[PRO.AO13.11.C1]

CAMERON, DUNCAN, settled in Mapleton, Albany County, NY, before
1776, a Loyalist and Ensign of the King's Royal Regiment of
NY.[PRO.AO13.12.3]

CAMERON, EVAN, Elisabethtown, NJ, a Loyalist in 1776 who moved to
Shelbourne, Nova Scotia, by 1786. [PRO.AO13.25.101]

CAMERON, HUGH, to America in 1774, settled on the Kingsborough
Patent, NY, a Loyalist in 1776, a soldier of the Royal Regiment of
NY, moved to Cornwall, Ontario. [DF.pp]

CAMERON, JAMES, from Islay, Argyll, in June 1739 bound for New
York and Wood Creek on the Hudson River. [HSBC]

CAMERON, JAMES, born in 1742, a farmer from Strathspey, from
Greenock to NY on the George in May 1774. [PRO.T47/12]

CAMERON, JAMES, born in 1750, a wright from Stirling, with his wife
   Janet, from Greenock to NY on the <u>Monimia,</u> in May 1775.
   [PRO.T47/12]
CAMERON, JAMES, born in 1753, a farmer from Blair Atholl, Perthshire,
   from Greenock to NY on the <u>Monimia,</u> in May 1775.[PRO.T47/12]
CAMERON, JANET, born in 1757, a servant from Loch Broom, Wester
   Ross, from Stornaway to Philadelphia on the <u>Clementina</u> in July
   1775.[PRO.T47/12]
CAMERON, JEAN, born in 1755, from Strathspey, from Greenock to NY
   on the <u>George</u> in May 1774. [PRO.T47/12]
CAMERON, JOHN, born during 1732, a deserter from Captain John de
   Garmo's Company in NY during 1764. [NY Mercury, 12.3.1764]
CAMERON, JOHN, of the Scotch Fusiliers, married Phoebe Duron of NY,
   there on 12 July 1769. [PCR]
CAMERON, JOHN, soldier in the French and Indian Wars, settled Bergen
   Co., NJ, Loyalist in 1776. [PRO.AO13.81.43]
CAMERON, JOHN, born in Glenmoriston, Inverness-shire, to America in
   1773, settled on the Kingsborough Patent, NY, a Loyalist who moved
   to Cornwall, Ontario, in 1785. [DFpp]
CAMERON, JOHN, born in 1741, a farmer from Beauly, Inverness-shire,
   from Stornaway to Philadelphia on the <u>Clementina</u> in July
   1775.[PRO.T47/12]
CAMERON, JOHN MCAFEE, born in Rannoch, Perthshire, during 1730,
   from Fort William, Inverness-shire, to NY on the <u>Pearl</u> in   1773,
   settled on the Kingsborough Patent, NY, a Loyalist and a soldier of
   the Royal Regiment of NY from 1776 to 1783, later settled in
   Fairfield, Lancaster, Glengarry County, Ontario. [DF.pp]
CAMERON, JOHN, born in 1753, a farmer from Strathspey, from
   Greenock to NY on the <u>George</u> in May 1774. [PRO.T47/12]
CAMERON, JOHN, settled on Johnson's Patent, Tryon County, NY, before
   1776, a Loyalist and soldier of the King's Royal Regiment of
   NewYork, who, with Ann his wife, moved to Montreal by 1786.
   [PRO.AO13.11.C1]
CAMERON, JOHN, settled in Tryon County, NY, before 1776, a Loyalist
   and a private soldier of the King's Royal Regiment of NY, who
   moved to Quebec. [PRO.AO13.11.C1]
CAMERON, MARY, born in 1772, from Beauly, Inverness-shire, from
   Stornaway to Philadelphia on the <u>Clementina</u> in July 1775.
   [PRO.T47/12]
CAMERON, MURDOCH, born in 1727, a farmer from Auchall, with his
   wife Mary and their children Ann, Bell, Jean, Mary, Ann, Kenneth,
   Murdoch, and Hector, from Stornaway, Isle of Lewis, to Philadelphia
   on the <u>Peace and Plenty,</u> in Nov. 1774. [PRO.T47/12]
CAMERON, SAMUEL, from Glen Urquhart, Inverness-shire, settled in
   Albany, New York, before 1776, a Loyalist and soldier of the 84th
   Regiment who moved to Bridgeville, Nova Scotia, in 1784.
   [TGS#53.457]

CAMERON, SIMON, born in 1746, a farmer from Beauly, Inverness-shire, from Stornaway to Philadelphia on the Clementina in July 1775. [PRO.T47/12]

CAMERON, WILLIAM, to America in 1774, settled on the Kingsborough Patent, NY, a Loyalist and soldier of the Royal Regiment of NY from 1776 to 1783, later settled in Charlottenburg, Ontario. [DFpp]

CAMERON, WILLIAM, settled in the Old Jerseys, NY, before 1776, a Loyalist who moved to Montreal by 1786. [PRO.AO13.11.C1]

CAMERON, WILLIAM, settled in Tryon County, NY, before 1776, a Loyalist who moved to Montreal by 1786. [PRO.AO13.11.C1]

CAMPBELL, ALEXANDER, from Islay, Argyll, aboard the Happy Return to NY in July 1738 to have settled at Wood Creek on the Hudson River, by 1763 he had settled in Perth Amboy, NJ. [HSPC][NY.Col.MS#72/170-171]

CAMPBELL, ALEXANDER, with his wife Margaret Campbell, and daughter Merran, from Islay, Argyll, aboard the Happy Return in Nov. 1740 bound for NY and Wood Creek on the Hudson River, dead by 1763 but two daughters living then. [HSBC][NY.Col.MS#72.170]

CAMPBELL, ALEXANDER, 'of the family of Landie', from Islay, Argyll, in Nov. 1740 aboard the Happy Return bound for NY and Wood Creek on the Hudson River, dead by 1763 when his daughter then in NY was granted 150 acres on the Argyle Patent, NY. [HSBC][NY.Col.MS#72/170]

CAMPBELL, ALEXANDER, born in Killin, Perthshire, on 14 Nov. 1734, son of James Campbell and Elizabeth Buchanan, as an officer of the Black Watch sent to NY during 1756, married (1) Catherine Vedder in NY on 12 Oct. 1765 and settled in Schenectady, (she died in 1767), (2) Magdalene Van Sice on 23 May 1768, later a merchant in Schoharie, NY, a Loyalist in 1776, in Montreal by 1783, settled in Ontario during 1785, died in 1800 and buried in New Johnstown, Edwardsburgh, Ontario. [CGS#432][PRO.AO13.12.9]

CAMPBELL, ALEXANDER, born in 1738, a farmer from Natiskir, Isle of Lewis, with his wife Margaret Morrison and children Neil and Isobel, from Stornaway to Philadelphia on the Friendship in May 1774. [PRO.T47/12]

CAMPBELL, ALEXANDER, settled at Fort Edward, Albany County, NY, before 1776, a Loyalist settled at the Bay of Quinte, Canada. [PRO.AO13.11.C1]

CAMPBELL, ANDREW, born in 1740, a shoemaker from Galloway, with his wife Agnes and children Jean and Mary-Ann, from Stranraer to NY on the Gale of Whitehaven,in May 1774. [PRO.T47/12]

CAMPBELL, ANGUS, with his son John, from Islay, Argyll, June 1739 on the Happy Return bound for NY and Wood Creek on the Hudson River. [HSBC]

CAMPBELL, ANNA, from Islay, Argyll, in Nov. 1740 aboard the Happy Return bound for NY and Wood Creek on the Hudson River, by 1763 she was married and living with six children, who lived in the Highlands of NY. [HSBC][NY.Col.MS#72/170]

CAMPBELL, ARCHIBALD, indentured servant, to East NJ 1684.
[NJSA.EJD.A195/D325]

CAMPBELL, ARCHIBALD, of Ardenton, from Islay, Argyll, in Nov.
1740 aboard the Happy Return bound for NY and Wood Creek on the
Hudson River, possibly the Archibald Campbell in NY who, as heir
to Dugald Campbell deceased, was granted 150 acres on the Argyle
Patent, NY in 1763. [HSBC][NY.Col.MS#72/170]

CAMPBELL, BARBARA, born in 1757, a servant from Ross-shire, from
Leith to Philadelphia on the Friendship of Philadelphia, in May
1775. [PRO.T47/12]

CAMPBELL, CATHERINE, from Islay, Argyll, in June 1739 on the
Happy Return bound for NY and Wood Creek on the Hudson River,
by 1763 she was living in the Highlands of NY.
[HSBC][NY.Col.MS#72/170]

CAMPBELL, COLIN, a Covenanter from Argyll, transported from Leith to
East NJ in 1685. [RPCS.11.329]

CAMPBELL, COLIN, born in 1707, son of Colin Campbell in Earnhill,
Nairnshire, a minister educated at Aberdeen University, to Nevis in
the West Indies 1737, later in PA and in NJ, died in Burlington, NJ,
9 Aug. 1766. [EMA#18]

CAMPBELL, COLIN, born in 1748, a smith from Breadalbane, via
Greenock to NY on the Commerce, in June 1775. [PRO.T47/12]

CAMPBELL, COLIN, born in 1751, a merchant from Perthshire, from
Greenock to NY on the Monimia, in May 1775. [PRO.T47/12]

CAMPBELL, COLIN, born in June 1752, son of David Campbell Writer to
the Signet, in Inveraray, Argyll, by 1782 he was a Notary Public in
NY and a Loyalist who moved to Shelbourne, Nova Scotia, in 1783.
[Clan Campbell Vol.IV, Edinburgh]

CAMPBELL, DANIEL, in NY, husband of Susanna, father of Jane,
Archibald, Mary, Margaret and Catherine, pro 20 Sep. 1779 NY.

CAMPBELL, DAVID, a Covenanter from Falkirk, Stirlingshire,
transported from Leith to East NJ on the Henry and Francis 11 Aug.
1685. [RPCS#11/145]

CAMPBELL, DAVID, from Greenock to NY 1735. [NAS.GD1.775.1]

CAMPBELL, DONALD, with his wife Mary McKay, and children Robert,
James, Margaret and Isabel, from Islay, Argyll, to NY aboard the
Happy Return in July 1738 to have settled at Wood Creek on the
Hudson River, in 1763 his widow and four children were granted 250
acres on the Argyle Patent, NY, his cousin Duncan Campbell in NY
acted as his trustee. [HSPC][NY.Col.MS#72/170-171]

CAMPBELL, DONALD, born in 1754, a Loyalist and British Army officer
from   1776 to 1783, married Margaret Campbell in NY on 2 Aug.
1815, died on 18 Aug.1825, probate 31 Aug.1825 NY.[Loyalists of
NJ in the Revolution, p.39]

CAMPBELL, DUGALD, settled in Little White Creek, Albany County,
NY, in 1762, a Loyalist who moved to Shelbourne, Nova Scotia.
[PRO.AO13.12.15]

CAMPBELL, DUNCAN, late of Boston, pro. 19 May 1704 NY. [Liber 3/4,
fo.386]

CAMPBELL, DUNCAN, with his wife Sarah Fraser, from Islay, Argyll, in June 1739 aboard the <u>Happy Return</u> bound for NY and Wood Creek on the Hudson River, in 1763 his widow, three sons and a daughter were granted 250 acres on the Argyle Patent, NY.
[HSBC][NY.Col.MS#72/170]

CAMPBELL, DUNCAN, 'of the family of Duntroon, from Islay, Argyll, in Nov. 1740 aboard the <u>Happy Return</u> bound for NY and Wood Creek on the Hudson River, in 1763 he, his wife, a son and three daughters, were granted 250 acres on the Argyle Patent, NY.
[HSBC][NY.Col.MS#72.170]

CAMPBELL, DUNCAN, with his wife Anna Campbell (Lenos), and their daughter Catherine, from Islay, Argyll, in Nov. 1740 aboard the <u>Happy Return</u> bound for NY and Wood Creek on the Hudson River. [HSBC]

CAMPBELL, DUNCAN, of Lochnel, from Islay, Argyll, in Nov. 1740 aboard the <u>Happy Return</u> bound for NY and Wood Creek on the Hudson River, by 1763 was married with children in NY and was granted 200 acres on the Argyle Patent, NY.
[HSBC][NY.Col.MS#72/170]

CAMPBELL, DUNCAN, of the family of Dunn, from Islay, Argyll, in Nov. 1740 aboard the <u>Happy Return</u> bound for NY and Wood Creek on the Hudson River. [HSBC]

CAMPBELL, DUNCAN, born in 1750, a farmer from Perthshire, from Greenock to NY on the <u>Monimia</u> in May 1775. [PRO.T47/12]

CAMPBELL, DUNCAN, in York near Albany, NY, a Loyalist in 1776, later in Montreal by 1786. [PRO.AO13.11.C1]

CAMPBELL, ESPIA, born in 1745, a servant from Beauly, Inverness-shire, from Stornaway to Philadelphia on the <u>Clementina</u> in July 1775. [PRO.T47/12]

CAMPBELL, GEORGE, a merchant in NY, from Scotland to NY in 1742 on the encouragement of Lauchlin Campbell, petitioned Governor Tryon on 10 May 1763.[NY.Col.MS#72/171]

CAMPBELL, GEORGE, a soldier, settled in NY before 1765.
[PC.Col.#4/818]

CAMPBELL, HUGH, born in 1730, a laborer from Perthshire, from Greenock to NY on the <u>Monimia</u> in May 1775. [PRO.T47/12]

CAMPBELL, JAMES, with his wife Anna McDougall, and their children Lauchlin, Archibald, Elizabeth and Janet, from Islay, Argyll, to NY in July 1738 on the <u>Happy Return</u> to have settled at Wood Creek on the Hudson River, by 1763 he was dead, his widow was granted 100 acres, Archibald was granted 50 acres, and Isabel (Elizabeth?) was granted 50 acres, on the Argyle Patent, NY.[HSPC]
[NY.Col.MS#72/170]

CAMPBELL, JAMES, born in 1734, a farmer from Perthshire, with his wife Jane Campbell, from Greenock to NY on the <u>Monimia</u> in May 1775. [PRO.T47/12]

CAMPBELL, JAMES, born in 1739, a farmer from Perthshire, from Greenock to NY on the <u>Monimia</u> in May 1775. [PRO.T47/12]

CAMPBELL, JAMES, late of Jamaica, now in NY, pro 25 July 1770 NY

CAMPBELL, JANET, from Greenock to NY on 21 Oct.1682.
[NAS.HH11]

CAMPBELL, JEAN, born in 1754, from Galloway, via Stranraer to NY on
the Gale of Whitehaven in May 1774.[PRO.T47/12]

CAMPBELL, JENNY, born in 1759, a servant from Edinburgh, from Leith
to Philadelphia on the Friendship of Philadelphia in May 1775.
[PRO.T47/12]

CAMPBELL, JOHN, settled in Perth Amboy, NJ, in 1684. [Insh#249]

CAMPBELL, JOHN, from Leith to East NJ in July 1685. [RPCS#11/329]

CAMPBELL, JOHN, of Ballinabie, and his wife Anna Campbell, from
Islay, Argyll, to NY in July 1738 aboard the Happy Return to have
settled at Wood Creek on the Hudson River, both dead by 1763.
[HSPC][NY.Col.MS#72/170]

CAMPBELL, JOHN, from Islay, Argyll, in Nov. 1740 aboard the Happy
Return bound for NY and Wood Creek on the Hudson River, by 1763
he was married and granted 200 acres on Argyle Estate, NY.
[HSBC][NY.Col.MS#72/170]

CAMPBELL, JOHN, born in 1715, a collier, enlisted in Captain William
Trent's Company of the PA Regiment on 27 June 1746.
[PaArch#5/1/8]

CAMPBELL, JOHN, born in 1738, a laborer, enlisted in Lt Colonel James
Burd's Company of the PA Regiment on 22 May 1757.
[Pa.Archives#5/1/190]

CAMPBELL, JOHN, a tailor in NY, son of John Campbell in New
Campbellton, 1766. [NAS.CS16.1.126]

CAMPBELL, JOHN, born in 1752, a tailor from Galloway, from Stranraer
to NewYork on the Gale of Whitehaven in May 1774. [PRO.T47/12]

CAMPBELL, JOHN, born in 1762, a servant from Stornaway, Isle of
Lewis, from Stornaway to Philadelphia on the Friendship May 1774.
[PRO.T47/12]

CAMPBELL, JOHN, an indentured servant who absconded from Walter
Beatty in Riding township, York County, PA, in 1771. [Pa.Chron:
19.9.1771]

CAMPBELL, Captain LAUGHLIN, of Leorin, brought immigrants from
Islay, Argyll, to settle at Wood Creek on the Hudson River, NY, in
1738, 1739 and 1740. [HSPC]

CAMPBELL, LILLIAS, born in 1758, a spinner from Paisley, from
Greenock to NY on the Commerce in Feb. 1774. [PRO.T47/12]

CAMPBELL, MALCOLM, from Islay, Argyll, in Nov. 1740 aboard the
Happy Return bound for NY and Wood Creek on the Hudson River,
a merchant in NY. [HSBC][NY.Col.MS#72/170]

CAMPBELL, MARY, from Islay, Argyll, aboard the Happy Return to
New York in July 1738 to have settled at Wood Creek on the Hudson
River.[HSPC]

CAMPBELL, MOSES, settled at Crown Point, NY, with his wife
Elizabeth, by 1776, Loyalists, he died in Feb. 1781.
[PRO.AO13.12.18]

CAMPBELL, NEIL, from Islay, Argyll, in June 1739 aboard the Happy Return bound for NY and Wood Creek on the Hudson River, settled on Jamaica by 1763 and his step-father Alexander Montgomery of Tappan offered to take up the grant in trust for said Neil. [HSBC][NY.Col.MS#72/170-171]

CAMPBELL, NEIL, from Islay, Argyll, in Nov. 1740 aboard the Happy Return bound for NY and Wood Creek on the Hudson River. [HSBC]

CAMPBELL, ROBERT, a Covenanter, transported from Leith to East NJ on the Henry and Francis Aug. 1685. [RPCS#11/145][NJSA.EJD.A225]

CAMPBELL, RONALD, from Islay, Argyll, aboard the Happy Return to NY in July 1738 to have settled at Wood Creek on the Hudson River, dead by 1763 and his kinsman George Campbell a pedlar in NY claimed his proportion. [HSPC][NY.Col.MS#72/170-171]

CAMPBELL, RONALD, born in 1739, a farmer from Perthshire, from Greenock to NY on the Monimia, in May 1775. [PRO.T47/12]

CAMPBELL, SAMUEL, born in Edinburgh or St Andrews during 1738, died in NY on17 Apr. 1813. [SM#75.639][EEC#1813] [NAS.CS17.1.26/10, 58] [NAS.B65.7.1.122]

CAMPBELL, SAMUEL, born in Edinburgh on 18 July 1765, son of Samuel Campbell a bookbinder and Catherine Taylor, a bookseller in NY, married (1) Eliza Duyckinck in 1786, and (2) Euphemia Duyckinck in 1799, died in NY 26 June 1836. [ANY#1.198]; bookseller in NY, 1794. [NAS.CS17.1.13,407]

CAMPBELL, SARAH, born in 1754, a maid-servant from Perthshire, from Greenock to NY on the Monimia in May 1775.[PRO.T47/12]

CAMPBELL, SARAH, born in 1759, a spinner from Paisley, from Greenock to NY on the Commerce in Feb. 1774. [PRO.T47/12]

CAMPBELL, WILLIAM, a Covenanter, transported from Leith to East NJ on the Henry and Francis of Newcastle in Aug. 1685. [RPCS#11/154]

CAMPBELL, ("Kemmel"), WILLIAM, born in England!?, married Aeltje Jeppes, (1697-1779) in 1717, buried in Tappan. [NYGBR#128/2/89]

CAMPBELL, WILLIAM, a joiner or wheelwright, from Islay, Argyll, aboard the Happy Return bound for NY in July 1738 to have settled at Wood Creek on the Hudson River, dead by 1763 when his cousin Mary Mackay of NYpetitioned the Governor for his grant.[HSPC][NY.Col.MS#72/171]

CAMPBELL, WILLIAM, a wheelwright, from Islay, Argyll, aboard the Happy Return bound for NY in July 1738 to have settled at Wood Creek on the Hudson River.[HSPC]

CAMPBELL, WILLIAM, from Islay, Argyll, aboard the Happy Return in Nov. 1740 bound for NY and Wood Creek on the Hudson River by 1763 he was dead but his children, who lived in the Highlands of NY, were granted 200 acres on the Argyle Patent, NY. [HSBC][NY.Col.MS#72/170]

CAMPBELL, WILLIAM, a mariner in NY, probate 17 Nov. 1767 NY

CAMPBELL, WILLIAM, born in 1758, a weaver from Paisley, from Greenock to NY on the Commerce in Feb. 1774. [PRO.T47/12]

CANNON, JAMES, born in Edinburgh, to America in 1763, graduated MA from the University of PA in 1767, a mathematics professor, died in Philadelphia on 28 Jan. 1782, buried in Christ churchyard. [AP#143]

CANT, CATHERINE, born in 1756, a servant from Edinburgh, from Leith to Philadelphia on the Friendship of Philadelphia in May 1775. [PRO.T47/12]

CARGILL, DAVID, from Islay, Argyll, aboard the Happy Return in Nov. 1740 bound for NY and Wood Creek on the Hudson River, by 1763 he was married and living in NY with his children when he was granted 200 acreson the Argyle Patent, NY. [HSBC][NY.Col.MS#72/170]

CARGILL, ELIZABETH, from Islay, Argyll, aboard the Happy Return in Nov. 1740 bound for NY and Wood Creek on the Hudson River, by 1763 she was married and living in Tappan when she was granted 150 acres on the Argyle Patent, NY. [HSBC][NY.Col.MS#72/170]

CARGILL, JAMES, from Islay, Argyll, aboard the Happy Return in Nov. 1740 bound for NY and Wood Creek on the Hudson River, by 1763 he was married and living in NY with his children when he was granted 200 acres on Argyle Patent [HSBC][NY.Col.MS#72/170]

CARGILL, JEAN, from Islay, Argyll, aboard the Happy Return in June 1739 bound for NY and Wood Creek on the Hudson River, by 1763 she had married Mr Van Vleck a merchant of NY, and was granted 150 acres on the Argyle Patent, NY. [HSBC][NY.Col.MS#72/170]

CARGILL, JOHN, from Islay, Argyll, aboard the Happy Return in Nov.1740 bound for NY and Wood Creek on the Hudson River, by 1763 he was married and living in NY with his children when he was granted 200 acres on the Argyle Patent, NY. [HSBC][NY.Col.MS#72/170]

CARGILL, MARGARET, from Islay, Argyll, aboard the Happy Return in Nov. 1740 bound for NY and Wood Creek on the Hudson River, by 1763 she was a widow with children, living in New Rochelle, and was granted 150 acres on the Argyle Patent, NY. [HSBC][NY.Col.MS#72/170]

CARMICHAEL, DONALD, and his wife Elizabeth McAlister, with their children John, Alexander, and Mary, from Islay, Argyll, aboard the Happy Return to NY in July 1738 to have settled at Wood Creek on the Hudson River, by 1763 he was dead and his children had left the colony.[HSPC][NY.Col.MS#72/170]

CARMICHAEL, DUGALD, with his wife Catherine McEuan, and their children Janet, Mary, Neil, and Catherine, from Islay, Argyll, aboard the Happy Return in June 1739 bound for NY and Wood Creek on the Hudson River, dead by 1763 when a son John was granted 200 acres on the Argyle Patent, NY. [HSBC][NY.Col.MS#72/170]

CARNE, JAMES, 5'9", a weaver, enlisted in the PA Regiment in Philadelphia on 3 May 1758. [Pa.Archives#5/1/363]

CARNEGIE, JAMES, an indentured servant who from Montrose, Angus, to East NJ on the Thomas and Benjamin in Nov. 1684. [NJSA.EJD.A184]

CARRE, ANDREW, in Del. 1 Jan. 1667. [NY.Hist.MS.Dutch.XX/XXI, p28]

CARSON, JAMES, born in 1755, a husbandman from Queenshill, from Stranraer to NY on the Gale in May 1774. [PRO.T47/12]

CARSON, JOHN, born in 1756, a laborer from Gatehouse, Kirkcudbrightshire, from Stranraer to NY on the Gale of Whitehaven in May 1774. [PRO.T47/12]

CARSON, THOMAS, born in 1738, a brewer from Gatehouse, Kirkcudbrightshire, from Stranraer to NY on the Gale of Whitehaven in May 1774. [PRO.T47/12]

CASSELS, ISOBEL, born in 1756, a servant from Edinburgh, from Leith to Philadelphia on the Friendship in May 1775. [PRO.T47/12]

CASSELS, JOHN, born in 1759, a servant from Edinburgh, from Leith to Philadelphia on the Friendship in May 1775. [PRO.T47/12]

CAVIE, CHRISTIAN, a Covenanter, transported from Leith to East NJ on the Henry and Francis in Aug. 1685. [RPCS#11/155]

CHALMERS, JOHN, born in 1750, a laborer from Partick, Glasgow, via Greenock to NY on the Lilly in Apr. 1775. [PRO.T47/12]

CHALMERS, ROBERT, indentured servant, to East NJ 1685. [NJSA.EJD.A225]

CHAMBERS, MARGARET, born 1681, indented for 6 years at Chester Court, PA, 1696. [Sgen.29.1.14]

CHEYNE, CHRISTIAN, emigrated to East NJ in 1685, married Archibald Silver. [NJSA.EJD.A226]

CHEYNE, JOHN, indentured in Edinburgh 12 Aug. 1685 for 4 years service in East NJ. [NJSA.EJD.A253]

CHILDS, ROBERT, born in 1747, a farmer from Sutherland, from Greenock to Philadelphia on the Sally in Oct. 1774. [PRO.T47/12]

CHISHOLM, ALEXANDER, to America in 1773, settled on the Kingsborough Patent, NY, a Loyalist and soldier of the Royal Regiment of NY from 1777 to 1783, later settled in Charlottenburg, Ontario. [DFpp]

CHISHOLM, ALEXANDER, settled on Johnson's Patent, Tryon County, NY, before 1776, a Loyalist. [PRO.AO13.11.C1]

CHISHOLM, GEORGE, in Aesopus County, NY, a Loyalist in 1776, in Shelbourne, Nova Scotia, by 1786. [PRO.AO13.25.19]

CHISHOLM, ALEXANDER, a merchant in Ticonderoga, NY, by 1776, a Loyalist who moved to Quebec by 1783 and to Montreal in 1787. [PRO.AO13.11.C1]

CHISHOLM, HUGH, settled in Johnson's Patent, Tryon County, NY, before 1776, a Loyalist who moved to Quebec by 1786. [PRO.AO13.11.C1]

CHISHOLM, JAMES, born in 1733, a farmer from Beauly, Inverness-shire, from Stornaway to Philadelphia on the Clementina July 1775.[PRO.T47/12]

CHISHOLM, JOHN, settled in Tryon County, NY, before 1776, a Loyalist
who settled at Niagara by 1786. [PRO.AO13.11.C1]
CHISHOLM, WILLIAM, settled on Johnson's Patent, Tryon County, NY,
before 1776, a Loyalist who settled in New Johnstown.
[PRO.AO13.11.C1]
CHRISTY, ALEXANDER, to NY aboard the Happy Return in 1738, by
1763 he was dead and his right to a grant on the Argyle Patent, NY,
was claimed by his cousin Mary Christy, his cousin and wife of
Duncan Campbell in NY. [NY.Col.MS#72/171]
CHRISTIE, DONALD, born in 1762, servant from Shather, via Stornaway
to Philadelphia on the Friendship in May 1774.[PRO.T47/12]
CHRYSTIE, GEORGE, born in Aberdeen around 1735, absconded from
George Burns, tavernkeeper, King's Head, NY, 26 Feb.1761.
[NYMerc.2.3.1761]
CHRISTY, JAMES, born in 1715, a weaver from Dunbarton, via Greenock
to Philadelphia on the Magdalene in Aug. 1774. [PRO.T47/12]
CHRISTIE, JAMES, born in Edinburgh on 13 Jan. 1750, son of John
Christie and Janet Clarkson, to Philadelphia in 1775, a US Army
officer from 1776/1783, later a merchant in NY, married Mary
Weygandt, died on 31 Mar. 1793. [ANY#1.160][Mathew's American
Armory & Blue Book, London, 1903]
CHRISTY, JOHN, with his wife Isabel McArthur, and daughters Hannah
and Mary, from Islay, Argyll, on the Happy Return in Nov. 1740
bound for NY and Wood Creek on the Hudson River, he was dead by
1763 when his widow, a son and daughter were granted 250 acres on
the Argyle Patent, NY. [HSBC][NY.Col.MS#72/170]
CHRISTY, JOHN, settled on the Kingsborough Patent, Tryon County, NY,
before 1776, a Loyalist who moved to Montreal by 1786.
[PRO.AO13.12.44]
CHRISTIE, JOHN, born in 1745, married Janet McGregor (1757-1852),
from Killin, Perthshire, to America, settled at Creek Road, Mumford,
New York, in 1797, died on 3 July 1843. ["Genealogy of Miller and
Tillotson",   Scottsville, NY, 1951]
CHRISTIE, JOHN, born in 1752, a smith from Glasgow, from Greenock
to NY on the Lilly in Apr. 1775. [PRO.T47/12]
CHRISTIE, MURDO, born in 1765, from Bregair, from Stornaway to
Philadelphia on the Friendship in May 1774. [PRO.T47/12]
CHRISTIE, PATRICK, a merchant, from Aberdeen to West NJ on the
Golden Hynd of London in July 1682. [NAS.E72.1.7]
CHRISTIE, WILLIAM, born in 1763, a wright from Glasgow, from
Greenock to Philadelphia on the Sally, master John Bruce, in Oct.
1774. [PRO.T47.12]
CLARK, ALEXANDER, married Femitje Van Borsum, in the Dutch
Reformed Church in NY on 13 Jan. 1714. [DRC]
CLARK, ANGUS, with his wife Mary McCollum and daughters Catherine
and Mary, from Islay, Argyll, aboard the Happy Return in Nov. 1740
bound for NY and Wood Creek on the Hudson River, by 1763 he and

his son Daniel were dead but the surviving two sons and a daughter
were granted 250 acres on the Argyle Patent, NY
[HSBC][NY.Col.MS#72/170]

CLARK, BENJAMIN, to East NJ 1684. [Insh#171/256]

CLARK, HUGH, settled in Tryon County, NY, before 1776, a Loyalist who
moved to Halifax, Nova Scotia, by 1786. [PRO.AO13.12.45]

CLARK, JAMES, indentured servant, to East NJ 1684. [NJSA.EJD.A195]

CLARK, JAMES, a waiter from Galloway, from Stranraer to NY on the
Gale in May 1774. [PRO.T47/12];{Possibly the 25 year old who
absconded from Tiddeman Hall, NY, 10 Sep.1774. [NYGaz-
Merc.19.9.1774]}

CLARK, JOHN, born in 1749, a farmer from Stirling, from Greenock to
NY on the Matty in May 1774. [PRO.T47/12]

CLARK, JOHN, born in 1746, a farmer from Inverness, with his wife Betty
and daughter Margaret, from Stornaway to Philadelphia on the
Clementina of Philadelphia, in July 1775. [PRO.T47/12]

CLARK, MARY, born in 1752, a servant from Aberdeen, from Leith to
Philadelphia on the Friendship in May 1775. [PRO.T47/12]

CLERK, MATTHEW, chief engineer in NY 1757.[NAS.GD18.4201-4]

CLARK, RICHARD, born 10 Feb.1663, settled in Matawan, East NJ, died
16 May 1733, buried in Old Scots graveyard, Marlboro. [OSC][MNJ]

CLARK, WILLIAM, born 1646, to East NJ 1684, settled in Freehold, died
26 May 1709. [NJSA.EJD.A195][Topanemus g/s]

CLARK, WILLIAM, born in 1754, a shoemaker from Glasgow, from
Greenock to NY on the Commerce. in Feb. 1774. [PRO.T47/12]

CLARK, WILLIAM, with his wife and son John, from Islay, Argyll,
aboard the Happy Return in June 1739 bound for NY and Wood
Creek on the Hudson River, in 1763 he, his wife, a son and a
daughter, were granted 250 acres on the Argyle Patent, NY.
[HSBC][NY.Col.MS#72/170]

CLARKSON, JAMES, possibly from Carstairs, Lanarkshire, then a
merchant in   Woodbridge, N.J., in 1697. [NAS.RD4.83.421]

CLARKSON, JOHN, born in 1738, son of John Clarkson in Craigmealon, a
minister in PA during 1772, at Muddy Creek, York County, from
1773, died on 30 Nov. 1811. [UPC#1.669]

CLEGHORN, ADAM, settled in NY by 1699. [DP#147]

CLERK, ANDREW, a schoolmaster, to NY in 1705. [EMA#20]

CLERK, HECTOR, 5'3", a laborer who enlisted into the PA Regiment in
Philadelphia on 3 May 1758. [Pa.Archives#5/1/154]

CLERK, JOHN, born in 1738, a servant from Findhorn, Morayshire, with
his wife Margaret and children John, Margaret, Janet and Jean, from
Stornaway to Philadelphia on the Clementina in July 1775.
[PRO.T47/12]

CLERK, JOHN, born in 1749, a farmer from Stirling, from Greenock to
NY on the Matty in May 1774. [PRO.T47/12]

CLERK, THOMAS, born in 1746, a farmer from Stirling, from Greenock
to NY on the Matty in May 1774. [PRO.T47/12]

CLOUSTON, GEORGE, indented in Chester Co., PA, 14 Dec.1698.
[Sgen.29.1.3]

CLOWNEY, WILLIAM, indented in Chester Co., PA, 5 Aug. 1697. [Sgen.29.1.13]

COCHRAN, RICHARD, Loyalist in Princeton, NJ, then in Glasgow 1780. [NAS.CS16.1.181][PRO.AO12.13.136]

COCHRAN, WILLIAM, in NJ, then in Glasgow 1782. [NAS.CS16.1.184]

COCK, WILLIAM, an indentured servant, from Scotland to Philadelphia on the Anne galley,Captain Houstoun, assigned to William David in Bucks County, PA, for four years from 20 Sep. 1745. [EP#64]

COCKBURN, JOHN, a mason from Kelso, via Leith to East NJ in 1684, settled in Perth Amboy. [Insh#276][NJSA.EJD.A196]

COCKBURN, THOMAS, a petitioner in NY 1701. [DNY.IV.934]

COLDEN, CADWALLADER, born in 1688, educated in Edinburgh and in London, to Philadelphia in 1710, a botanist, settled in NY during 1718, Governor of NY, died on Long Island 28 Sep. 1776.

COLLINS, CORNELIUS, from Islay, Argyll, in June 1739 aboard the Happy Return bound for NY and Wood Creek on the Hudson River, by 1763 he was living in NJ. [HSBC][NY.Col.MS#72/170]

COMRIE, ALEXANDER, born in Perthshire, married Christine McIntyre in Breadalbane, Perthshire, to NY by 1776, settled in Johnstown, NY. [SPW]

COMRY, ALEXANDER, born in 1750, a farmer from Stirling, from Greenock to NY on the Matty in May 1774. [PRO.T47/12]

CONNEL, JOHN, born in 1735, a weaver from Paisley, with wife Barbara, children Robert, Margaret, Jean, John and James, from Greenock to NY on the Commerce in Feb. 1774. [PRO.T47/12]

CONNELL, ROBERT, born in 1736, a laborer, with wife Elizabeth, via Greenock to NY on the Commerce in Feb. 1774. [PRO.T47/12]

CONNER, MARGARET indented in Chester Court, PA, 14 July 1697. [Sgen.29.1.12]

COOPER, ANN, born in 1753, a spinner from Wick, from Greenock to NY on the Commerce in Feb. 1774. [PRO.T47/12]; a servant who absconded from Thomas Steele, Beekman St., NY, 27 May 1775. [NYGaz-Merc.29.5.1775]

COOPER, JAMES, born in 1772, from New Luce, Wigtownshire, from Stranraer to NY on the Jackie of Glasgow, on 31 May 1775. [PRO.T47/12]

COOPER, THOMAS, born in 1771, from New Luce, Wigtownshire, from Stranraer to NY on the Jackie of Glasgow on 31 May 1775. [PRO.T47/12]

COPELAND, GEORGE, born in Shetland, a grocer who settled in NY before 1785, died there on 25 Dec. 1820. [ANY#1.377]

CORBETT, ANDREW, a Covenanter, transported from Leith to East NJ on the Henry and Francis of Newcastle in Aug. 1685. [RPCS#11.154]

CORBETT, JOHN, a Covenanter, transported from Leith to East NJ on the Henry and Francis of Newcastle in Aug. 1685.[RPCS#11.154]

CORHEAD, AGNES, a Covenanter, transported from Leith to East NJ on Henry and Francis of Newcastle Aug. 1685. [RPCS#11.154]

CORMUTT, DANIEL, born 1685, indented in Chester Court, PA, 14 July 1697. [Sgen.29.1.12]

CORRIE, GEORGE, indentured servant, to East NJ 1685.
[NJSA.EJD.A225]

CORSAN, JOHN, a Covenanter, transported from Leith to East NJ on the
Henry and Francis of Newcastle in Aug. 1685. [RPCS#11.154]

CORSE, ELIZABETH, a Covenanter, transported from Leith to East NJ on
the Henry and Francis of Newcastle in Aug. 1685. [RPCS#11.166]

COUGHTRY, MARY, born in 1759, from Gatehouse, Kirkcudbrightshire,
from Stranraer to NY on the Gale in May 1774. [PRO.T47/12]

COUTTS, JAMES, a merchant in Philadelphia, 1699, admitted as a burgess
of Montrose Angus, in 1709. [SPAWI.1699.138/1][MBR]

COWAN, ALEXANDER, born in 1754, a weaver from Glasgow, from
Greenock to NY on the Matty in May 1774. [PRO.T47/12]

COWAN, BARBARA, a Covenanter, transported from Leith to East NJ on
the Henry and Francis in Aug. 1685. [RPCS#11.154]

COWAN, JOHN, born in 1756, a laborer from Breadalbane, Perthshire,
from   Greenock to NY on the Lilly in May 1775. [PRO.T47/12]

COWAN, MARJORY, a Covenanter, transported from Leith to East NJ on
the Henry and Francis in Aug. 1685. [RPCS#11.154]

CRAIG, ANDREW, indentured servant, to East NJ in 1684.
[NJSA.EJD.A266/B351]

CRAIG, ANN, born in 1756, a servant from Anstruther, Fife, from Leith to
Philadelphia on the Friendship in May 1775. [PRO.T47/12]

CRAIG, ARCHIBALD, born 1677, indentured servant, to East NJ on the
Henry and Francis in 1685, died Matawan 6 March 1750.
[NJSA.EJD.A225]

CRAIG, GEORGE, from Elgin, Morayshire, an Episcopal minister
educated at King's College, Aberdeen, around 1750, to Philadelphia
in 1751, died after 1783 in Marcus Hook, PA.
[EMA#22][NAS.GD1.495/35]

CRAIG, GRISELDA, indentured servant, to East NJ in 1685.
[NJSA.EJD.A225]

CRAIG, JAMES, indentured servant, to East NJ in 1685.
[NJSA.EJD.A225]

CRAIG, JAMES, sr., born in Scotland during 1717, a merchant in
Philadelphia, died there on 9 Oct. 1793. [AP#152]

CRAIG, JOHN, indentured servant,with wife Ursula, children Archibald,
James and Ursula, to East NJ in 1685 on Henry and Francis, settled in
Middlesex Co. [NJSA.EJD.A225/B321]

CRAIG, JOHN, born in 1755, a weaver from Stoneykirk, Wigtownshire,
from Stranraer to NY on the Jackie on 31 May 1775. [PRO.T47/12]

CRAIG, MARGARET, born in 1755, a spinner from Paisley, via Greenock
to NY on the Commerce in Feb. 1774. [PRO.T47/12]

CRAWFORD, HENRY, born in 1749, a weaver from Paisley, via Greenock
to NY on the Matty in May 1774. [PRO.T47/12]

CRAWFORD, JAMES, in Del., 1 Jan. 1669, 1667 and 1671.
[NY.Hist.MS.Dutch.XX/XXI,28]

CRAWFORD, JEAN, born 1747, spinner from Paisley, with son John via
Greenock to NY on Commerce in Feb. 1774. [PRO.T47/12]

CRAWFORD, JOHN, in Middletown, East NJ, 27 June 1685.
[NJSA.EJD.B134]

CRAWFORD, JOHN, born in 1739, a weaver from Paisley, with his wife
Margaret and children Lawrence, Margaret and John from Greenock
to NY on the Commerce in Feb. 1774. [PRO.T47/12]

CRAWFORD, PATRICK, a merchant, via London to NY by 1699.
[DP#153]

CRAWFORD, THOMAS, a minister, to Dover, Del., in 1709.
[SCHR#14/144]

CRAWFORD, WILLIAM, a cooper in NY, probate 2 May 1773 NY

CRICHTON, JOHN, a Covenanter from Dalry, Ayrshire, transported from
Leith to East NJ on the Henry and Francis in Aug. 1685.
[RPCS#11/154]

CRIGHTON, ANN, born in 1746, a servant from Stornaway, Isle of Lewis,
from Stornaway to Philadelphia on the Friendship in May 1774.
[PRO.T47/12]

CRIGHTON, JAMES, settled in East NJ by 1689. [NJSA.EJD.B138]

CROCKER, HUGH, born in 1744, a farmer from Lochwinnoch, via
Greenock to Philadelphia on the Sally in Oct. 1774.[PRO.T47/12]

CROMERY, JAMES, born in 1747, a shoemaker from Breadalbane,
Perthshire, from Greenock to NY on the Commerce in June
1775.[PRO.T47/12]

CROMERY, PATRICK, born in 1752, a wright from Breadalbane,
Perthshire, from Greenock to NY on the Commerce in June 1775.
[PRO.T47/12]

CROSS, JOHN, a minister, to Philadelphia in 1732, died there on 9 Aug.
1766. [APC#274][SM#28.558]

CROSS, ROBERT, clerk, a Presbyterian in NY 1724. [NAS.CH1.2.49.55]

CRUIKSHANK, Captain GEORGE, and his daughter Clementina, from
Aberdeen, settled at Clifton Hall, Philadelphia, before 1768.
[AP#311]; in Haverford, PA, then in Elgin, cnf 13 Aug. 1785
Commissariat of Moray. [NAS]

CULLENS, DAVID, born in 1754, a laborer from Dundee, from Greenock
to NY on the Lilly in May 1775. [PRO.T47/12]

CULLINGS, JOHN, son of James Cullings in Dunblane, Perthshire, to
America in 1775, settled in Albany County, NY, married Ann
Lennox [TV#15.16]

CUMMING, ALEXANDER, born in 1745, a farmer from Strathspey, from
Greenock to NY on the George in May 1774. [PRO.T47/12]

CUMMING, DONALD, born in 1729, a farmer from Strathspey, with his
wife Espa and children Mary, Alexander, Peter, John and Margery,
from Greenock to NY on the George in May 1774. [PRO.T47/12]

CUMMING, ELIZABETH, wife of Andrew McFarlane from Dunbarton,
settled in NY before 1755. [NAS.RS10.9.3]

CUMMING, GEORGE, and wife Margaret Burness, emigrated to East NJ
in 1685. [NAS.SQR.U3/20]

CUMMING, JAMES, born in 1755, a farmer from Strathspey, from
Greenock to NY on the George in May 1774. [PRO.T47/12]

CUMMING, JOHN, born in 1740, a farmer from Strathspey, from
   Greenock to NY on the George, in May 1774. [PRO.T47/12]
CUMMING, JOHN, born in 1748, a tailor from Ayr, from Stranraer to NY
   on the Gale of Whitehaven in May 1774. [PRO.T47/12]
CUMMING, JOHN, born in 1758, a farmer from Strathspey, from
   Greenock to NY on the George in May 1774. [PRO.T47/12]; settled
   in Oswald Field, Catskill,Albany County, NY. [PRO.AO12.20.53]
CUMMING, KATHERINE, born in 1764, from Strathspey, from
   Greenock to NY on the George in May 1774. [PRO.T47/12]
CUMMING, MARY, born in 1768, from Strathspey, from Greenock to NY
   on the George of Greenock in May 1774. [PRO.T47/12]
CUMMING, WILLIAM, born in 1722, a farmer from Strathspey, with his
   wife Isobel and children Barbara, Margery, Isobel, Alexander,
   Katherine and John, from Greenock to NY on the George in May
   1774. [PRO.T47/12]
CUNNINGHAM, AGNES, born in 1750, a farmer from Inverness, from
   Greenock to NY on the George in May 1774. [PRO.T47/12]
CUNNINGHAM, DAVID, married Elisabeth Elsworth, in the Dutch
   Reformed Church of NY on 4 Apr. 1712. [DRC]
CUNNINGHAM, DAVID, a baker in NY, a Loyalist in 1776 who moved to
   Digby, Nova Scotia, by 1783. [PRO.AO13.26.74]
CUNNINGHAM, JAMES, born in 1732, a weaver from Paisley, with
   Elizabeth his wife and children Elizabeth, Catherine, Donald, James
   and Sarah, from Greenock to NY on the George of Greenock in May
   1774. [PRO.T47/12]
CUNNINGHAM, JANET, indentured servant, to East NJ in 1685.
   [NJSA.EJD.A225]
CUNNINGHAM, PATRICK, a Covenanter, transported from Leith to East
   NJ on the Henry and Francis, in Aug. 1685. [RPCS#11/289]
CUNNINGHAM, WILLIAM, a Covenanter from Ashinyards, Ayrshire,
   transported from Leith to East NJ on the Henry and Francis of
   Newcastle, in Aug. 1685. [RPCS#11/159][NAS.HH11]
CUNNINGHAM, WILLIAM, born in 1740, a farmer from Dunblane,
   Perthshire, from Greenock to NY or GA on the Christy in May
   1775.[PRO.T47/12]
CURRIE, DAVID, in NY, 1781. [NAS.CS16.1.181]
CURRY, NEIL, born in 1723, a cooper who enlisted in the PA Regiment on
   22 May 1758. [Pa.Archives#5/1/187]
CURRIE, Reverend WILLIAM, born in Glasgow around 1710, educated
   at Glasgow University, to America before 1730, a tutor in Virginia, a
   minister in Newcastle, Del., from 1734, later in Perkiomen, PA, died
   in Radnor, Chester Valley, PA, on 26 Oct. 1803. [AP#159][EMA#23]
CURRY, ROBERT, born in 1749, a weaver from Kilsyth, Stirlingshire,
from Greenock to NY on the Monimia May 1775. [PRO.T47/12]
CUTHBERT, JAMES, born 1755, a blacksmith from Lanark, with wife
   Margaret, from Greenock to Philadelphia on the Magdalene Aug.
   1774. [PRO.T47/12]

CUTHBERT, MARY, born in 1756, a servant from Edinburgh, from Leith
  to Philadelphia on the Friendship in May 1775. [PRO.T47/12]

DALGLEISH, ALEXANDER, a Covenanter from Kilbride, transported
  from Leith to East NJ on the Henry and Francis in Aug. 1685.
  [RPCS#11/154]

DAVIDSON, GEORGE, from Albany, married Jannetje Lopers from NY,
  in the Dutch Reformed Church in NY on 9 Dec. 1674. [DRC.Reg.]

DAVIDSON, JAMES, born in 1755, a sailor from Kirkholm, from
  Stranraer to NY on the Jackie in May 1775. [PRO.T47/12]

DAVIDSON, JEAN, born in 1753, from Kirkholm, from Stranraer to
  NY on the Jackie of Glasgow in May 1775.[PRO.T47/12]

DAVIDSON, JOHN, from Fort Orange, married Lysbeth Lucas from NY,
  in the Dutch Reformed Church in NY on 4 Oct. 1673. [DRC.Reg.]

DAVIDSON, JOHN, born around 1687, an indentured servant in Chester
  County, PA, 14 Dec. 1698. [Sgen.29.1.13]

DAVIDSON, WILLIAM, indentured servant, to East NJ in 1684.
  [NJSA.EJD.Liber A187]

DAVIESON, WILLIAM, indentured servant, to East NJ in 1685.
  [NJSA.EJD.Liber A302]

DEMPSTER, ALEXANDER, born in 1757, a gardener from Perthshire,
  from Leith to Philadelphia on the Friendship in May 1775.
  [PRO.T47/12]

DEMPSTER, LILLY, born in 1759, a servant from Edinburgh, from Leith
  to Philadelphia on the Friendship in May 1775. [PRO.T47/12]

DENISTON, MARGARET, born 1738, from Kirkcudbright, from
  Dumfries to NY on the Gale in May 1774. [PRO.T47/12]

DENNISTON, SAMUEL, born in 1749, a tailor from Auchincairn, from
  Kirkcudbright to NY on the Adventure in May 1774. [PRO.T47/12]

DICK, ARCHIBALD, born in Edinburgh during 1715, son of Thomas
  Dick, settled in PA before 1771, died in 1782. [BLG#2997]

DICK, CATHERINE, born in 1754, a servant from Breton, from Leith to
  Philadelphia on the Friendship in May 1775. [PRO.T47/12]

DICK, THOMAS, born in 1747, a wright from Stirling, from Greenock
  to NY or GA on the Christy in May 1775. [PRO.T47/12]

DICK, Sir WILLIAM, Captain of the NY Independent Company of Foot,
  died at Albany 19 Dec.1737, cnf 9 Oct. 1747.
  [NAS.CC8.8.111][Zenger's NY Wkly Journal,.26.12.1737]

DICKSON, ANDREW, born in 1746, a laborer from Edinburgh, from
  Greenock to NY on the Lilly, in Apr. 1775. [PRO.T47/12]

DICKSON, DAVID, born in 1754, a laborer from Glasgow, from Greenock
  to NY on the Matty in May 1774. [PRO.T47/12]

DICKSON, MARGARET, indentured servant, to East NJ in 1684.
  [NJSA.EJD.A]

DICKSON, WILLIAM, born in Whitslaid, Berwickshire, during 1719, to
  Jamaica in 1748, later settled in Philadelphia, PA, during 1763.
  [BLG#2659]

DINGWALL, ARTHUR, born on 25 Feb. 1752, son of John Dingwall of
  Rainieston and Mary Lumsden, a merchant in NY and later in St
  John, NB, died in 1824. ['Thanage of Fermartyn', p.546]

DISHINGTON, JOHN, born 1655, arrived in NY via Barbados 3 June 1689. [DNY#3/586]

DOBIE, JAMES, to East NJ in 1684. [Insh#249]

DOIG, CHARLES, born in 1754, a weaver from Perthshire, from Leith to Philadelphia on the Friendship in May 1775. [PRO.T47/12]

DONALD, ALEXANDER, born in 1738, a laborer from Killearn, Stirlingshire, from Greenock to NY or GA on the Christy, in May 1775. [PRO.T47/12]

DONALDSON, JOHN, from Galloway, married Elizabeth Rodenburg, widow of Ephriam Hermas, in the Dutch Reformed Church in NY on 24 Mar 1692. [DRC.Reg.]

DONALDSON, JOHN, a merchant, probate 8 Apr. 1702 Newcastle, Del..

DONALDSON, MARY, born in 1758, a servant from Alloa, Clackmannanshire, from Leith to Philadelphia on the Friendship in May 1775. [PRO.T47/12]

DONALDSON, ROBERT, a shipmaster in NY, 1765. [NAS.CS16.1.122]

DOUGAL, JAMES, born in 1755, a weaver from Paisley, via Greenock to NY on the Commerce in Feb. 1774. [PRO.T47/12]

DOUGALL, WALTER, born in 1757, a weaver from Paisley, from Greenock to NY on the Commerce in Feb. 1774. [PRO.T47/12]

DOUGLAS, ALEXANDER, born in 1723, a laborer from Perth, from Leith to Philadelphia on the Friendship in May 1775. [PRO.T47/12]

DOUGLAS, CHARLES, a Covenanter, transported from Leith to East NJ on the Henry and Francis in Aug. 1685. [RPCS#11.154]

DOUGLAS, DUNCAN, born in 1725, a laborer, enlisted in Captain John Shannon's Company of the PA Regiment on 1 July 1746. [PaArch#5/1/11]

DOUGLAS, GEORGE, born around 1685, an indentured servant 'sold' by James Trent, in Burlington, N.J., 21 July 1697. [Sgen.29.1.14]

DOUGLAS, ISABELLA, born around 1682, an indentured servant in Chester County, PA, 14 Dec. 1698. [Sgen.29.1.14]

DOUGLAS, PATRICK, born in 1740, a mason from Perthshire, from Greenock to NY on the Monimia in May 1775. [PRO.T47/12]

DOUGLAS, THOMAS, born in 1765, married Rebecca Myers in NJ on 13 July 1790, died on 2 June 1822. [Sgen#9.81]

DOUGLAS, WILLIAM, ("Willem Doukles"), in Fort Amsterdam, New Netherlands, in 1658. ['Laws & Writs of Appeal, 1647-1663', C.T.Gehrins,(Syracuse, 1991)]

DOUGLAS, WILLIAM, a clerk in Bergen, N.J., 1679/1686. [NJSA.EJD.B16/366]

DOUGLAS, WILLIAM, a Covenanter from the Bridge of Ken, transported from Leith to East NJ on the Henry and Francis in Aug. 1685. [RPCS#11.154]

DOUGLAS, WILLIAM, a merchant in Philadelphia, reference in 1698. [NY Wills, Liber 3/4, fo.280]

DOW, ALEXANDER, in Perth Amboy, N.J., 1686. [NJSA.EJD.B159]

DOW, JOHN, born 1732(?), former soldier, settled as a merchant in Philadelphia in 1763, Loyalist in 1776. [PRO.AO12.4.319]

DRIVER, JAMES, born around 1679, a servant imported by Maurice Trent
and indentured in Chester County, PA, on 3 Oct. 1693.
[Sgen.29.1.11]

DRUMMOND, GEORGE, Customs officer in Philadelphia 1769-1777,
Loyalist. [PRO.AO12.101.151]

DRUMMOND, JOB, a petitioner in NY 1701. [DNY.IV.934]

DRUMMOND, JOHN, born in 1755, a weaver from Paisley, via Greenock
to NY on the <u>Commerce</u> in Feb. 1774. [PRO.T47.12]

DRUMMOND. ROBERT, in East NJ 1689. [NJSA.EJD.B138][Insh#263]

DRUMMOND, WILLIAM, born in 1749, a laborer from Renfrew, from
Greenock to Philadelphia on the <u>Sally</u> in Oct. 1774. [PRO.T47.12]

DUFFIE, DUNCAN, born in Edinburgh, married Mary Thomson, to NY
before 1763. [ANY#1.298]

DUGGAN, JOHN, born in 1723, a laborer, enlisted in Captain William
Trent's Company of the PA Regiment on 9 July 1746. [PaArch#5/1/8]

DUGDALE, WILLIAM, married Jane Prevoost, in the Dutch Reformed
Church in NY on 25 June 1715. [DRC]

DUGALL, ALEXANDER, born in 1753, a farmer from Duffus,
Morayshire, from Stornaway to Philadelphia on the <u>Clementina</u> in
July 1775. [PRO.T47/12]

DUN, JAMES, born in 1746, a farmer from Breadalbane with his wife
Katherine, from Greenock to NY on the <u>Commerce</u> in June 1775.
[PRO.T47.12]

DUN, JAMES, born in 1747, a fiddler from Glencoe with wife Mary Crerar
and son John, from Greenock to NY on the <u>Commerce</u> in Feb. 1775.
[PRO.T47.12]

DUN, JOHN, born in 1749, a fiddler from Breadalbane, Perthshire, from
Greenock to NY on the <u>Commerce</u> in June 1775. [PRO.T47.12]

DUNBAR, DAVID, born in 1762, from Wick, Caithness, from Leith to
Philadelphia on the <u>Friendship</u> in June 1775. [PRO.T47.12]

DUNBAR, GEORGE, a merchant from Edinburgh, settled in NY before
1782. [NAS.RD2.235.17]; in NY, 1787. [NAS.CS17.1.6]

DUNBAR, THOMAS, indentured servant, to East NJ in 1684.
[NJSA.EJD.Liber A195]

DUNCAN, ANN, born in 1744, from Strathspey, from Greenock to NY on
the <u>George</u> in Mar. 1774. [PRO.T47.12]

DUNCAN, CHARLES, possibly from Dundee, in NY, 1776.
[NAS.CS16.1.168]

DUNCAN, GYLES, indentured servant, to East NJ in 1685.
[NJSA.EJD.Liber A225]

DUNCAN, ISOBEL, born in 1745, from Strathspey, from Greenock to NY
on the <u>George</u> in Mar. 1774. [PRO.T47.12]

DUNCAN, JAMES, master of the <u>Margaret of New York</u>, 50 tons, 7 man
crew, from NY via England to Holland, at Dover on return voyage in
Oct. 1692. [CTB#IX.IV.1865]

DUNCAN, JAMES, born in 1759, a storekeeper from Hawthorndean,
Midlothian, from Leith to Philadelphia on the <u>Friendship</u> in May
1775.[PRO.T47.12]

DUNCAN, JAMES, born in 1760, a storekeeper from Falkirk, Stirlingshire, from Greenock to NY on the <u>Lilly</u> in Apr. 1775. [PRO.T47.12]

DUNCAN, JAMES, born in 1772, from Strathspey, from Greenock to New York on the <u>George</u> in May 1774. [PRO.T47.12]

DUNCAN, JEAN, born in 1757, from Strathspey, from Greenock to NY on the <u>George</u> in May 1774. [PRO.T47.12]

DUNCAN, JOHN, born 1684, indented in Bucks Co. Court, PA, in Sept. 1697. [Sgen.29.1.14]

DUNCAN, JOHN, born in 1730, a farmer from Strathspey, from Greenock to NY on the <u>George</u> in May 1774. [PRO.T47.12]

DUNCAN, KATHERINE, born in 1769, from Strathspey, from Greenock to NY on the <u>George</u> in May 1774. [PRO.T47.12]

DUNCAN, MARGARET, inventory, 20 Mar. 1703. [NY Wills, liber 3/4, fo.311]

DUNCAN, THOMAS, a merchant in Philadelphia, 1767. [NAS.CS16.1.130]

DUNCAN, THOMAS, sutler to the Army in NY 1784. [NAS.CS17.11.3/212]

DUNCAN, THOMAS ERSKINE, son of Charles Duncan in NY, 1779. [NAS.CS16.1.175]

DUNCAN, WILLIAM, born in 1773, from Strathspey, from Greenock to NY on the <u>George</u> in May 1774. [PRO.T47.12]

DUNDAS, JAMES, a merchant, from Leith to East NJ on the <u>Henry and Francis</u> in Aug. 1685. [NAS.E72.15.32]

DUNLOP, AGNES, indentured servant, to East NJ 1685. [NJSA.EJD.A225]

DUNLOP, JOHN, indentured servant, to East NJ, 1685. [NJSA.EJD.A225]

DUNLOP, JOHN, married Rachel Grant, in the Dutch Reformed Church in NY on 26 May 1713. [DRC]

DUNLOP, MATTHEW, 5'6", a carpenter, enlisted in the PA Regiment on 11 May 1758 in Philadelphia. [Pa.Arch.5/1/154]

DUNLOP, WILLIAM, indentured servant, to East NJ 1685. [NJSA.EJD.Liber A225]

DUNMORE, NELLY, born in 1748, a spinner from Paisley, from Greenock to NY on the <u>Commerce</u> in Feb. 1774.[PRO.T47.12]

DUNN, ALEXANDER, indentured servant, to East NJ 1684. [NJSA.EJD.A195]

DUNSMUIR, HUGH, born in 1734, a weaver from Paisley via Greenock to NY on the <u>Commerce</u> in Feb. 1774.[PRO.T47.12]

DURIE, ISOBEL, a Covenanter, transported from Leith to East NJ on the <u>Henry and Francis</u> in Aug. 1685. [RPCS#11.154]

EATON, ROBINA, born in 1750, from Greenock to NY on the <u>Lilly</u> in Apr. 1775. [PRO.T47.12]

EATON, THOMAS, born in 1746, a chapman from Edinburgh, from Greenock to Philadelphia on the <u>Magdalene</u> in Aug. 1774. [PRO.T47.12]

EDGAR, MARGARET, indentured servant, to East NJ 1685. [NJSA.EJD.A225]

ELDER, JOHN, born on 26 Jan. 1706, son of Robert Elder and Eleanor Elder, a minister educated at Edinburgh University, emigrated 1736, settled in Paxton and Pennsburg, PA, died in Swatara, PA, on 17 July 1792. [F#7.663]

ELDER, JOHN, born in 1752, a smith from Glasgow, from Greenock to NY on the Lilly in May 1775. [PRO.T47.12]

ELL, JOHN, born in 1734, a laborer from Cavin, from Stranraer to New York on the Gale of Whitehaven in May 1774.[PRO.T47.12]

ELLICE, GEORGE, settled in Philadelphia, probate 1753 PCC

ELLIOT, ANDREW, born in Edinburgh during 1728, son of Sir Gilbert Elliot, settled in Philadelphia during 1747 as a merchant, married Eleanor McCall in 1754 and Elisabeth Plumstead in 1759, Customs Collector of NY in 1764, Lieutenant Governor of NY in 1780, returned to Scotland, admitted as a burgess of Montrose, Angus, in 1789, died at Mount Teviot, Roxburghshire, on 25 May 1797. [AP#168][MBR]

EMIRY, JAMES, born in 1754, a weaver from Paisley, via Greenock to NY on the Commerce, in Feb.1774. [PRO.T47.12]; absconded from Alexander Robertson in NY city 1 Nov.1774. [NYGaz-Merc.7.11.1774]

ENNIS, ROBERT, born in 1736, a weaver who enlisted in the PA Regiment on 3 May 1758. [Pa.Archives#5/1/187]

ERSKIN, Mrs JANE, widow of Sergeant John Erskin, late in Del., 1678, Newcastle, Del. [NY Hist.MS.Dutch XX/XXI,367]

ERSKIN, JOHN, quit rent in Del., 1 Jan. 1667. [NY Hist.MS.Dutch XX/XXI,28]

EWART, AGNES, born 25 Sep. 1755, daughter of Rev. John Ewart and Mary Corrie, married John Carson, a merchant in Philadelphia, on 4 Aug. 1784.[F#2.303]

EWING, JOHN, a petitioner in NY 1701. [DNY.IV.934]

EWING, Reverend JOHN, a minister in Philadelphia, admitted as a burgess of Montrose in 1774. [MBR]

FAIRLIE, JAMES, a merchant in NY and Virginia before 1783, then in Kingston, Jamaica, and after in Kilmarnock, Ayrshire, [NAS.NRAS.0396.TD248/2][NAS.CS17.1.3/375]

FALCONER, JOHN, son of David Falconer in Edinburgh, land grant in Amboy, East NJ 23 Nov.1682. [NJSA.EJD.A105]

FALCONER, PATRICK, to America in 1684, settled in Elisabethtown, N.J. [Insh#245][NJSA.EJD.B174]

FALCONER, PETER, a merchant in Woodbridge, East NJ, 1688. [NJSA.EJD.Liber B174/420]

FARQUHAR, HUGH, petitioner in NY 30 Dec.1701, a witness in Westchester parish, NY, on 6 Dec. 1702. [DNY.IV.934][NY Wills, liber 7, fo.86]

FARQUHAR, WILLIAM, born around 1703, a physician, settled in NJ around 1730, later in NY, Loyalist in 1776. [PRO.AO12.99.321]

FARQUHARSON, ALEXANDER, a minister educated at King's College, Aberdeen, in 1705, to NJ. [EMA#27]

FARQUHARSON, JAMES, a minister, to PA in 1712. [EMA#27]

FENWICK, JAMES, a Covenanter, transported from Leith to East NJ on the Henry and Francis in Aug. 1685. [RPCS#11.154]

FERGUS, JAMES, born in 1750, a weaver from Glasgow, from Greenock to NY on the Matty in May 1774. [PRO.T47.12]

FERGUSON, ALEXANDER, settled on Johnson's Patent, Tryon County, NY, before 1776, a Loyalist. [PRO.AO13.12.92]

FERGUSON, DONALD, with Flory Shaw his wife, and a child of their own plus Catherine and Anna Ferguson his brother's children, from Islay, Argyll, aboard the Happy Return in June 1739 bound for NY and Wood Creek on the Hudson River, dead by 1763 when his daughter and a niece were granted150 acres on the Argyle Patent, NY. [HSBC][NY.Col.MS#72/170]

FERGUSON, DONALD, born in 1754, a farmer from Stirling, from Greenock to   NY on the Matty in May 1774. [PRO.T47.12]

FERGUSON, DUNCAN, born in 1739, a farmer from Falkirk, Stirlingshire, from Greenock to NY or GA on the Christy, in May 1775. [PRO.T47.12]

FERGUSON, ELIZABETH, born in 1747, a spinner from Paisley, from Greenock to NY on the Commerce, master John Mathie, in Feb. 1774. [PRO.T47.12]

FERGUSON, ELSPETH, a Covenanter, transported from Leith to East NJ on the Henry and Francis of Newcastle, in Aug. 1685. [RPCS#11.155]

FERGUSON, HENRY HUGH, late of Philadelphia, now in Kilmarnock, Ayrshire, 1787. Loyalist. [NAS.CS17.1.6,164][PRO.AO12.38.04]

FERGUSON, JAMES, born in 1743, a wright from Breadalbane, Perthshire, with Jean McGregor his wife and children Mary, Robert, Helen, and Ann, fromGreenock to NY on the Commerce in June 1775.[PRO.T47.12]

FERGUSON, JAMES, born in 1754, a farmer from Stirling, from Greenock to   NY on the Matty in May 1774. [PRO.T47.12]

FERGUSON, JAMES, born in 1755, a farmer from Blair Atholl, Perthshire, from Greenock to NY on the Monimia in May 1775.[PRO.T47.12]

FERGUSON, JANET, a Covenanter, transported from Leith to East NJ on the Henry and Francis in Aug. 1685. [RPCS#11.155]

FERGUSON, JANET, wife of …. McDonald, and son Alexander McDonald, from Islay, Argyll, aboard the Happy Return to NY in July 1738 to have settled at Wood Creek on the Hudson River, dead by 1763 and her son Alexander McDonald then a ropemaker living in NY was granted 150 acres on the Argyle Patent, NY.[HSPC][NY.Col.MS#72/170-171]

FERGUSON, JANET, born in 1743, from Paisley, via Greenock to NY on the Lilly in Apr. 1775. [PRO.T47.12]

FERGUSON, JOHN, born in 1747, a weaver from Paisley, from Greenock to NY on the George in May 1774. [PRO.T47.12]

FERGUSON, MARY, married Thomas Lawrence, a widower, in the Dutch Reformed Church in NY on 9 Nov. 1692. [DRC.Reg.]

FERGUSON, PETER, settled on Johnson's Patent, Tryon County, NY, before 1776, a Loyalist. [PRO.AO13.12.397]

FIFE, ISOBEL, born in 1748, from Paisley, from Greenock to NY on the Lilly in May 1775. [PRO.T47.12]

FIMISTER, ALEXANDER, born in 1759, a servant from Morayshire, from Stornaway to Philadelphia on the <u>Clementina</u> July 1775. [PRO.T47.12]

FIMISTER, ELSPIA, born in 1761, a servant from Morayshire, from Stornaway to Philadelphia on the <u>Clementina</u> July 1775. [PRO.T47.12]

FIMISTER, JOHN, born in 1765, a servant from Avis, from Stornaway to Philadelphia on the <u>Clementina</u> in July 1775. [PRO.T47.12]

FIMISTER, MARGARET, born in 1763, a servant from Morayshire, from Stornaway to Philadelphia on the <u>Clementina</u> in July 1775. [PRO.T47.12]

FIMISTER, WILLIAM, born in 1729, a farmer from Avis, with Elizabeth his wife from Stornaway to Philadelphia on the <u>Clementina</u> July 1775. [PRO.T47.12]

FINLAY, JOHN, born in 1727, a laborer, enlisted in Captain Richard Gardiner's Company of the PA Regiment in 6 May 1749. [PaArch#5/1/29]

FINLAY or SINCLAIR, MARY, born 1684, indented in Chester Co., PA, 14 July 1697. [Sgen.29.1.12]

FINNELSTONE, JOHN, born in 1741, a wright from Paisley, via Greenock to Philadelphia on the <u>Sally</u> in Oct. 1774. [PRO.T47.12]

FISHER, ADAM, a merchant and mariner in NY, son of James Fisher a merchant in Inveraray, Argyll, 1755. [NAS.CS16.1.95/125/148][NAS.RD4.178.596]

FISHER, ARCHIBALD, born in 1740, a farmer from Breadalbane, from Greenock to NY on the <u>Lilly</u> in May 1775. [PRO.T47.12]

FISHER, DONALD, born in 1749, a farmer from Breadalbane, from Greenock to NY on the <u>Lilly</u> in May 1775. [PRO.T47.12]

FISHER, FINLAY, born in 1751, a farmer from Breadalbane, from Greenock to NY on the <u>Lilly</u> in May 1775. [PRO.T47.12]

FISHER, JOHN, born in 1730, a farmer from Breadalbane, from Greenock to NY on the <u>Lilly</u> in May 1775. [PRO.T47.12]

FITCHETT, JAMES, indentured servant, to East NJ 1684. [NJSA.EJD.A196]

FLEMING, WILLIAM, born in 1758, a weaver from Glasgow, via Greenock to NY on the <u>Commerce</u> in Feb.1774. [PRO.T47.12]

FLETT, ROBERT, indented in Chester Co., PA, Sept. 1695. [Sgen.29.1.11]

FORBES, ALEXANDER, a merchant in Philadelphia, son of James Forbes in Badyfurrow, Aberdeenshire, 1748. [NAS.CS16.1.80/85]

FORBES, ARTHUR, a merchant, from Aberdeen to East NJ on the <u>Exchange of Stockton</u> in Aug. 1683. [NAS.E72.1.10]

FORBES, GILBERT, a merchant in NY, probate 20 Apr. 1769 NY

FORBES, HUGH, a merchant in Philadelphia, admitted as a burgess of Montrose in 1764. [MBR]

FORBES, JANET, born in 1757, a servant from Inverness, from Stornaway to Philadelphia on the <u>Clementina</u> in July 1775. [PRO.T47.12]

FORBES, JOHN, from Barnla, Aberdeenshire, to East NJ in 1684, settled in Perth Amboy. [Insh#263][NJSA.EJD.Liber A249]

FORBES, JOHN, in Flushing, NY, husband of Margaret ...,
    will subscribed 20 Aug. 1666. [NY Wills, liber 7, fo.425]

FORBES, JOHN, in Hempstead, Queens Co., NY, wife Ann, children
    Alexander, William, Robert, and Agnes, probate 11 Mar. 1766 NY

FORBES, General JOHN, born at Pittencrieff, Fife, during 1710, died in
    Philadelphia on 11 Mar. 1759, buried in Christ Church, Philadelphia.
    [Christ Church g/s] [Pa.Gaz, 15.3.1759][AP#168]

FORBES, WILLIAM, to East NJ 1684. [NJSA.EJD.Liber A]

FORBES, WILLIAM, a widower, married Marytje Palding of NY, in the
    Dutch Reformed Church in NY on 29 Apr. 1713. [DRC]

FORD, GEORGE, indentured servant, to East NJ 1685. [NJSA.EJD.A226]

FORD, JOHN, a Covenanter, from Leith to East NJ on the Henry and
    Francis of Newcastle, in Aug. 1685. [RPCS#11.154]

FORFAR, MARGARET, born in 1756, a servant from Perthshire, from
    Leith to Philadelphia on the Friendship in May 1775. [PRO.T47.12]

FORMAN, JOHN, a Covenanter, transported from Leith to East NJ on the
    Henry and Francis in Aug. 1685. [RPCS#11.154]

FORREST, JAMES, son of Marion Forrest and brother of Margaret from
    Cambusnethan, a Covenanter, from Leith to East NJ in 1685.
    [RPCS.11.155]

FORREST, MARGARET, a Covenanter, daughter of Marion Forrest in
    Cambusnethan, Lanarkshire, transported from Leith to East NJ on
    the Henry and Francis of Newcastle in Aug. 1685. [RPCS#11.155]

FORRESTER, ANDREW, born in Dundee, claimed Long Island on behalf
    of Sir William Alexander, Earl of Stirling, there in Sep. 1647.
    [NYHM, Dutch#IV.442-446]

FORRET, MARY, from Leith to East NJ on the Henry and Francis in 1685.
    [NWI.1.422]

FORSTER, THOMAS, born in 1739, a shoemaker from Perthshire, with his
    wife Janet Tasie, from Greenock to NY on the Monimia in May
    1775. [PRO.T47.12]

FORSYTH, ARCHIBALD, born in 1753, a farmer from Duffus,
    Morayshire, from Stornaway to Philadelphia on the Clementina in
    July 1775. [PRO.T47.12]

FORSYTH, JAMES, a Covenanter from Annandale, Dumfriesshire, from
    Leith to East NJ on the Henry and Francis in Aug. 1685.
    [RPCS#11.154]

FORTUNE, WILLIAM, born in 1745, a saddler from Edinburgh, from
    Greenock to NY on the Monimia in May 1775. [PRO.T47.12]

FRANK, WILLIAM BOUGH, born in 1735, son of James Frank of
    Boughbridge, Colonel and Collector of NY, died in 1810. [Eccles g/s,
    Berwickshire]

FRASER, ALEXANDER, soldier of the 42nd Regiment, married Elinor
    Eiger, in NY on 7 Apr. 1763. [PCR]

FRASER, ALEXANDER, a soldier who settled in NY before 1773.
    [PCCol.1773/597]

FRASER, ANDREW, indented in Chester Co., PA, Sept. 1695.
    [Sgen.29.1.11]

FRASER, AUGUSTUS, a petitioner in NY 1701. [DNY.IV.934]

FRASER, CATHERINE, from Islay, Argyll, to NY aboard the Happy Return in July 1738 to have settled at Wood Creek on the Hudson River, by 1763 she was dead leaving a daughter named Elizabeth in NY for whom her cousin Robert Campbell in NY acted.[HSPC][NY.Col.MS#72/171]

FRASER, CHRISTIAN, born in 1749, a servant from Stornaway, Isle of Lewis, from Stornaway to Philadelphia on the Friendship in May 1774. [PRO.T47.12]

FRASER, DONALD, born in 1760, a servant from Dunbalich, from Stornaway to Philadelphia on the Clementina in July 1775. [PRO.T47/12]

FRASER, ELIZABETH, born in 1755, a servant from Ross-shire, from Stornaway to Philadelphia on the Friendship of Philadelphia in May 1774. [PRO.T47.12]

FRASER, GEORGE, a minister who was educated at Marischal College, Aberdeen, around 1728, to PA in 1732. [EMA#28]

FRASER, HUGH, a soldier, married Elizabeth Clark, in NY on 24 Feb.1763. [PCR]

FRASER, HUGH, a former Captain of the 78th [Fraser Highlanders] Regiment, land grant in NY on 26 Aug. 1773. [PCCol.#5.597]

FRASER, ISOBEL, born in 1754, a servant, from Stornaway to Philadelphia on the Friendship of Philadelphia in May 1774. [PRO.T47.12]

FRASER, JAMES, born in Inverness during 1739, a laborer, deserted from the 22nd Foot in NY during Apr. 1761.[NY.Merc. 11.5.1761]

FRASER, JAMES, acting Paymaster of the Royal Artillery in NY, 1782. [NAS.RD4.237.887][NAS.RS38.PR14/217]

FRASER, JANET, born in 1757, a servant from Inverness, from Stornaway to Philadelphia on the Clementina in July 1775. [PRO.T47/12]

FRASER, JEAN, born in 1750, a servant from Beauly, Inverness-shire, from Stornaway to Philadelphia on the Clementina in July 1775. [PRO.T47/12]

FRASER, Reverend JOHN, of Pitcalzean, born in 1658, a Covenanter, transported from Leith to East NJ on the Henry and Francis of Newcastle in Aug. 1685, settled in Woodsbury, Connecticut, married Jean Moffat, father of John,James, Catherine and Isobel, returned to Scotland in 1691, died on 7 Nov. 1711 in Alness, Ross and Cromarty.[RPCS#11.154][F#7.663][F#7.26]

FRASER, JOHN, indented in Chester Co., PA, 14 Dec.1698. [Sgen.29.1.13]

FRASER, JOHN, a former Captain of the 78th [Fraser Highlanders] Regiment, land grant in NY on 26 Aug. 1773. [PCCol.#5.597]

FRASER, JOHN, born in 1735, a farmer from Kinmily, with Christian his wife and children Janet, Margaret, William and Jean, from Stornaway to Philadelphia on the Clementina of Philadelphia in July 1775. [PRO.T47/12]

FRASER, MARY, from Islay to NY in 1739 aboard the Happy Return, by 1763 she was married and living in NY. [NY.Col.MS#72/171]

FRASER, MARY, born in 1757, a servant from Park, from Stornaway to Philadelphia on the Clementina of Philadelphia July 1775. [PRO.T47/12]

FRASER, MARY, born in 1758, a servant from Beauly, Inverness-shire, from Stornaway to Philadelphia on the Clementina in July 1775. [PRO.T47/12]

FRASER, ROBERT, with his wife Mary McLean, and children Charles, Colin, Sarah, Catherine, Mary and Isabel, from Islay, Argyll, aboard the Happy Return in June 1739 bound for NY and Wood Creek on the Hudson River, the surviving children were granted 250 acres on the Argyle Patent, NY, in 1763. [HSBC][NY.Col.MS#72/170]

FRASER, SIMON, son of William Fraser of Guisachan, Strathglass, Inverness-shire, and Margaret McDonnell, a former Captain of the 78th [Frasers Highlanders], settled in Bennington, NY, by 1773, married Isabella Grant, father of William, Angus and Simon, died in Albany, NY, during the 1770s. [HOFL][PCCol.5/597]

FRASER, WALTER, from Falshope, Selkirkshire, a tailor in NY, married Jemima Carter 1784, died in May 1793. [ANY#1.703]

FRASER, WILLIAM, born in 1743, educated at Marischal College, Aberdeen, from 1760 to 1764, a minister, to NJ in 1766, died in Trenton, New Jersey, on 6 July 1795. [EMA#28][MCA]

FRASER, WILLIAM, born in 1749, a wright from Inverness, with his wife Anne, from Stornaway to Philadelphia on Clementina in July 1775. [PRO.T47/12]

FRASER, WILLIAM, born in Inverness on 13 Mar. 1753, died in Troy, NY, on 25 Apr. 1826. [Old Troy g/s]

FRISSELL, ALEXANDER, indented in Chester Co., PA, 14 Dec.1698. [Sgen.29.1.13]

FROST, ROBERT, indentured servant, to East NJ 1684. [NJSA.EJD.A195]

FROST, THOMAS, indentured servant, to East NJ 1684. [NJSA.EJD.A195]

FROST, WILLIAM, indentured servant, to East NJ 1684. [NJSA.EJD.A195]

FULLARTON, JAMES, in Perth Amboy, East NJ 1696. [ActsPCCol.II.641]

FULLARTON, ROBERT, from Kinnaber, Montrose, Angus, from Montrose to East NJ on the Thomas and Benjamin in June 1684, settled in New Caesarea, NJ. [Insh#250][NAS.E72.16.13]

FULLARTON, THOMAS, from Kinnaber, Montrose, to East NJ in 1684. [NJSA.EJD.A187]

FULLARTON, Captain WILLIAM, born in Scotland, a master mariner in NY for 20 years, died in NY 5 Feb.1783, buried in Trinity Churchyard. [NY Gaz-Merc.10.2.1783]

FULTON, JAMES, born in 1753, a farmer from Inverness, from Greenock to NY on the George in May 1774. [PRO.T47.12]

FYFFE, GABRIEL, born at Loch Fannich, Ross and Cromarty, to America in 1783, settled in Albany, NY. [BLG#2865]

GAIRDNER, JOHN, a Covenanter from Monklands, Lanarkshire, transported to NY on 16 May 1684. [RPCS.8.516]

GALBREATH, JOHN, from Edinburgh, indented for 4 year's service in East NJ 12 August 1685. [NJSA.EJD.A252]

GALBRAITH, MARION, from Islay, Argyll, to NY aboard the Happy Return in 1739, by 1763 she was dead and her heir Duncan Reid claimed her right to a grant on the Argyle Patent, NY. [NY.Col.MS#72/171]

GALBREATH, THOMAS, a merchant from Glasgow or Knockdaw, Ayrshire, to NY by 1776, in London 1784.[NAS.CS17.1.3/114] [GA#B10.12.4][NAS.RD2.242/2.4][NAS.CS16.1.170]

GALLOWAY, ANDREW, landowner in East NJ 1683. [NJSA.EJD.A85/B321]

GALLOWAY, JOHN, born in 1749, a weaver from Paisley, via Greenock to Philadelphia on the Sally, master John Bruce, in Oct.1774. [PRO.T47.12]

GALLOWAY, JOHN, born in 1752, a joiner from Galloway, from Stranraer to NY on the Gale in May 1774. [PRO.T47.12]

GALLOWAY, PETER, husband of Isbell Rother, father of 9 month old Hannah, letters of administration, 20 June 1702 NY.

GALLOWAY, SARAH, born in 1754, from Galloway, from Stranraer to NY on the Gale of Whitehaven in May 1774.[PRO.T47.12]

GAMMEL, DAVID, Scottish resident of NY, drowned off Staten Island 17 Aug.1763, buried at Constable Point, NJ.[NY Merc. 29.8.1763]

GARDNER, JAMES, born in 1739, a farmer from Stirling, from Greenock to NY on the Lilly in Apr. 1775. [PRO.T47.12]

GARDNER, MATTHEW, 5'3", a carpenter, enlisted in the PA Regiment in Philadelphia on 11 May 1758. [Pa.Arch#5/1/154]

GARDNER, WILLIAM, born in 1750, a wright from Glasgow, from Greenock to Philadelphia on the Sally in Oct. 1774. [PRO.T47.12]

GARLAND, GEORGE, born in 1750, a barber from Glasgow, from Greenock to NY on the Lilly in Apr. 1775. [PRO.T47.12]

GAULEY, JEAN, born in 1749, from Dailly, Ayrshire, from Stranraer to NY on the Gale of Whitehaven in May 1774. [PRO.T47.12]

GEDDES, CHARLES, a watchmaker, son of James Geddes in Edinburgh, settled in NY before 1781. [NAS.RD2.232.86]

GEDDES, JOHN, to East NJ in 1684. [Insh#242][NJSA.EJD.A196]; took the Oath of Association in NY on 26 May 1696. [PRO.C213:OR470]; a petitioner in NY 1701. [DNY.IV.934]

GEDE, WILLIAM, from Burntisland, Fife, died on the Henry and Francis of Newcastle bound from Leith to East NJ during 1685, probate 31 Oct. 1685, Middlesex, NJ. [N.J. Archives 21/93]

GELLATLY, ALEXANDER, born in 1720, a minister from Perth, to America in Apr. 1753, settled in Octara, PA, died in Warwick, PA, on12 Mar. 1761. [SM#15.203][AP#278][UPC#654]

GELLIBRAND, ANDREW, minister, to NY on 9 June 1690 [Rawl.MS.A306.142]

GEMMELL, DAVID, merchant in NY, died in 1763. [N.Y.Postboy, 15 Sep. 1763]

GEMMILL, GRISSELL, a Covenanter, transported from Leith to East NJ on the <u>Henry and Francis of Newcastle</u> in Sep. 1685. [RPCS#11.154]

GENTLEMAN, MARGARET, from Montrose to East NJ on the <u>Thomas and Benjamin</u> in 1684. [NJSA.EJD.A196/B159]

GHAINE, CHRISTINE, indentured servant, to East NJ in 1685. [NJSA.EJD.A236]

GIBB, JOHN, transported from Leith to NY on 16 May 1684. [RPCS#8.709]

GIBB, JOHN, transported from Leith to East NJ on 30 July 1685. [RPCS#11.136][NJSA.EJD.A226]

GIBB, MARGARET, indentured servant, to East NJ 1685. [NJSA.EJD.A226]

GIBB, ROBERT, a merchant, Leith to NY on the <u>Hope</u> July 1681. [NAS.E72.15.32]

GIBB, ROBERT, indented in Chester County, PA, 14 Dec.1698. [Sgen.29.1.13]

GIBSON, COLIN, born in 1749, a tailor from Paisley, with his wife Janet, from Greenock to NY on the <u>Commerce</u> in Feb. 1774. [PRO.T47.12]

GIBSON, JOHN, born in 1755, a farmer from Galloway, from Stranraer to NY on the <u>Gale of Whitehaven</u> in May 1774. [PRO.T47.12]

GIBSON, MARGARET, born in 1750, from Galloway, from Stranraer to NY on the <u>Gale of Whitehaven</u> in May 1774. [PRO.T47.12]

GIBSON, MARGARET, born in 1758, a spinner from Paisley, via Greenock to NY on the <u>Commerce</u> in Feb. 1774. [PRO.T47.12]

GIBSON, WILLIAM, born in 1748, a weaver from Paisley,via Greenock to NY on the <u>Lilly</u> in Apr.1775. [PRO.T47.12]

GIBSON, WILLIAM, born in 1755, a weaver from Paisley,via Greenock to NY on the <u>Commerce</u> in Feb. 1774. [PRO.T47.12]

GIFFORD, ANDREW, born in Loanhead, Midlothian, during 1761, wife Margaret Noble, a cabinetmaker who settled NY in 1784, later a manufacturer and timber merchant in NY, died on 28 Nov. 1846. [ANY#2.299/97]

GILCHRIST, ALEXANDER, from Islay, Argyll, to NY in July 1738 aboard the <u>Happy Return,</u> to have settled at Wood Creek on the Hudson River, later settled in the Highlands of NY, in 1763 he was granted 200 acres on the Argyle Patent, NY. [HSPC][NY.Col.MS#72/170]

GILCHRIST, DUNCAN, with his wife Florence McAlister, and daughter Mary, from Islay, Argyll, aboard the <u>Happy Return</u> to NY in July 1738 to have settled at Wood Creek on the Hudson River, in 1763, he, his wife, and six children were granted 400 acres on the Argyle Patent. [HSPC][NY.Col.MS#72/170]

GILCHRIST, JAMES, Berkely Co., Carolina, pro. 16 Aug. 1693 NY

GILCHRIST, JOHN, from Islay, Argyll, to NY in July 1738 to have settled at Wood Creek on the Hudson River, later settled in the Highlands of NY, granted 200 acres on the Argyle Patent, NY, in 1763. [HSPC][NY.Col.MS#72/170]

GILCHRIST, Mrs MARION, a widow in Woodbridge, Middlesex County, NJ, probate 17 July 1745 NJ. [NJSA: Liber D/307]

GILCHRIST, MARGARET, by 1763 was living in NY when she was granted 150 acres on the Argyle Patent, NY. [NY.Col.MS#72/170]

GILCHRIST, ROBERT, a Covenanter from Dalgarnock, Nithsdale, Dumfries-shire,from Leith to East NJ on the Henry and Francis in Sep. 1685. [RPCS#11.154]

GILCHRIST, ROBERT, Woodbridge, Middlesex County, NJ, probate 25 Jan. 1733 NJ. [NJSA:Liber B/481]

GILDART, RICHARD, born in 1744, a dyer, from Whitehaven to NY on the Golden Rule in June 1774. [PRO.T47.12]

GILFILLAN, JOHN, a Covenanter, transported from Leith to East NJ on the Henry and Francis of Newcastle in Sep. 1685. [RPCS#11.154]; a witness in Woodbridge, NJ, 1697. [NAS.RD4.83.421]

GILKERSON, GAVIN, a Covenanter from Monklands, Lanarkshire, transported from Leith to NY on 16 May 1684. [RPCS#8.516]

GILLESPIE, GEORGE, born in Glasgow during 1683, a minister educated at Glasgow University from 1700 to 1704, in 1712, settled in New England, then NJ and finally at White Creek, Del., died on 2 Jan. 1760. [AP#171][SA#102][F#7.663]

GILLESPIE, NEIL, with his wife Mary McIlpheder, and sons Gilbert and Angus, from Islay, Argyll, in June 1739 bound for NY and Wood Creek on the Hudson River, in 1763 he, his wife and a daughter were granted 350 acres on the Argyle Patent, NY. [HSBC][NY.Col.MS#72/170]

GILLESPY, NEIL, yeoman on the Wallkill Precinct, Ulster County, NY, probate 31 Mar. 1769 NY

GILLESPIE, WILLIAM, a petitioner in NY 1701. [DNY.IV.934]

GILLESPIE, WILLIAM, born in 1754, a farmer from Stirling, from Greenock to NY on the Matty in May 1774. [PRO.T47.12]

GILLILAND, JOHN, a Covenanter, transported from Leith to East NJ in July 1685. [RPCS#11.329]

GILMOUR, ALEXANDER, born in 1729, a weaver from Glasgow, from Greenock to Philadelphia on the Magdalene, in Aug. 1774. [PRO.T47.12]

GIRVAN, CATHERINE, a Covenanter, transported from Leith to East NJ on the Henry and Francis in Aug. 1685. [RPCS#11.154]

GLASS, WILLIAM, born in 1758, a servant from Stornaway, Isle of Lewis, from Stornaway to Philadelphia on the Friendship in May 1774. [PRO.T47.12]

GLEN, ALEXANDER, born in 1738, a weaver from Paisley, with his wife Ann, from Greenock to NY on the Commerce in Feb. 1774. [PRO.T47.12]

GLEN, JOHANNES, a yeoman, Schenectady County, NY, pro. 26 Sep. 1706 NY. [Liber 7, fo.425]

GLEN, SANDER LEENDERTSEN, alias Alexander Lindsay, via Holland to the New Netherlands in 1639. [NYGBR.XIV]

GLENCROSS, WILLIAM, a merchant in NY, probate 9 Dec.1713 NY

GOODWIN, ROBERT, a Covenanter from Glasgow, transported from Leith to East NJ on the Henry and Francis of Newcastle, in Sep. 1685. [RPCS#11.155]

GORDON, ADAM, born in 1738, a laborer from Barwhinnoch, Twynholm, Kirkcudbrightshire, with his wife Ann Bryce and children Hugh, Agnes, and Mary, from Kirkcudbright to NY on the Adventure May 1774. [PRO.T47.12]

GORDON, ADAM, born in 1757, a farmer from Aberdeen, from Leith to Philadelphia on the Friendship of Philadelphia in May 1775. [PRO.T47.12]

GORDON, AGNES, born in 1754, from Queenshill, from Stranraer to NY on the Gale of Whitehaven in May 1774. [PRO.T47.12]

GORDON, ANNABELL, a Covenanter, transported from Leith to East NJ on the Henry and Francis of Newcastle in Sep. 1685. [RPCS#11.154]

GORDON, BESSIE, a Covenanter, transported from Leith to East NJ on the Henry and Francis of Newcastle in Sep. 1685. [RPCS#11.164]

GORDON, CHARLES, from Straloch, Aberdeenshire, to America in 1684, settled in Woodbridge, N.J., died 1698. [Insh#255][NJSA.EJD.A248]

GORDON, GEORGE, a merchant, from Leith to East NJ on the America Merchant of Stockton in Aug. 1685. [NAS.E72.15.32]; a planter in Perth Amboy, N.J., 1685. [NJSA.EJD.A248]

GORDON, JEAN, born 1680, indented in Chester County, PA, 1696. [Sgen.29.1.14]

GORDON, JOHN, DD, HM Chaplain in NY, was appointed as Bishop of Galloway on 4 Feb. 1688. [NAS.CH3.12.426]

GORDON, JOHN, son of Reverend Patrick Gordon and Marie Howie in Aberdeen, minister of Wilmington, died in 1705. [F#7.368]

GORDON, JOHN, Captain of an Independent Company in NY, 1763. [NAS.CS16.1.115]

GORDON, PATRICK, son of Patrick Alexander Gordon in Coull, Aberdeenshire, a minister who was educated at Marischal College, Aberdeen, around 1658, via Cowes, Isle of Wight, to NY on 28 Apr. 1702, died in Jamaica, Long Island, NY, during July 1703. [SCHR#14.145][EMA#30][SNQ#2.60]

GORDON, ROBERT, to America in 1684, settled in Elisabethtown, NJ. [Insh#251]; a petitioner in NY 1701. [DNY.IV.934]

GORDON, THOMAS, to East NJ in 1684, settled in Perth Amboy and in Elisabethtown, NJ. [Insh#264][NJSA.EJD.Liber A248]

GORDON, THOMAS, a Sergeant of the 55th Regiment, married Martha Needham, in New York on 29 Jan. 1763. [PCR]

GORDON, THOMAS, born around 1727, a former schoolmaster who escaped from Elizabeth jail, NJ, 11 May 1767. [NYMerc.18.5.1767]

GORDON, THOMAS, watchmaker, son of James Gordon in Garmouth, Morayshire, before 1770, settled in NY. [NAS.SH,18..5.1770]

GORDON, WILLIAM, born in 1752, a laborer from Twynholm, Kirkcudbright, from Kirkcudbright to NY on the Adventure in May 1774. [PRO.T47/12]

GORDON, ..., "a young gentleman from the Scottish Highlands", to NY on the Pearl died in NY City on 27Oct. 1773. [NYGaz.&Wkly.Mercury, 1.11.1773]

GORRIE, ROBERT, indentured servant, to East NJ 1684. [NJSA.EJD.A225]

GRAEME, Dr THOMAS, born on 20 Oct. 1688 at Balgowan, Perthshire, to
Philadelphia in 1717, married Ann Diggs in Christ Church,
Philadelphia, on12 Nov. 1719, a physician, Customs Collector of
Philadelphia, Chief Justice of PA, died on 4 Sep. 1772. [AP#176]

GRAEME, THOMAS, a soldier, to America before 1765, settled in NY.
[PCCol#4.818]

GRAHAM, ALEXANDER, a Covenanter, transported from Leith to East
NJ in Aug. 1685. [RPCS#11.136]

GRAHAM, ALEXANDER, from Islay, Argyll, to NY in July 1738 to have
settled at Wood Creek on the Hudson River, dead by 1763 but his
two sons in NY were granted 200 acres on the Argyle Patent, NY.
[HSPC][NY.Col.MS#72/170]

GRAHAM, ANGUS, in Albany, NY, 1676. [SPAWI.1698;988/iii]

GRAHAM, ANGUS, from Islay, Argyll, in Nov. 1740 bound for NY and
Wood Creek on the Hudson River, by 1763 he had settled with two
sons and three daughters in NY. [HSBC][NY.Col.MS#72/170]

GRAHAM, ARCHIBALD, from Islay, Argyll, in Nov. 1740 bound for NY
and Wood Creek on the Hudson River. [HSBC]

GRAHAM, AUGUSTINE, born in Edinburgh during 1672, son of James
Graham, Colonel of a Militia Regiment in NY in 1700.
[NY.Col.Docs.#1/362][SPAWI.1698/919]

GRAHAM, CATHERINE, from Islay, Argyll, in Nov. 1740 bound for
NY and Wood Creek on the Hudson River. [HSBC]

GRAHAM, EDWARD, took the Oath of Association in NY on 26 May
1696. [PRO.C213:OR470]

GRAHAM, EDWARD, NY, carpenter on the <u>Adventure</u> probate 11 Nov.
1715 NY

GRAHAM, EDWARD, with his wife Jean Fraser, from Islay, Argyll,in
Nov. 1740 bound for NY and Wood Creek on the Hudson River,
dead by 1763. [HSBC][NY.Col.MS#72.170]

GRAHAM, HUGH, son of Anne Graham in Westhall, Dunsyre,
Lanarkshire, to America, died Philadelphia, pro 1727 PCC

GRAHAME, ISOBEL, born 1757, a servant from Stornaway, Isle of Lewis,
to NY on the <u>Peace and Plenty</u> Nov. 1774. [PRO.T47.12]

GRAHAM, JAMES, born in Edinburgh during 1650, son of James Graham
and Isabella Auchenleck, from London on the <u>Blossom</u> on 27 May
1678, arrived in NY on 7 Aug. 1678, Attorney General of NY,
Assemblyman 1691-1699, Speaker from 1695 to 1699, Colonel of the
Westchester Regiment, as Recorder of NY he took the Oath of
Association in NY on 26 May 1696, [PRO.C213: OR470], died in
Westchester March 1701, pro. 3 Apr. 1701 NY

GRAHAM, JOHN, born in 1749, a farmer from Stirling, from Greenock to
NY on the <u>Matty</u> in May 1774. [PRO.T47.12]

GRAHAM, JOHN, born in 1752, a tailor from Glasgow, from Greenock to
NY on the <u>Lilly</u> in Apr. 1775. [PRO.T47.12]

GRAHAME, MARGARET, born in 1756, a servant from Stornaway, Isle
of Lewis, from Stornaway to NY on the <u>Peace and Plenty</u> in Nov.
1774. [PRO.T47.12]

GRAHAM, MARY, from Islay, Argyll, to NY in July 1738 to have settled at Wood Creek on the Hudson River, dead by 1763 when her children then living on the Manor of Livingston, NY, were granted 200 acres on the Argyle Patent, NY. [HSPC][NY.Col.MS#72/170]

GRAHAM, PEGGY, born in 1754, a servant from Caithness, from Leith to Philadelphia on the Friendship in May 1775. [PRO.T47.12]

GRAHAM, RICHARD, a merchant in NY, 1782. [NAS.CS17.1.1]

GRAHAM, THOMAS, a Covenanter from Skirling, Peebles-shire, transported from Leith to East NJ on the Henry and Francis in Sep. 1685. [RPCS#11.173]

GRANT, ALEXANDER, born in 1722, enlisted in Lieutenant Colonel James Burd's Company of the 2nd Battalion, the PA Regiment, on 3 Oct. 1757.   [Pa.Archives#5/1/190]

GRANT, ALEXANDER, born in 1733 son of Patrick Grant in Glenmoriston, Inverness-shire, to America as a soldier in 1754, later settled in Charlotte County, NY, marrried Therese Barthe, died at Gross Point, Detroit, on 18 Nov. 1813. [EA#5197][MAA]

GRANT, ALEXANDER, born in 1745, a farmer from Strathspey, from Greenock to NY on the George in May 1774. [PRO.T47.12]

GRANT, ALEXANDER, born in 1749 a farmer from Strathspey, from Greenock to NY on the George in May 1774. [PRO.T47.12]

GRANT, ALEXANDER, born in 1752, a cooper from Stirling, from Greenock to Philadelphia on the Sally in Oct. 1774. [PRO.T47.12]

GRANT, ALAN, born in 1752, a farmer from Strathspey, from Greenock to NY on the George of Greenock in May 1774.[PRO.T47.12]

GRANT, ANDREW, indentured servant, to East NJ 1685. [NJSA.EJD.A225]

GRANT, ANGUS, to America in 1774, settled on the Kingsborough Patent, NY, a Loyalist and soldier of the Royal Regiment of NY, later settled in Charlottenburg, Ontario. [DF.pp]

GRANT, ANN, widow of (1) Donald Grant and (2) Alexander McPherson, mother of Catherine McPherson, Farquhar McPherson, and Colin McPherson late Quartermaster of the 42nd Regiment, probate 3 Dec. 1770 NY

GRANT, ANN, born in 1756, from Strathspey, from Greenock to NY on the George of Greenock in May 1774. [PRO.T47.12]

GRANT, ARCHIBALD, to America in 1774, settled on the Kingsborough Patent, NY, a Loyalist and soldier of the Royal Regiment of NY from 1776 to 1783, later settled in Charlottenburg, Ontario. [DF.pp]

GRANT, DAVID, born in 1728, a farmer from Strathspey, from Greenock to NY on the George of Greenock in May 1774.[PRO.T47.12]

GRANT, DONALD, to America in 1773, settled on the Kingsborough Patent, NY, a soldier of the Royal Regiment of NY from 1776 to 1783, later settled in Charlottenburg, Ontario.[DF.pp]

GRANT, DONALD, a weaver in Croskey, to America in 1773, settled on the Kingsborough Patent, NY, a Loyalist and soldier of the Royal Regiment of NY from 1776 to 1783, later settled in Charlottenburg, Ontario. [DF.pp]

GRANT, DUNCAN, to America in 1773, settled on the Kingsborough Patent, NY, a Loyalist soldier of the Royal Regiment of NY from 1776 to 1783, later settled in Charlottenburg, Ontario. [DF.pp]

GRANT, FINLAY, to America in 1773, settled on the Kingsborough Patent, NY, a Loyalist soldier of the Royal Regiment of NY from 1776 to 1783, later settled in Charlottenburg, Ontario. [DF.pp]

GRANT, FRANCIS, at Albany and at Fort Edward, NY, in 1756-1758. [NAS.GD248.box 49, bundle 1]

GRANT, GEORGE, born in 1750, a farmer from Strathspey, from Greenock to NY on the George in May 1774. [PRO.T47.12]

GRANT, JAMES, born in 1727, a farmer from Strathspey, with his wife Ann and children Janet, Ann, James, Sally, Margery and Peter, from Greenock to NY on the George in May 1774. [PRO.T47.12]

GRANT, JAMES, born in 1727, a farmer from Strathspey, with his children Swithin, Betty, Mary, and Francis, from Greenock to NY on the George of Greenock in May 1774. [PRO.T47.12]

GRANT, JAMES, born in 1747, a farmer from Strathspey, from Greenock to NY on the George of Greenock in May 1774. [PRO.T47.12]

GRANT, JAMES, born in 1751, a farmer from Strathspey, from Greenock to NY on the George in May 1774. [PRO.T47.12]

GRANT, JEAN, born in 1757, from Strathspey, from Greenock to NY on the George in May 1774. [PRO.T47.12]

GRANT, JOHN, a soldier, married Mary Conner, in NY on 8 Jan. 1763. [PCR]

GRANT, JOHN, born in 1732, a farmer from Strathspey, with his wife Margery and children Peter, Donald, Elizabeth, Elspa, Nelly, Alexander and Janet, from Greenock to NY on the George in May 1774. [PRO.T47.12]

GRANT, JOHN, born in 1755, a farmer from Strathspey, from Greenock to NY on the George in May 1774. [PRO.T47.12]

GRANT, JOHN, to America in 1773, settled on the Kingsborough Patent, NY, a Loyalist and soldier of the Royal Regiment of NY, died in Canada during 1777. [DF.pp]

GRANT, JOHN DOW, a horse-thief from Perthshire, was transported from Greenock to NJ in Nov. 1764. [NAS.B59.26.116.39]

GRANT, LEWIS, born in 1742, a farmer from Strathspey, from Greenock to NY on the George in May 1774. [PRO.T47.12]

GRANT, MARGARET, born in 1760, a servant from Holm, Isle of Lewis, from Stornaway to Philadelphia on the Friendship in May 1774. [PRO.T47.12]

GRANT, MARY, born in 1762, a farmer from Strathspey, from Greenock to NY on the George in May 1774. [PRO.T47.12]

GRANT, NEIL, born 1684, indented in Bucks County, PA, Sept. 1697. [Sgen.29.1.14]

GRANT, PATRICK, born in 1745, a farmer from Strathspey, from Greenock to NY on the George in May 1774. [PRO.T47.12]

GRANT, PETER, to America in 1774, settled on the Kingsborough Patent, NY, a Loyalist soldier of the Royal Regiment of NY from 1776 to 1783, later settled in Charlottenburg, Ontario. [DF.pp]

GRANT, ROBERT, born 1727, a farmer from Strathspey, with his wife Mary and children Margaret, Ellen, Alexander, Elizabeth, Peter, Katherine and Donald, from Greenock to NY on the George in May 1774. [PRO.T47.12]

GRANT, ROBERT, born in 1745, a farmer from Strathspey, from Greenock to NY on the George in May 1774. [PRO.T47.12]

GRANT, VIOLET, from Kilmalcolm, via Greenock to Philadelphia on the Sally in Oct. 1774. [PRO.T47.12]

GRANT, WILLIAM, born in 1722, a farmer from Strathspey, with his wife Ann and children Barbara, William, Peter, Ann, Margery, Janet, John and Robert, from Greenock to NY on the George in May 1774. [PRO.T47.12]

GRANT, WILLIAM, a farmer from Glen Urquhart, Inverness-shire, from the Isle of Mull to NY on the Moore of Greenock in July 1774. [SM#36.445]

GRANT, ..., daughter of Reverend William Grant and Janet Grant [1743-1764] in Elgin, Morayshire, settled in Pittsburg, PA. [Rothes g/s, Morayshire]

GRAY, DANIEL, born in 1743, a farmer from Breadalbane, Perthshire, via Greenock to NY on the Lilly in May 1775. [PRO.T47.12]

GRAY, ISOBEL, born in 1749, servant from Coiduch, via Stornaway to NY on the Peace and Plenty in Nov. 1774. [PRO.T47.12]

GRAY, JAMES, former soldier during the French and Indian Wars, settled in Essex County, NJ, and later in Albany County, NY, Loyalist in 1776. [PRO.AO12.14.180]

GRAY, JAMES, born 1753, a blacksmith from Argyll, from Greenock to Philadelphia on the Magdalene in Aug. 1774. [PRO.T47.12]

GRAY, JOHN, from Leith to East NJ on the Henry and Francis in September 1685. [NWI.1.422]

GRAY, JOHN, a soldier, married Christian McDonald, in NY on 22 Jan. 1763. [PCR]

GREEN, PETER, from Islay, Argyll, in June 1739 bound for NY and Wood Creek on the Hudson River. [HSBC]

GREENLEES, JAMES, in Princeton, NJ, around 1769. [Hugh Simm papers, Princeton University]

GREIG, JENNY, born 1751, from Edinburgh, via Leith to Philadelphia on the Friendship of Philadelphia in May 1775. [PRO.T47.12]

GREIG, JOHN, a minister, to America 1766, settled in PA.[UPC#655]

GREIR, FERGUS, Covenanter from Dalry, transported from Leith to East NJ on the Henry and Francis in Sep. 1685. [RPCS#11.154]

GREIR, JAMES, a Covenanter, transported from Leith to East NJ on the Henry and Francis of Newcastle in Sep. 1685. [RPCS#11.154]

GRIERSON, WILLIAM, born in 1751, a smith from Galloway, from Greenock to Philadelphia on the Sally in May 1775. [PRO.47.12]

GRIEVE, ANN, born in 1758, from Edinburgh, from Greenock to NY on the Lilly in Apr. 1775. [PRO.T47.12]

GRIEVE, GEORGE, born 1684, indented in Chester Co., PA, 14 July 1697. [Sgen.29.1.12]

GRIGORSON, DUGALD, born1743, a farmer from Perthshire, with his wife Jane Blue, from Greenock to NY on the <u>Monimia</u> in May 1775. [PRO.T47.12]

GRISE, MARTHA, indentured servant, from Montrose to East NJ in 1684. [NJSA.EJD.A184]

GRUBB, THOMAS, and wife Jean, indentured servants to East NJ in 1684. [NJSA.EJD.A187/B351]

GUIN, CHRISTIAN, born in 1761, a servant from Galsik, Isle of Lewis, from Stornaway to Philadelphia on the <u>Friendship</u> in May 1775. [PRO.T47.12]

GUIN, JOHN, born in 1771, from Galsik, Isle of Lewis, from Stornaway to Philadelphia on the <u>Friendship</u> in May 1775. [PRO.T47.12]

GUTHRIE, JOHN, indentured servant, to East NJ 1684. [NJSA.EJD.A184]

GUTHRIE, SAMUEL, Woodbridge, NJ, administration 10 May 1686. [NJ Archives: EJD, Liber A/265]

HAGGART, DONALD, born 1714, a farmer from Glen Coe, with his wife Katherine Kippen, from Greenock to NY on the <u>Commerce</u> in Feb. 1775. [PRO.T47.12]

HAGGART, DONALD, born in 1749, a tailor from Glen Coe, Argyll, from Greenock to NY on the <u>Commerce</u> in Feb.1775. [PRO.T47.12]

HAGGART, DUNCAN, born 1743, a smith from Glen Coe, Argyll, via Greenock to NY on the <u>Commerce</u> in Feb. 1775. [PRO.T47.12]

HAGGART, JAMES, born 1685, indented in Burlington, N.J. 21 July 1697. [Sgen.29.1.14]

HAGGART, JAMES, born 1754, weaver from Glen Coe, Argyll, from Greenock to NY on the <u>Commerce</u> in Feb. 1775.[PRO.T47.12]

HAGGART, JOHN, born in 1751, a smith from Glen Coe, Argyll, from Greenock to NY on the <u>Commerce</u> in Feb. 1775,settled on the Kingsborough Patent, NY, and later, as a Loyalist, in Charlottenburg, Ontario . [PRO.T47.12]

HAGGART, KATHERINE, born 1759, servant from Glen Coe, Argyll, Greenock to NY on the <u>Commerce</u> in Feb.1775. [PRO.T47.12]

HAGGART, ROLAND, [?], {"Roelant Hackwaert"}, a tobacco planter in NY on 3 July 1638, [NY Hist.MS.Dutch; Register of the Provincial Secretary, 1638-1642]; a young man from "Brandtfort in Schotland" who married Janneken Jans from Amsterdam in the Reformed Dutch Church, New Amsterdam, 4 Nov. 1640.[DRC]

HAGGART, WILLIAM, officer of the 77th Foot in the French and Indian wars, land grant near Albany, NY, in 1765. [NAS.GD237.21.21]

HAIG, Mrs MARY, indentured servant, to East NJ 1684. [NJSA.EJD.A]

HAIG, OBADIAH, in NY in 1699. [NAS.RD2.82.739/RD4.85.1]

HAIG, REBECCA, indentured servant, to East NJ 1684.[NJSA.EJD.A]

HAIG, WILLIAM, born on 28 Mar. 1646, second son of David Haig of Bemersyde, Berwickshire, married Mary Lawrie, daughter of Gavin Lawrie in London during 1673, died in West NJ on 29 July 1688. ['Haigs of Bemersyde', p.441,Edinburgh, 1881]

HALDANE, DAVID, to NY as a soldier, settled there in 1765. [PCCol.1765/818]

HALL, DAVID, born in Edinburgh during 1714, a printer who settled in Philadelphia by 1743, partner of Benjamin Franklin, died on 24 Dec. 1772. [DAB#8.123][AP#187]

HALLIDAY, THOMAS, a minister, educated at Edinburgh University in 1702, to East NJ in 1710, settled there and in Del., dead by May 1722. [EMA#31]

HALYBURTON, MARGARET, indentured servant, to East NJ 1684. [NJSA.EJD.A195]

HALYBURTON, WILLIAM, a minister who to Virginia in 1766, later in NY. [EMA#32][PCCol.4.819]

HAMILTON, ANDREW, to East NJ 1685, Deputy Governor ENJ 1687-1692, Gov. of NJ 1692-1703, Dep. Gov, of PA, 1701-1703, died 26 April 1703. [Insh#179]

HAMILTON, ANDREW, to America 1700, lawyer in PA. [AP]

HAMILTON, ARCHIBALD, to America as a soldier, settled in NY during 1765. [PCCol.1765/818]

HAMILTON, JAMES, born in 1733, a farmer from Paisley, via Greenock to NY on the George of Greenock in May 1774, possibly settled in New Perth north of Albany. [PRO.T47.12][Hugh Simm papers, Princeton University]

HAMILTON, JAMES, son of William Hamilton in Smailholemill, a surgeon in NY, cnf 22 Mar. 1781. [NAS.CC8.8.126]

HAMILTON, JOHN, ("Johan Hamelton"), a soldier from Hamelton (Hamilton, Lanarkshire, Scotland?), from the Netherlands to the New Netherlands (later NY) on the Spotted Cow on 15 Apr. 1660. [NYGBR, Vol.94][NYCol.MS#XIII/88]

HAMILTON, JOHN, a gypsy who was transported from Greenock to NY on 21 Oct. 1682. [NAS.HH11]

HAMILTON, ROBERT, Middletown, East NJ, 1680s. [NJSA.EJD/A]

HAMILTON, WILLIAM, a merchant from NY trading in Del. 1676. [NY.Hist.MS.Dutch.XX/XXI, 102]

HAMILTON, WILLIAM, born in 1745, a farmer from Kilbride, from Greenock to Philadelphia on the Sally in Oct. 1774. [PRO.T47.12]

HAMMEL, ARCHIBALD, from Islay, Argyll, in Nov. 1740 bound for NY and Wood Creek on the Hudson River. [HSBC]

HAMMEL, MARY, from Islay, Argyll, in Nov. 1740 bound for New York and Wood Creek on the Hudson River, by 1763 she was dead but her daughter living in the Highlands of NY was granted 150 acres on Argyle Estate, N.Y. [HSBC][NY.Col.MS#72/1170]

HAMMEL, MERRAN, from Islay, Argyll, to NY in July 1738 to have settled at Wood Creek on the Hudson River.[HSPC]

HAMMEL, MURDOCH, from Islay, Argyll, to NY in July 1738 to have settled at Wood Creek on the Hudson River, by 1763 he had settled on the Island of Jamaica. [HSPC][NY.Col.MS#72/170]

HAMPTON, JANET, born 1668, daughter of John Hampton, to East NJ 1684. [NJSA.EJD.A183]

HAMPTON, JOHN, jr., married Martha Brown in Shrewsbury, ENJ, 1687. [NJSA.EJD]

HANCOCK, JOHN, a gardener from East Lothian, from Leith to East NJ in 1683. [NJSA.EJD.Liber A256/280/434]; pro.1702 NJ

HANCOCK, JOHN, from Edinburgh, died at sea, pro.18 Nov. 1686 NJ.

HANNA,WILLIAM, a Covenanter from the Borders, was transported from Leith to East NJ aboard the <u>Henry and Francis</u> on 5 Sep. 1685. [RPCS#11.94]

HANNAH, JAMES, born in 1757, a tailor from Gatehouse, Kirkcudbrightshire, from Stranraer to NY on the <u>Gale of Whitehaven</u> in May 1774. [PRO.T47.12]

HANNAY, ANDREW, born during 1733 in Galloway, a cooper from Gatehouse, Kirkcudbrightshire, with his wife Catherine and children Elizabeth, John,James, and Andrew, from Stranraer to NY on the <u>Gale</u> 7 May 1734, died in Albany County, NY, during 1808. [PRO.T47.12][HS#192]

HARDIE, ALEXANDER, son of Robert Hardie in Aberdeen, indentured servant to East NJ 1684. [Insh#252][NJSA.EJD.A]

HARDIE, ROBERT, a merchant from Aberdeen, to America in 1684, settled in Elisabethtown, East NJ, father of William, Alexander, John, Elspeth, James and Andrew. [Insh#252/263]

HARDIE, WILLIAM, son of Robert Hardie in Aberdeen, to East New Jersey in 1684, died 1684. [Insh#252][NJSA.EJD.A]

HARLEY, ADAM, born in 1763, a weaver from Glasgow, from Greenock to NY on the <u>Commerce</u> in Feb. 1774. [PRO.T47.12]

HARPER, JOHN, a Covenanter from Fenwick, Ayrshire, tranported to NY(?) in 1684. [RPCS.8.516/710]

HARPER, THOMAS, indented in Chester County, PA, 5 Aug.1697. [Sgen.29.1.13]

HARRIS, JOHN, from Leith to East NJ on the <u>Henry and Francis</u> in 1685. [NWI.1.423]

HARRIS, ROBERT, from Edinburgh, married Maria Van Huysen from Albany, in the Dutch Reformed Church, NY, 7 Dec. 1695. [DRC]

HARDIE, ROBERT, born on 18 Feb. 1727, married Martha Cogill, died in Philadelphia on 23 Dec. 1798. [AP#203]

HARRIS, ROBERT, from Ayr then in Philadelphia, 1771. [NAS.CS16.1.146]

HART, JOHN, a merchant in Salem, possibly from Glasgow, probate 27 Apr. 1726 NJ. [NJ Archives, Liber 2/334]

HART, JOHN, born in 1743, a mason from Glasgow, from Greenock to NewYork on the <u>Monimia</u> in May 1775. [PRO.T47.12]

HARVEY, ALEXANDER, born 1746, a farmer from Gargunnock, Stirlingshire, Greenock to NY on the <u>Matty</u> in May 1774, landed in NY on 22 July 1774, settled in Barnet, NH. [PRO.T47.12]

HARVEY, DANIEL, born 1744, a gardener, with his wife Mary, via Liverpool to Philadelphia on the <u>Boston Packet</u> in May 1774. [PRO.T47.9/11]

HARVIE, JOHN, a Covenanter from Dalserf, Lanarkshire, husband of Marion Forrest, was transported from Leith to East NJ on the <u>Henry and Francis of Newcastle</u> on 5 Sep. 1685. [RPCS#11.329]

HARVEY, WILLIAM, a merchant skipper in NY from 1756 to 1775, a Loyalist who moved to Shelbourne, Nova Scotia, in Nov. 1783. [PRO.AO13.24.254/261]

HASTIE, ROBERT, a merchant from Glasgow then in NY by 1781, cnf 4 Aug. 1796 Edinburgh. [NAS.CC8.8.-] [NAS.CS16.1.183]

HATMAKER, MAGDALENE, indentured servant, to East NJ 1685. [NJSA.EJD.A225]

HATTRICK, PETER, born around 1755, a merchant from Greenock, in NY 1795, died in there on 11 June 1832. [DGC:31.7.1832][NAS.RS54.PR36/1231]

HAUTON, ANDREW, to East NJ by 1688. [NJSA.EJD.B403]

HAY, HENRY, born in 1739, a joiner from Stirling, from Greenock to NY on the Lilly in May 1775. [PRO.T47.12]

HAY, JAMES, born in 1758, a joiner from Edinburgh, from Leith to Philadelphia on the Friendship in May 1775. [PRO.T47.12]

HECKLE, ROBERT, born in 1740, a mason from Kirkcudbright, with his wife Margaret McKitteich, and children David, William, Thomas and Robert, from Kirkcudbright to NY on the Adventure May 1774. [PRO.T47.12]

HENDERSON, ALEXANDER, born in 1751, a tailor from Morayshire, from Stornaway to Philadelphia on the Clementina of Philadelphia in July 1775. [PRO.T47.12]

HENDERSON, JAMES, born in 1722, a tailor, enlisted in Captain John Shannon's Company of the PA Regiment on 11 July 1746. [PaArch#5/1/11]

HENDERSON, JAMES, a wright, from Greenock to NY on the Matty on 25 Mar. 1773, settled in Ryegate, NH.[PRO.T47.12]

HENDERSON, JAMES, son of William Henderson in Smailholmill, a surgeon of the Royal Artillery of NY, cnf 22 Mar. 1781Edinburgh.

HENDERSON, JOHN, Covenanter from Ruchoard, from Leith to East NJ on the Henry and Francis 5 Sep. 1685, landed 7 Dec.1685. [RPCS#11.164/289]

HENDERSON, JOHN, born in 1709, to America as a soldier before 1762, settled in Fishkill, NY, died there on 13 Dec. 1811. [SM#74.316]

HENDERSON, MATTHEW, born on 25 Apr. 1735, son of Matthew Henderson in Orwell, Kinross-shire, a minister, in 1758, settled in Del. and in Charteris, PA, died in Pittsburgh, Washington County, PA on 2 Oct. 1795. [UPC#654][GM#65/1112]

HENDERSON, ROBERT, born in 1749, a gentleman from Lasswade, from Greenock to NY on the Monimia in May 1775. [PRO.T47.12]

HENDRY, ALEXANDER, born in 1745, a saddler from Edinburgh, via Greenock to NY on the Monimia in May 1775. [PRO.T47.12]

HENDRIE, GEORGE, a merchant, from Leith to East NJ on the Henry and Francis of Newcastle in Aug. 1685. [NAS.E72.15.32]

HENDRY, JAMES, born in 1755, a servant from Morayshire, from Stornaway to Philadelphia on the Clementina in July 1775. [PRO.T47.12]

HENDRY, ROBERT, born in 1752, a tailor from Dundee, from Greenock to NY on the George in May 1774. [PRO.T47/12]

HEPBURN, JOHN, indentured servant, to East NJ 1684.
[NJSA.EJD.A/B403]

HERCULES, JAMES, indented in Chester County, PA, 3 Oct.1693.
[Sgen.29.1.11]

HERCULES, WILLIAM, born 1750, a weaver from Paisley, via Greenock
to NY on the Commerce in Feb. 1774. [PRO.T47.12]

HERIOT, DAVID, indentured servant, to East NJ 1685. [NJSA.EJD.A225]

HERRIOT, WILLIAM, born 1753, a baker from Gorbals, Glasgow,
Greenock to NY or GA on Christy in May 1775. [PRO.T47.12]

HERRON, JAMES, born 1734, a mason from Gatehouse of Fleet, with
children Samuel, Robert, James and John, from Dumfries to NY on
the Gale of Whitehaven, in May 1774. [PRO.T47.12]

HODGE, JOHN, a Covenanter and an armorer, son of Robert Hodge in
Glasgow, was transported from Leith to East NJ on the Henry and
Francis of Newcastle, on 5 Sep. 1685. [RPCS#11.155]

HODGE, ROBERT, born in Edinburgh during 1746, to Philadelphia in
1770, later a bookseller in NY, died 23 Aug. 1813.[ANY#1.170]

HODGZART, WILLIAM, a merchant in NY, 1783. [NAS.CS17.1.2]

HOGG, ANDREW, a gypsy, was transported from Greenock to NY on 21
Oct. 1682. [NAS.HH11]

HOGG, GRISSELL, indentured servant, to East NJ 1685.
[NJSA.EJD.A225]

HOGG, JOHN, indentured servant, to East NJ 1685. [NJSA.EJD.A225]

HOGG, ROBERT, born in East Lothian, to North Carolina in 1756, a
merchant in Wilmington, a Loyalist who died in NY during 1779.
[James Hogg Papers, Southern Historical Collection, Uni.NC]

HOGIE, JANET, born in 1760, a spinner from Paisley, from Greenock to
NY on the Commerce in Feb. 1774.[PRO.T47.12]

HOLLAND, GABRIEL, to East NJ in 1684. [NJSA.EJD.B159]

HOLLIDAY, THOMAS, indentured servant, to East NJ 1684.
[NJSA.EJD.A255]

HOLMES, FRANCIS, a petitioner in NY 1701.[DNY.IV.934]

HOME, CHARLES, a merchant in NY during 1730s. [NAS.GD1.384.3]

HONEYBULL, ANN, born in 1741, a spinner from Glasgow, from
Greenock to NY on the Commerce in Feb. 1774. [PRO.T47.12]

HONEYMAN, ROBERT, son of Rev. James Honeyman in Kinneff,
Kincardineshire, a minister who in 1702, settled in NY. [F#7.663]

HOOD, ADAM, a Covenanter who was transported from Leith to East NJ
on the Henry and Francis of Newcastle on 5 Sep. 1685, landed 7
Dec.1685.   [RPCS#11.154][NWI.1.423]

HOOD, PETER, born 1687, indented i Chester County, PA, 14 July 1697.
[Sgen.29.1.2]

HOOKS, JANE, indentured servant, to East NJ 1684. [NJSA.EJD.A187]

HOOKS, ROBERT, indentured servant, to East NJ 1684.
[NJSA.EJD.A187]

HOPE. ARCHIBALD, son of Henry Hope a Scots merchant in the
Netherlands, settled in PA 1677. [PA. Hist. Soc. Ms]

HORNE, SOPHIA, from Edinburgh, settled in NJ before 1747.
[NJSA.EJ.Deeds, liber E, fo.101]

HOSSACK, JANET, indented in Chester County, PA, 14 Dec.1698. [Sgen.29.1.13]

HOSSACK, SIMON, born in Avoch, Ross-shire, a minister, educated at Aberdeen University in 1779, to NY, married Catherine Carr (1767-1795) in Goshen, NY, settled in Johnstown, NY, during 1790. ["Some Pioneer Women of Johnstown", Johnstown, 1937]

HOUSTOUN, JAMES, born in 1747, a farmer from Strathspey, from Greenock to NY on the George in May 1774. [PRO.T47.12]

HOUSTOUN, WILLIAM, a merchant burgess of Whithorn, Kirkcudbrightshire, and a burgess and guildsbrother of Glasgow, a merchant in Newcastle, Del., died 1707, probate 11 Dec. 1711 Newcastle, Del.. [DSA.Misc.1/178]

HOWET, MARY, born in 1749, a spinner from Glasgow, from Greenock to NY on the Commerce in Feb. 1774. [PRO.T47.12]

HOWIE, ALEXANDER, son of Reverend John Howie in Birse, Aberdeenshire, a minister who was educated at Marischal College, Aberdeen, around 1719, to PA in 1730. [EMA#34]

HOWIE, DAVID, born in 1737, a farmer who from Greenock to NY or GA on the Christy in May 1775. [PRO.T47.12]

HUE, THOMAS, an indentured servant, to East NJ 1684. [NJSA.EJD.A196]

HUGHIN, JOHN, indented in Chester County, PA, 14 Dec.1698. [Sgen.29.1.13]

HULL, RICHARD, a merchant in Philadelphia, admitted as a burgess and guilds-brother of Edinburgh on 25 July 1744. [EBR]

HUME, CATHERINE, an indentured servant, to East NJ 1684. [NJSA.EJD.A196]

HUME, JANE, an indentured servant, to East NJ 1684. [NJSA.EJD.A196]

HUME, JOHN, an indentured servant, to East NJ 1684. [NJSA.EJD.A196]

HUME, ROBERT, an indentured servant, to East NJ 1684. [NJSA.EJD.A196]

HUNTER, ALEXANDER, with Anna Anderson his wife, and children William, Alexander, and Janet, from Islay, Argyll, in June 1739 bound for NY and Wood Creek on the Hudson River, dead by 1763 when his son and daughter were granted 200 acres on the Argyle Patent, NY.[HSBC][NY.Col.MS#72/170]

HUNTER, DAVID, born in 1751, a shipmaster from Ayr, from Greenock to Philadelphia on the Sally in Oct. 1774. [PRO.T47.12]

HUNTER, JAMES, born in 1746, a housewright from Kirkmichael, with Janet McKinnel his wife and son John, from Stranraer to NY on the Jackie of Glasgow, on 31 May 1775. [PRO.T47.12]

HUNTER, ROBERT, an Army officer and administrator, Governor of NY from 1710 to 1719, died in 1734.[NAS.GD135/141/1/126]

HUNTER, SAMUEL, born in Dumfries during 1685, an indentured servant who absconded from William Bradford in NY during 1735. [NY Gaz., 2.6.1735]

HUNTER, SANDY, born ca1680, indented in Chester County, PA 1696. [Sgen.29.1.4]

HUSK, THOMAS, born in 1719, enlisted as a drummer in Captain Richard Gardiner's Company of the PA Regiment on 10 May 1749. [PaArch#5/1/29]

HUTCHEON ALEXANDER, born in 1750, a wright from Stirling, from Greenock to NY on the <u>Monimia</u> in May 1775. [PRO.T47.12]; a wright in NY 1796. [NAS.CS17.1.15/343]

HUTCHISON, DANIEL, shipmaster in NY around 1752, grandson of Robert Tennant, shoemaker in Leith. [NAS.RD3.211/2.196][NAS.CS16.1.88]

HUTCHISON, Mr JOHN, a prisoner in Edinburgh Tolbooth, exiled to Holland on 8 July 1682, died at Sandy Hook, NJ (?), in 1684. [NAS.HH11]

HUTCHESON, JOHN, a farmer and a Covenanter from Hairlaw, Dumfries-shire, husband of Marion Weir, was transported from Leith to East NJ on the <u>Henry and Francis of Newcastle</u>, on 5 Sep. 1685. [RPCS#11.155]

HUTCHISON, JOHN, a sergeant of the 55th Regiment, married Jane Neal, a widow, in NY on 15 July 1763. [PCR]

HUTCHISON, JOHN, born in 1754, a weaver from Paisley, via Greenock to NY on the <u>Commerce</u> in Feb. 1774. [PRO.T47.12]

HUTCHISON, WILLIAM, born 1744, baker from Nairn, fromStornaway to Philadelphia on the <u>Friendship</u> in May 1774. [PRO.T47.12]

HUTCHING, JOHN, a petitioner in NY 1701. [DNY.IV.934]

HUTTON, ALEXANDER, in East NJ by 1690. [NJSA,EJD.B132]

HYSLOP, ROBERT, a merchant in NY by 1773, died 22 Sept.1798. [ANY.2.63]

IMBRIE, JOHN, a merchant in Falkland, Fife, then in NY, 1778. [NAS.CS16.1.174]

INGLIS, JOHN, an indentured servant, to East NJ 1685. [NJSA.EJD.A226]

INGLIS, JOHN, born in Scotland during 1708, via Nevis in the West Indies to Philadelphia in 1736, a merchant and public official there, married Catherine McCall on 16 Oct. 1736, died on 20 Aug. 1753 and was buried in Christ Church graveyard, Philadelphia. [PaGaz: 23.8.1775][PA#210]

INGLIS, JOHN, sutler and merchant in NY around 1780. [NAS.GD1.46/20-1]

INGLIS, THOMAS, a Presbyterian in NY 1724. [NAS.CH1.2.49.55]

INNES, ALEXANDER, from Aberdeenshire, a schoolmaster educated at Aberdeen University, military chaplain in NY 1686, [SPAWI.1686/896]; in 1693 to New England, died in Elisabethtown, NJ, in Aug. 1713.[APB#2.118]; a cleric in Monmouth County, NJ, pro. 27 July 1713 N.J.

INNES, GILBERT, from Aberdeen. Pro.1685 NJ. [NJSA.EJD.A261]

INNES, GYLLES, a widow in Perth Amboy, NJ, Administration 13 Oct.1687 NJ. [NJ Archives 21/102]

INNES, KATHERINE, born in 1755, a servant from Caithness, from Leith to Philadelphia on the <u>Friendship of Philadelphia</u> in May 1775. [PRO.T47.12]

INNES, or JOHNSTON, MARGARET, late of Newburgh, Aberdeenshire, probate 25 Jan. 1727 NJ [NJ Archives, Liber B/24]

IRELAND, DAVID, a smith, with his family, from Wigtown to PA in 1773. [PRO.T1.500/234]

IRVING, WILLIAM, born in Shapinsay, Orkney Islands, on 31 Aug. 1731, married Sarah Sanders on 18 May 1761, settled in NY in 1763, father of Ebenezer and Washington. [BLG#2762]

JACK, ISOBEL, born in 1761, servant from Kilsain, via Stornaway to Philadelphia on the Clementina in July 1775.[PRO.T47/12]

JACK, JANET, born in 1752, a servant from Morayshire, from Stornaway to Philadelphia on the Clementina in July 1775. [PRO.T47/12]

JACK, JOHN, born in 1745, a servant from Morayshire, from Stornaway to Philadelphia on the Clementina in July 1775.[PRO.T47/12]

JACK, ROBERT, born 1684, indented in Chester County, PA, 14 July 1697. [Sgen.29.1.12]

JACKSON, ANNABEL, a Covenanter, transported from Leith to East NJ on the Henry and Francis on 5 Sep.1685. [RPCS#11.154]

JACKSON, MARGARET, born in 1754, from Edinburgh, from Greenock to NY on the Lilly in Apr. 1775. [PRO.T47.12]

JACKSON, THOMAS, a Covenanter, transported from Leith to East NJ on the Henry and Francis on 5 Sep. 1685. [RPCS#11.159]

JACKSON, WILLIAM, a Covenanter imprisoned in Edinburgh Tolbooth, transported from Leith to East NJ on the Henry and Francis on 5 Sep. 1685; took the Oath of Association in New York on 26 May 1696; a cordiner in NY by 1702.
[RPCS#11.159][NAS.HH11][PRO.C213.OR470] [WMQ#47.1.75]

JAFFREY, JOHN, from Stirling, a merchant in Salem Town, probate 24 Feb. 1704 NJ. [NJ Archives, Liber 1/11]

JAMIESON, ARCHIBALD, transported from Leith to East NJ in July 1685. [RPCS#11.131]

JAMIESON, DANIEL, a will witness in NY on 25 Apr. 1700, [NY Wills, Liber 1/346]

JAMIESON, DAVID, a Covenanter, transported from Leith to NY on 19 May 1684. [RPCS#8.516]; clerk to the Secretary, married Maria Hardenbroeck from NY, in the Dutch Reformed Church in NY on 7 May 1692.[DRC.Reg.]; took the Oath of Association on 26 May 1696. [PRO.C213: OR469/1]; a petitioner in NY 1701. [DNY.IV.934]

JAMIESON, JOHN, from Thornhill, Dumfries-shire, a minister in Bathgate, West Lothian, from 1776 to 1783, to America, a minister in Newville, PA, from 1784 to 1792, and in Hannastown, PA, from 1792 to 1797, died on 1 July 1821. [UPC#1.599]

JAMIESON, MARY, born in 1750, a spinner from Paisley, via Greenock to NY on the Commerce in Feb. 1774. [PRO.T47.12]

JANS [?], MARGARET, from Scotland, married Jean du Pre Van Coma, in the Dutch Reformed Church in NY on 28 May 1655. [DRC]

JEFFREY, WILLIAM, son of James Jeffrey in Perth, with his daughter Jean to Philadelphia, died there in 1758. [NAS.SH.30.9.1758]

JOHNSON, Mrs EUPHAM, Middlesex County, NJ, probate 13 Nov. 1764
NJ. [NJSA: Liber H/379]

JOHNSON, JAMES, indented in Chester County, PA, Sep.1695.
[Sgen.29.1.11]

JOHNSTON, ANDREW, a councillor, died in Amboy, NJ, on 24 June 1762
[SM#24.451]

JOHNSTON, ARCHIBALD, with his wife Christine Johnston, from Islay,
Argyll, to NY in July 1738 to have settled at Wood Creek on the
Hudson River, by 1763 he was dead, his widow had married Daniel
McAlpine, Malcolm Johnston a son and his brother and three sisters
were allocated 250 acres on the Argyle Patent, NY. [HSPC]

JOHNSTON, GEORGE, a Covenanter from Midcalder, Midlothian, from
Leith to East NJ aboard the Henry and Francis on 5 Sep. 1685.
[RPCS#11.154]

JOHNSTON, GEORGE, from Kirriemuir, Angus, was sought for in
NYduring 1782. [NY.Gaz.& Wkly.Merc., 20.5.1782]

JOHNSTON, ISABEL, indentured servant, to East NJ 1684.
[NJSA.EJD.A187]

JOHNSTONE, JAMES, from Spotswood, Berwickshire, to East NJ in
1684, settled in Pitscataway, NJ. [Insh#264][NJSA.EJD.A249]

JOHNSTON, JEREMIAH, in NY 1809. [NAS.CS17.1.28/482]

JOHNSTON, JOHN, an apothecary in Edinburgh, son of William Johnston
of Labrioblan, from Leith to East NJ on the Henry and Francis of
Newcastle on 5 Sep. 1685.
[Insh#242][NAS.RD4.67.97][NJSA.EJD.B326]

JOHNSTON, JOHN, married Elizabeth Lamb, in the Dutch Reformed
Church in NY on 6 July 1712. [DRC]

JOHNSTON, JOHN, born in 1749, a cooper from Coupar Angus,
Perthshire, from Greenock to Philadelphia on the Magdalene in Aug.
1774.[PRO.T47.12]

JOHNSTON, WILLIAM, born 1681, indented in Chester County, PA,
1696. [Sgen.29.1.14]

JOND[?], JAMES, from Scotland, married Jeanne Nicols, widow of James
Jenkin, in the Dutch Reformed Church in NY on 28 Sep. 1688.[DRF]

KEIR, ALEXANDER, born 1713, absconded from J. Warrell in Trenton,
NJ, in 1737. [NYGaz.12.12.1737]

KEITH, ALEXANDER, was transported from Greenock to NY on 21 Oct.
1682. [NAS.HH11]

KEITH, GEORGE, born during 1638 in Peterhead, Aberdeenshire, a
minister who was educated at Marischal College, Aberdeen, around
1658, to Philadelphia, settled in Perth Amboy, NJ, and in Maryland,
died in England during 1714.
[Insh#171][SNQ.1.60][NJSA.EJD.A236/B321]

KEITH, ISABEL, to East NJ in 1684. [NJSA.EJD.A]

KEITH, JAMES, born in 1719, a gentleman who enlisted in Captain
Richard Gardiner's Co. of the PA Regiment on 5 May 1749.
[PaArch#5/1/29]

KELLY, ALEXANDER, born in 1752, a laborer from Galloway, from Stranraer to NY on the <u>Gale</u> in May 1774. [PRO.T47.12]

KELLY, ANNE, born in 1760, a servant from Contin, Ross and Cromarty, from Stornaway to Philadelphia on the <u>Clementina</u> in July 1775. [PRO.T47.12]

KELLIE, JOHN, a Covenanter from Dunbar, was transported from Leith to East NJ on the <u>Henry and Francis of Newcastle</u>, on 5 Sep. 1685. [RPCS#10.129]

KELLIE, KATHERINE, a Covenanter, was transported from Leith to East NJ on the <u>Henry and Francis of Newcastle,</u> on 5 Sep. 1685. [RPCS#11.154]

KELLY, PETER, born in 1734, from Glen Luce, Wigtownshire, with his wife Ann Adair and children Jean, Elizabeth, and Alexander, from Stranraer to New York on the <u>Gale </u>in May 1774. [PRO.T47.12]

KELLY, ROBERT, born in 1736, from Galloway, with his wife Mary and Margaret, James and Jean their children, from Stranraer to NY on the <u>Gale of Whitehaven,</u> in May 1774. [PRO.T47.12]

KEMP, WILLIAM, born in 1757, a servant from Morayshire, from Stornaway to Philadelphia on the <u>Clementina</u> in July 1775. [PRO.T47.12]

KENNAN, JOHN, a tailor in NY, probate 24 June 1767 NY

KENNEDY, ALEXANDER, born in 1762, a servant from Wester Leys, from Stornaway to Philadelphia on the <u>Clementina</u> in July 1775. [PRO.T47.12]

KENNEDY, ANGUS, born in 1749, a farmer from Breadalbane, Perthshire, from Greenock to NY on the <u>Commerce</u> in June 1775.[PRO.T47.12]

KENNEDY, ANNE, born in 1735, a servant from Wester Keys, with Margaret her daughter from Stornaway to Philadelphia on the <u>Clementina of Philadelphia,</u> in July 1775. [PRO.T47.12]

KENNEDY, ANNE, born in 1764, a servant from Wester Leys, from Stornaway to Philadelphia on the <u>Clementina of Philadelphia,</u> in July 1775. [PRO.T47.12]

KENNEDY, ARCHIBALD, born in 1685, son of Alexander Kennedy of Kilhenzie and Helen Monteith, settled in Pavonia, Second River, Hoboken, NY, Receiver General of Customs, married (1) .... Massam, (2) Maria Walter Schuyler, father of James, Robert, Archibald, Thomas and Catherine, died in NY on 14 June 1763. [SP#2.494][SM#25/415][NAS.GD25.sec.9, box 44]

KENNEDY, ARCHIBALD, late of NY, Captain in the Royal Navy, 1782. [NAS.GD25.sec.9, box 79]

KENNEDY, DONALD, born in 1755, a servant from Wester Leys, from Stornaway to Philadelphia on the <u>Clementina</u> in July 1775. [PRO.T47.12]

KENNEDY, JAMES, indented in Chester County, PA, 1693. [Sgen.29.1.11]

KENNEDY, JOHN, born in 1752, a laborer from Galloway, from Stranraer to NY on the <u>Gale of Whitehaven</u> in May 1774. [PRO.T47.12]

KENNEDY, JOHN, born in 1758, a servant from Wester Leys, from Stornaway to Philadelphia on the <u>Clementina of Philadelphia</u> in July 1775. [PRO.T47.12]

KENNEDY, MARY, born in 1765, a servant from Wester Leys, from Stornaway to Philadelphia on the <u>Clementina of Philadelphia</u> in July 1775. [PRO.T47.12]

KENNEDY, QUINTIN, of Knockdour, Ayrshire, a shipwright in NY, husband of Catherine, father of Walter and Janet, pro. 1777 NY

KENNEDY, ROBERT, drowned in NY on 17 Aug. 1763. [NY Weekly Postboy, 18.8.1763]

KENNEDY, SAMUEL, born in 1720, a minister educated at Edinburgh University, after 1740, settled at Basking Ridge, NJ. [SA#102]

KENNEDY, WILLIAM, born in 1739, a servant from Wester Leys, from Stornaway to Philadelphia on the <u>Clementina</u> in July 1775. [PRO.T47.12]

KENNEDY, WILLIAM, born in 1762, a servant from Wester Leys, from Stornaway to Philadelphia on the <u>Clementina</u> in July 1775. [PRO.T47.12]

KENNIE, JOHN from Leith to East NJ on the <u>Henry and Francis</u> in 1685. [NWI.1.423]

KERR, WALTER, a Covenanter who was transported from Leith to East NJ on the <u>Henry and Francis of</u> Newcastle 5 Sep. 1685. [RPCS#11.173][NJSA.EJD.B142]

KIDD, WILLIAM, born in Dundee 1654, son of John Kidd and Bessie Butchart, a master mariner and privateer who settled in NY during 1688. [PRO.HCA.Vol.81, Jackson & Jacobs, v. Noell, 1695]; gentleman in NY, issued a licence to marry Sarah, widow of John Oort a late merchant of NY on 16 May 1691. [NY Wills, liber 3/4, fo.195, 329, 375]

KILGOUR, JAMES, in East NJ 1688. [NJSA.EJD.B139]

KILPATRICK, ROBERT, a minister, to Newfoundland in 1730, settled at Trinity Bay there, and later in New Windsor, NY, died at Trinity Bay in Aug. 1741. [EMA#39][SPG#.22]

KINCAID, JOHN, a Covenanter from Chalcarrock who was transported from Leith to East NJ on the <u>Henry and Francis</u> 5 Sep. 1685. [RPCS#11.154]

KIMMINGS, ALEXANDER, from Stranraer, Wigtownshire, settled in Upper Freehold, Monmouth County, NJ, pro 13.1.1784 [NJSA.Liber#26/342]

KING, CHRISTIAN, born in 1757, a servant from Perth, from Leith to Philadelphia on the <u>Friendship</u> in May 1775. [PRO.T47.12]

KING, JAMES, a merchant in NY, dead by 1789. [NAS.CS17.1.8,24]

KING, JOHN, a Covenanter who was transported from Leith to East NJ on the <u>Henry and Francis</u> on 5 Sep. 1685. [RPCS#11.155][NJSA.EJD/A]

KING, PATRICK, born in 1750, a wright from Edinburgh, from Greenock to NY on the <u>Lilly</u> in Apr. 1775. [PRO.T47.12]

KINNEAR, JOHN, born in 1744, a porter from Kirkcudbright, with his wife Nichola and children Anthony, Elizabeth and Nicola, from

Kirkcudbright to NY on the <u>Adventure of Liverpool</u> in May 1774.
[PRO.T47.12]

KIRKWOOD, JAMES, a Covenanter who was transported from Leith to
East NJ on the <u>Henry and Francis</u> on 5 Sep. 1685. [RPCS#11.154]

KNOX, ISABEL, born in 1754, a servant from Stirling, from Leith to
Philadelphia on the <u>Friendship of Philadelphia</u> in May 1775.
[PRO.T47.12]

KNOX, JAMES, born in 1753, a weaver from Paisley, via Greenock to NY
on the <u>Commerce</u> in Feb. 1774. [PRO.T47.12]

KNOX, JOHN, son of David Knox in Edinburgh, settled in NY before
1750.   [NAS.SH/27.7.1750]

KNOX, ROBERT, from Paisley to NY 1773. [Hugh Simm pp, Princeton]

LAIDLIE, ARCHIBALD, born in Kelso, Roxburghshire, educated at
Edinburgh, University around 1730, a Dutch Reformed minister in
NY from 1734 to 1776, died at Red Hook, NY, in 1779. [CCMC]

LAING, ALEXANDER, born in 1754, a servant from Morayshire, from
Stornaway to Philadelphia on <u>Clementina of Philadelphia</u> in July
1775. [PRO.T47.12]

LAING, JOHN, from Craigforthie, in NJ by 1688.
[NAS.SQR.Kinmuck#11/20]

LAING, ROBERT, a minister in 1722, settled in Philadelphia.
[AP#193][F.7.664]

LAING, WILLIAM, a Covenanter from Hawick, Roxburghshire, who was
transported from Leith to NY on 19 May 1684. [RPCS#8.216]

LAING, WILLIAM, a planter in Freehold, NJ, probate 27 Feb. 1711NJ.
[NJ Archives, Liber 1/305]

LAING, WILLIAM, a minister from Aberdeenshire who settled in
Freehold, Monmouth County, NJ, died before 1739, cnf 1739
Edinburgh.   [NAS.CC8.8.101]

LAING, WILLIAM, born in 1760, a weaver from Paisley, from Leith to
Philadelphia on the <u>Friendship</u> in May 1775. [PRO.T47.12]

LAMB, ("Lam"), ALEXANDER, from Scotland, married Lysbeth
Koningk of New York, in the Dutch Reformed Church in NY on 14
Dec. 1688. [DRF.Reg.]

LAMB, JAMES, 5'6", a gardener who enlisted in the PA Regiment on 6
May 1758. [Pa.Archives#5/1/162]

LAMONT, JANET, born in 1757, from Edinburgh, from Greenock to NY
on the <u>Lilly,</u> in Apr. 1775. [PRO.T47.12]

LANDER, JOHN, born in 1755, a husbandman from Edinburgh, from
London to Philadelphia on the <u>Mary</u> in Oct. 1774. [PRO.T47.9/11]

LANG, JOHN, born 1744, weaver from Paisley, wife Margaret, from
Greenock to NY on the <u>Commerce</u> in Feb. 1774. [PRO.T47.12]

LAW, ANDREW, a petitioner in NY 1701. [DNY.IV.934]

LAWRIE, GAVIN, in Elizabethtown, NJ, late Governor of East New
Jersey, Probate 7 Oct. 1696 PCC [NJSA.EJD.A183/190]

LAWRIE, JAMES, son of Governor Gavin Lawrie of NJ, 1699.
[NAS.RD2.82.418]

LAWRIE, JOHN, born 1747, servant from Kinross, from Leith to
Philadelphia on the <u>Friendship of Philadelphia</u>, in May 1775.
[PRO.T47.12]

LAWRIE, REBECCA, daughter of Gavin Lawrie, to East NJ 1684.
[NJSA.EJD.A]

LAWRIE, THOMAS, to East NJ 1683, settled in Freehold.
[NAS.RD2.82.418]

LAWSON, AGNES, indentured servant, to East NJ 1685.
[NJSA.EJD.A225]

LAWSON, CICELLA, indentured servant, to East NJ 1685.
[NJSA.EJD.A225]

LAWSON, MARION, from Edinburgh, was transported from Greenock to
New York on 21 Oct. 1682. [NAS.HH11]

LAWSON, ROBERT, a minister educated at Edinburgh University in 1693,
from Torthorwald, Dumfries, settled in Monikinie and Wicomico,
PA, died in Nov. 1712. [F#7.664]

LEACY, GEORGE, indented in Chester County, PA, 3 Oct.1693.
[Sgen.29.1.11]

LEARMONTH, ALEXANDER, indentured servant, to East NJ 1685.
[NJSA.EJD.A225/B420]

LEARMONTH, B., born in 1754, a servant from Ratho, Midlothian, from
Leith to Philadelphia on the <u>Friendship</u> in May 1775. [PRO.T47.12]

LEARMONTH, EUPHAME, born in 1752, a servant from Ratho,
Midlothian, from Leith to Philadelphia on the <u>Friendship</u> in May
1775. [PRO.T47.12]

LEARMONTH, JOHN, son of Alexander Learmonth in Edinburgh, settled
in Lewiston, PA, by 1766; formerly a pilot in Philadelphia, sought by
Dr William Moore, Wall Street, NY, in 1781. [NAS.CS16.1.125]
[NY.Gaz.&Wkly.Merc.,8.1.1787] [NAS.RD4.236.762]

LECKIE, ANDREW, born in 1756, a laborer from Anderston, Glasgow,
Greenock to NY on <u>Lilly</u> in Apr. 1775. [PRO.T47.12]

LEE, JAMES, born in St Andrews, Fife, settled in NY, wife Mary
Crookshank, died in NY on 9 Oct. 1795.   [ANY#2.83]

LEGET, WILLIAM, a soldier, married Catherine Boswin, in NY on 18
Feb. 1763. [PCR]

LEITH, MARGARET, widow of John Buchanan of Galstone, in
Philadelphia by 1751. [NAS.CS16.1.85]

LEITH, ROBERT, former baillie of Pittenweem, Fife, in Philadelphia by
1751.[NAS.CS16.1.85]

LEIPER, Dr JAMES, born in 1676, educated at Edinburgh University,
settled in Prince George County, Maryland, buried in the
Presbyterian Churchyard, Arch Street, Philadelphia, in Feb. 1771.
[Pa.Chron:12.1.1771]

LEIPER, THOMAS, born in Strathaven, Lanarkshire, on 15 Dec. 1745,
third son of Thomas Leiper and Helen Hamilton, to Maryland in
1763, a merchant in Philadelphia, settled in Strathaven, Avondale,

Delaware County, PA, died in Philadelphia on 6 July 1825.
[AP#218][The Aurora,8.7.1825]

LEITCH, ROBERT, born in 1746, a farmer from Glasgow, from Greenock
to NY on the Commerce in Feb. 1774. [PRO.T47.12]

LEITH, ALEXANDER, a merchant who died in Philadelphia before 1750,
cnf 17 July 1750 Edinburgh. [NAS.CC8.8.113]

LEMMONS, FRANCIS, a transported rebel, absconded from Ranier
Vanhist, Salem NJ, in May 1720. [American Weekly Mercury,
18.5.1720]

LENNOX, ANN, to America in 1775, married James Cullings, settled in
Albany County, NY, died in New Scotland, Albany County, on 14
Mar. 1850. [TV#15.16]

LENNOX, ROBERT, born in Kirkcudbright on 31 Dec. 1759, son of James
Lennox and Elizabeth Sproat, to America in 1770, settled in New
York by 1783, a merchant who died there on 13 Dec. 1839.
[ANY#1.173][NAS.RGS.196/1]

LESSLY, CATHERINE, from Islay, Argyll, to NY in July 1738 to have
settled at Wood Creek on the Hudson River.[HSPC]

LESLEY, DAVID, born in 1750, a joiner, from Hull to NY on the
Adventure of Liverpool in July 1774.[PRO.T47.9/11]

LESLIE, JOHN, born in 1760, a servant from Sutherland, from Leith to
Philadelphia on the Friendship in May 1775. [PRO.T47.12]

LESLIE, MARGARET, a Covenanter, transported from Leith to East NJ
on the Henry and Francis on 5 Sep. 1685. [RPCS#11.154]

LEWIS, ANDREW, indented in Chester County, PA, 14 July 1697.
[Sgen.29.1.13]

LIDDEL, JOSEPH, a Presbyterian in NY 1723. [NAS.CH1.2.49.55]

LILLIE, JOHN, in NY, graduated Doctor of Divinity from Edinburgh
University on 6 Jan. 1755. [CEG]

LINDSAY, ALEXANDER, (Sander Leendertse Glen), born 1610 in Dysart,
via Amsterdam to the New Netherlands on the Harinck in 1639, with
his wife Catherine Duncanson (Catalyn Jacobs or Donckers) from
Ellon, settled at Fort Nassau later at Fort Orange, died 13 Nov.1685.
[DP][NWI.1.119]

LINDSAY, DONALD, and his wife Mary McQuarrie, and their children
Richard, Duncan, Effie and Christian, from Islay, Argyll, aboard the
Happy Return in June 1739 bound for NY and Wood Creek on the
Hudson River, in 1763 they were granted 250 acres on the Argyle
Patent, NY.[HSBC] [NY.Col.MS#72/170]

LINDSAY, JOHN, born on 2 July 1694 in Crail, Fife, son of John Lindsay
of Wormiston and Margaret Haliburton, a merchant who settled in
Philadelphia in 1729, granted 3000 acres in Cherry Valley and at
Little Falls on the Mohawk River, NY, appointed as Lieutenant
Governor of Fort Oswego in 1748, died in Albany, NY, on 12 Oct.
1751. [SP#5.415][NAS.GD203]

LINDSAY, JOHN, in Canongate, Edinburgh, formerly in Virginia, 1752.
[NAS.RD2.172.514]

LINDSAY, WILLIAM, born in 1758, a cabinetmaker from Boreland, Colvend, Kirkcudbrightshire, from Kirkcudbright to NY on the Adventure of Liverpool in May 1774. [PRO.T47.12]

LINDSAY, Captain ....., born in Edinburgh, settled in NY by 1758, sought there in 1782. [NY.Gaz.& Wkly.Merc., 18.3.1782]

LINN, GEORGE, indented in Chester County, PA, 14 July 1697. [Sgen.29.1.13]

LINN, WILLIAM, born in 1753, a laborer from Galloway, Stranraer to NY on the Gale of Whitehaven in May 1774. [PRO.T47.12]

LINTRON, JANET, a Covenanter, from Leith to East NJ on the Henry and Francis of Newcastle on 5 Sep. 1685. [RPCS#11.164]

LITTLE, ARCHIBALD, in Oxford, Cornwall Precinct, Orange County, NY, husband of Sarah, father of James, Timothy, Archibald, Joseph, John and Sarah, probate 1 Jan. 1779 NY.

LITTLEJOHN, DUNCAN, born 1737, a wright from Breadalbane, from Greenock to NY on Commerce in June 1775. [PRO.T47.12]

LIVINGSTON, DONALD, with his wife Isabel McCuarg, and sons John and Duncan, from Islay, Argyll,on the Happy Return in June 1739 bound for NY and Wood Creek on the Hudson River, in 1763 his widow and daughters were granted 150 acres on the Argyle Patent, NY. [NY.Col.MS#72/170] [HSBC]

LIVINGSTON, JAMES, from Islay, Argyll, aboard the Happy Return bound for NY in July 1738 to have settled at Wood Creek on the Hudson River, by 1763 he was dead and his widow and children were living in Trenton, NJ. [HSPC][NY.Col.MS#72/170]

LIVINGSTONE, JOHN, a petitioner in NY 1701. [DNY.IV.934]

LIVINGSTON, ROBERT, born in Ancrum, Roxburghshire, on 13 Dec. 1654, son of Rev. John Livingston and Janet Fleming, to America in 1673, settled in Charlestown, Mass., and later in Albany, NY, collector of excise and quit rents, town clerk, clerk of the peace and clerk of the Court of Common Pleas in Albany, NY, on 6 Jan. 1695, a merchant in NY, admitted a burgess of Edinburgh 3 Aug. 1705, died 1 Oct. 1728. [CTP.vol.36] [CF#6.334] [EBR]

LIVINGSTONE, WILLIAM, transported from Leith to East NJ on the Henry and Francis 5 Sep. 1685. [RPCS#11.165][NAS.HH11]

LIVISTON, GEORGE, born in 1752, a mason from Gatehouse of Fleet, from Stranraer to NY on the Gale in May 1774. [PRO.T47.12]

LOCHHEAD, HUGH, born in 1736, a farmer from Perthshire, his wife Isobel Bruce, from Greenock to NY on the Monimia, May 1775. [PRO.T47.12]

LOCKHART, BETTY, born in 1760, a servant from Foubriggs, from Leith to Philadelphia on Friendship in May 1775. [PRO.T47.12]

LOCKHART, GAVIN, a Covenanter, from Leith to East NJ on the Henry and Francis on 5 Sep. 1685.[RPCS.11.162]

LOCKHART, GEORGE, a surgeon in NY, died intestate, letters of administration 18 Mar. 1698. [NY Wills, liber 3/4, fo.224]

LOCKHART, JANET, born in 1759, a servant from Edinburgh, from Leith to Philadelphia on the Friendship in May 1775. [PRO.T47.12]

LOCKHART, ROBERT, born in 1753, a farmer from Kilbarchan, from Greenock to Philadelphia on the Sally in Oct. 1774. [PRO.T47.12]

LOGAN, GEORGE, a shipmaster in Philadelphia, 1753. [NAS.CS16.1.103]

LOGAN, HUGH, born in 1734, enlisted in Captain John Haslet's Company of the PA Regiment 18 May 1758. [Pa.Arch#5/1/149]

LOGAN, JAMES, born in 1756, a wright from Paisley, from Greenock to NY on the Lilly in May 1775. [PRO.T47.12]

LOGAN, WALTER, Customs Controller in Perth Amboy, NJ, 1766, Loyalist in 1776. [PRO.AO.12.104.12]

LOGAN, WILLIAM, in Philadelphia, with his wife Hannah, 1773. [NAS.GD1.384.2]

LOGGAT, JOHN, a shipmaster in Philadelphia, cnf 15 June 1785. [NAS.CC8.8.126]

LONG, HENRY, a laborer from Galloway, from Stranraer to NY on the Gale of Whitehaven in May 1774. [PRO.T47.12]

LORIMER, HUGH, born in 1753, a laborer from Ayr, from Greenock to NY on the Lilly in Apr. 1775. [PRO.T47.12]

LOVE, ROBERT, 5'8", 'smooth faced', enlisted in the PA Regiment on 5 May 1758. [Pa.Arch#5/1/146]

LOW, ALEXANDER, born in 1755, a laborer from Kilbirnie, Ayrshire, from Greenock to Philadelphia on the Sally in Oct. 1774. [PRO.T47.12]

LOW, JAMES, born in 1750, a weaver from Glasgow, from Greenock to NY on the Christy in Oct. 1774. [PRO.T47.12]

LOWRIE, ALEXANDER, born in 1751, a laborer from Monklands, Lanarkshire, via Greenock to Philadelphia on the Sally in Oct. 1774 [PRO.T47.12]

LUNAN, ALEXANDER, a merchant in Philadelphia, died there on 24 July 1770, buried in St Peter's Churchyard.[AP#228][Pa.Gaz. 2.8.1770]

LUNDIE, ARCHIBALD, born in 1750, a merchant from Edinburgh, from Greenock to NY on the Georgia in July 1775. [PRO.T47.12]

LYELL, DAVID, a petitioner in NY 1701. [DNY.IV.934]

LYLE, DAVID, born in 1746, a laborer from Edinburgh, from Greenock to NY on the Lilly in Apr. 1775. [PRO.T47.12]

LYLE, JOHN, born in 1748, a farmer from Caithness, from Greenock to NY on the Lilly in Apr. 1775. [PRO.T47.12]

MCADAM, JOHN LOUDOUN, eldest son of James McAdam of Waterhead, a merchant in NY, 1782. [NAS.CS17.1.1/286]

MCADAM, WILLIAM, born 1746, a tailor from Boreland, balmaghie, Kirkcudbrightshire, via Kirkcudbright to NY on the Adventure in May 1774. [PRO.T47/12]

MCADAM, WILLIAM, a merchant in NY around 1772, [his will refers to his wife Anne and his brothers James and Gilbert in Ayrshire], probate 2 Oct.1779 NY. [NAS.GD174.159/160]

MCALISTER, ANGUS, from Islay, Argyll, on board the Happy Return bound for NY in July 1738 to have settled at Wood Creek on the Hudson River, by 1763 he was in SC.[NYCol.ms72/170][HSPC]

MCALISTER, CHARLES, and his wife Catherine McInnish, with their children John and Margaret, from Islay, Argyll, aboard the Happy Return in June 1739 bound for NY and Wood Creek on the Hudson River, in 1763 his two sons were granted 200 acres on the Argyle Patent, NY.[HSBC][NY.Col.MS#72/170]

MCALISTER, DUNCAN, and his wife Effie Keith, from Islay, Argyll, in June 1739 aboard the Happy Return bound for NY and Wood Creek on the Hudson River, dead by 1763 when his son and two daughters were granted 200 acres on the Argyle Patent, NY. [HSBC][NY.Col.MS#72/170]

MCALLISTER, HUGH, from Argyll, emigrated before 1732, settled in Lancaster County, PA, married ...Harbison, father of John, died in 1769.[BLG#2800]

MCALESTER, JOHN, born in 1745, a coppersmith from Edinburgh, from Greenock to NY or GA on the Christy in May 1775. [PRO.T47.12]

MCALLISTER, JOHN, born in Glasgow during Feb. 1753, to NY in July 1775, a manufacturer in Philadelphia from 1781, died there on 12 May 1830.[AP#234]

MCALISTER, MARGARET, from Islay, Argyll, aboard the Happy Return in Nov. 1740 bound for NY and Wood Creek on the Hudson River, by 1763 she was married and living at Livingstone Manor when she was granted 150 acres on the Argyle Patent, NY. [HSBC][NY.Col.MS#72/170]

MCALLASTER, THOMAS, born 1754, shoemaker in Glasgow, from Greenock to NY on the Commerce in Feb. 1774. [PRO.T47.12]

MCALLAN, JOHN, born 1735, farmer from Lorne, Argyll, with Janet his wife and children Janet, Donald, Anne and Katherine, from Greenock to NY on the Monimia in May 1775. [PRO.T47.12]

MCALPINE, DONALD, settled in Saratoga, Tryon County, NY, a Loyalist in 1776, wife Elizabeth, a Captain of the Royal North Carolina Rangers, died in SC after 1781. [PRO.AO13.131.1-14]

MCALPINE, DUGALD, with his wife Mary McPhaden, and children Donald and Mary, from Islay, Argyll, aboard the Happy Return bound for NY in July 1738 to have settled at Wood Creek on the Hudson River.[HSPC]

MCALPIN, JAMES, born in Glasgow during Aug. 1761, to VA, later a tailor in Philadelphia, died there on 20 July 1847. [AP#236]

MCALPIN, PETER, born 1726, farmer from Inverness, with his wife Eliza via Greenock to NY on George in May 1774. [PRO.T47.12]

MCALPINE, ROBERT, from Islay, Argyll, in Nov. 1740 aboard the Happy Return bound for bound for NY and Wood Creek on the Hudson River, by 1763 he had settled in NY with a family of five sons and two daughters, and was granted 200 acres on the Argyle Patent, NY. [HSBC][NY.Col.MS#72/170]

MCARTHUR, ALEXANDER, and his wife Catherine McArthur, with their children John, Donald, Duncan, Catherine and Florence, from Islay, Argyll, aboard the Happy Return bound for to NY in July 1738 to have settled at Wood Creek on the Hudson River, by 1763 he was dead as was son John, survivors granted 350 acres on the Argyle Patent, NY. [HSPC][NY.Col.MS#72/170]

MCARTHUR, ALEXANDER, with his wife Catherine Gillies, and their children Flora and Duncan, from Islay, Argyll, in June 1739 aboard the Happy Return bound for bound for NY and Wood Creek on the Hudson River, in 1763 his widow and a son were granted 200 acres on the Argyle Patent, NY. [HSBC][NY.Col.MS#72/170]

MCARTHUR, ANN, from Islay, Argyll, in Nov. 1740 aboard the Happy Return bound for NY and Wood Creek on the Hudson River, by 1763 she was married and living in Albany when she was granted 150 acres on the Argyle Patent, NY. [HSBC][NY.Col.MS#72/170]

MCARTHUR, CHARLES, his wife and family had intended to emigrate from Islay, Argyll, aboard the Happy Return in 1738 but had taken a ship from Ireland a couple of weeks later and had arrived in NY earlier than the main party, in 1763, and had settled there. [NY.Col.MS#72/171]

MCARTHUR, DONALD, born in 1716, a farmer from Breadalbane, with Katherine McNaughton his wife, and children John, Donald, Katherine and Archibald, from Greenock to NY on the Commerce in June 1775. [PRO.T47.12]

MCARTHUR, DUNCAN, and his wife Anna McUin, with their children Mary, Margaret, Anna and John, from Islay, Argyll, aboard the Happy Return bound for NY in July 1738 to have settled at Wood Creek on the Hudson River, by 1763 he was dead but his widow, two sons and two daughters were granted 250 acres on the Argyle Patent, NY.[HSPC][NY.Col.MS#72/170]

MCARTHUR, DUNCAN, born in 1723, a farmer from Breadalbane, Perthshire, Eliza McEwan his wife, and children John, Donald, Peter, John and Donald, from Greenock to NY on the Commerce in June 1775. [PRO.T47.12]

MCARTHUR, DUNCAN, born in 1755, a weaver from Breadalbane, Perthshire, from Greenock to NY on the Commerce in June 1775 [PRO.T47.12]

MCARTHUR, ISOBEL, born in 1747, from Crawfordyke, via Greenock to NY on the George in May 1774. [PRO.T47.12]

MCARTHUR, JOHN, with his son John and daughter Christian, from Islay, Argyll, aboard the Happy Return in Nov. 1740 bound for NY and Wood Creek on the Hudson River, he was dead by 1763 when his son and daughter were granted 150acres on the Argyle Patent, NY. [NY.Col.MS#72/170][HSBC]

MCARTHUR, JOHN, born in 1727, a farmer from Breadalbane, Perthshire, with Mary Fletcher his wife, and daughter Christian from Greenock to NY on the Commerce in June 1775. [PRO.T47.12]; (possibly) settled in Charlotte County, NY, a Loyalist in 1776, later in New Carlisle, Bay of Chaleur, 1786. [PRO.AO13.18.180]

MCARTHUR, MARGARET, wife of Archibald McCollum in NY, with their two daughters Anna and Mary, from Islay, Argyll, aboard the Happy Return in Nov. 1740 bound for NY and Wood Creek on the Hudson River. [HSBC]

MCARTHUR, NEIL, and his wife Mary Campbell, with their children
     Alexander, John and Christian, from Islay, Argyll, aboard the Happy
     Return bound for NY in July 1738 to have settled at Wood Creek on
     the Hudson River.[HSPC]
MCARTHUR, PATRICK, with his wife Mary McDougall, and children
     Charles, Colin,and Janet, from Islay, Argyll, aboard the Happy
     Return bound for NY in July 1738 to have settled at Wood Creek on
     the Hudson River, he was dead by 1763 and his widow and five
     surviving children were granted 300 acres on the Argyle Patent,
     NY.[HSPC][NY.Col.MS#72/170]
MCARTHUR, PETER, born 1757, weaver from Breadalbane, Perthshire,
     from Greenock to NY on the Commerce in June 1775. [PRO.T47.12]
MCAULLA, CHRISTIAN, from Islay, Argyll, in June 1739 aboard the
     Happy Return bound for bound for NY and Wood Creek on the
     Hudson River. [HSBC]
MCAULAY, KENNETH, born in 1757, a servant from Bayble, Isle of
     Lewis, from Stornaway to Philadelphia on the Friendship in May
     1774.[PRO.T47.12]
MCAULAY, NORMAN, born in 1746, a farmer from Bayble, Isle of
     Lewis, with Isobell McLeod his wife, from Stornaway to
     Philadelphia on the Friendship in May 1774. [PRO.T47.12]
MCBEAN, DONALD, a former Captain of the 78th [Frasers Highlanders],
     granted land in NY in 1773. [PCCol.5.597]
MCBRIDE, DUNCAN, born in 1729, a farmer from Stirling, with his wife
     Marion Donaldson, from Greenock to NY on the Monimia in May
     1775. [PRO.T47.12]
MCCALL, GEORGE, born around 1700 son of Samuel McCall a merchant
     in Glasgow, settled in Philadelphia as a merchant, died 13 Oct. 1740
     and was buried in Christ Church. [AP#237]
MCCALLACHY, ROBERT, born in 1746, a watchmaker from Dundee,
     Angus, from Greenock to NY on the Christy in May
     1775.[PRO.T47.12]
MCCALLUM, HUGH, born in 1743, a farmer from Angus, from
     Greenock to NY on the Lilly in May 1775. [PRO.T47.12]
MCCALLUM, JOHN, a Covenanter from Argyll, was transported from
     Leith to East NJ on the Henry and Francis on 5 Sep. 1685.
     [RPCS#11.126]
MCCALLUM, JOHN, born 1756, laborer from Stornaway, Isle of Lewis,
     from Greenock to NY on the Lilly in Apr. 1775. [PRO.T47.12]
MCCALLUM, JOHN, Amenia Precinct, Duchess County, NY, pro.11 Apr.
     1781 NY
MCCALLUM, PETER, born in 1748, a farmer from Breadalbane,
     Perthshire, from Greenock to NY on the Commerce in June
     1775.[PRO.T47.12]
MCCALMAN, WILLIAM, a Covenanter from Culbrattoun, was
     transported from Leith to East NJ on the Henry and Francis on 5 Sep.
     1685. [RPCS#10.612]
MCCANN, WILLIAM, born 1739, weaver from Galloway, with wife Jean
     and children Sarah, John and Janet, from Stranraer to NY on the

Gale of Whitehaven in May 1775. [PRO.T47.12]

MCCARR, JOHN, born in Newton Stewart, Wigtownshire, during 1757, a merchant tailor in NY, died there in 1843. [ANY#1.306]

MCCARTY, JEREMIAH, born in 1736, a wigmaker, enlisted in Captain John Haslet's Company of the PA Regiment on 10 May 1758. [Pa.Arch.#5/1/149]

MCCARTNEY, WILLIAM, born 1754, husbandman from Queenshill, via Stranraer to NY on the Gale in May 1775. [PRO.T47.12]

MCCAUL, JAMES, born in 1754, a farmer from Inverness, from Greenock to NY on the George, in May 1774. [PRO.T47.12]

MCCEUN, Captain ..., born in 1743, a mariner via London to NY on the Earl Dunmore in Feb. 1774. [PRO.T47.12]

MCCHRISTEN, ALEXANDER, from Islay, Argyll, in June 1739 aboard the Happy Return bound for NY and Wood Creek on the Hudson River. [HSBC]

MCCLAVRAN, JOHN, born in Argyll during 1738, a laborer and a soldier of Captain John Haslet's Company of the PA Regiment enlisted on 10 May 1758. [Pa.Archives#5/1/149,285]

MCCLELLAND, ANDREW, a Covenanter who was transported from Leith to East NJ on the Henry and Francis on 5 Sep. 1685. [RPCS.11.154]

MCCLELLAND, ROBERT, a Covenanter who was transported from Leith to East NJ on the Henry and Francis on 5 Sep. 1685. [RPCS.11.154]

MCCLUMPHA, THOMAS, born 1748, farmer from Galloway, with Jean his wife and son John, from Stranraer to NY on the Gale in May 1774. [PRO.T47.12]

MCCLURE, WILLIAM, born in 1747, a merchant from Ayr, from Greenock to Friendship on the Sally in Oct. 1774. [PRO.T47.12]

MCCOLL, JOHN, from Islay, Argyll, aboard the Happy Return bound for NY in July 1738 to have settled at Wood Creek on the Hudson River.[HSPC]

MCCOLL, JOHN, from Glasgow, to NY on the Ruby in 1781. [NAS.GD170]; John McColl of Glassdrum merchant in Glasgow now in NY, 1786, 1787. [NAS.CS17.1.5/92; CS17.1.6, 369]

MCCOLLUM, ARCHIBALD, with his wife Merran McLean, and their children Donald, John, Margaret, Mary and Allan, from Islay, Argyll, aboard the Happy Return in June 1739 bound for NY and Wood Creek on the Hudson River, in 1763 he, his two sons and a daughter were granted 250 acres on the Argyle Patent, NY. [HSBC][NY.Col.MS#72/170]

MCCOLLUM, ARCHIBALD, with his wife Flory McEacheon, and sons Hugh and Duncan, from Islay, Argyll, aboard the Happy Return in Nov. 1740 bound for NY and Wood Creek on the Hudson River, in 1763 Archibald, a son and daughter were granted 250 acres on the Argyle Patent, NY. [HSBC][NY.Col.MS#72/170]

MCCOLLUM, DUNCAN, from Islay, Argyll, aboard the Happy Return in Nov. 1740 bound for NY and Wood Creek on the Hudson River. [HSBC]

MCCOMB, ALEXANDER, born in 1753, a husbandman from Glen Luce,

Wigtownshire, from Stranraer to NY on the Gale in May 1774. [PRO.T47.12]

MCCOY, DANIEL, born in the Highlands during 1738, a tailor and indentured servant who absconded from James Richey in Kingston, Ulster County, NY, in 1768. [NY Gaz.&Wkly. Mercury, 20.11.1768]

MCCRA, ANNE, born in 1752, a servant from Inverness, via Stornaway to Philadelphia on the Clementina in July 1775. [PRO.T47.12]

MCCRA, DONALD, born in 1766, a servant from Kinmily, via Stornaway to Philadelphia on the Clementina in July 1775. [PRO.T47.12]

MCCRA, HUGH, born in 1764, a servant from Kinmily, via Stornaway to Philadelphia on the Clementina in July 1775. [PRO.T47.12]

MCCRACKEN, JAMES, born in 1747, a tailor from Stonykirk, Wigtownshire, via Stranraer to NY on the Jackie of Glasgow in May 1775. [PRO.T47.12]

MCCRAE, THOMAS, born 1747, from Paisley, with wife Elizabeth, Greenock to NY on the Commerce in Feb. 1774. [PRO.T47.12]

MCCRAN, ANN, born in 1747, a servant from Loch Broom, Ross-shire, via Stornaway to NY on the Peace and Plenty in Nov. 1774. [PRO.T47.12]

MCCRAN, MARY, born in 1749, a servant from Loch Broom, Ross-shire, via Stornaway to NY on the Peace and Plenty in Nov. 1774. [PRO.T47.12]

MCCREA, HUGH, a laborer from Galloway, via Stranraer to NY on the Galeof Whitehaven in May 1774.[PRO.T47.12]

MCCREADY, JOHN, born 1744, a blacksmith and currier, an indentured servant who arrived from the Isle of Whithorn, Wigtownshire, aboard the Golden Rule, and later absconded from Patrick McMiking in 1774. [NYMerc. 5.9.1774]

MCCREDDIE, JANE, born around 1750, a servant from Greenock in 1774, absconded from John Myford, Little Dock Street, Coenties Market, New York city, 1 Jan.1775. [NY Gaz-Merc.2.1.1775]

MCCREE, GEORGE, in NY, 1781. [NAS.CS16.1.181]

MCCRINNEL, WILLIAM, born in 1716, a laborer who enlisted in Captain Samuel Perry's Company of the PA Regiment on 27 July 1746. [PaArch#5/1/14]

MCCULLOCH, ALEXANDER, born in 1750, a servant from Braen, via Stornaway to Philadelphia on the Clementina in July 1775. [PRO.T47.12]

MCCULLOCH, JOHN, born in 1753, a weaver from Paisley, to NY on the Commerce, in Feb. 1774.[PRO.T47.12]

MCDANIEL, ANN, born in 1732, an indentured servant who absconded from John Holliday, a shoemaker in Baltimore, in 1772. [Pa.Chron:25.5.1772]

MCDANIEL, DANIEL, indented in Chester County, PA, 3 Oct.1693. [Sgen.29.1.11]

MCDANIELL, WILLIAM, indented in Chester County, PA, 5 Aug.1697. [Sgen.29.1.13]

MCDERMOD, HUGH, a drummer in NY, husband of Grizel Colvill in New Greyfriars parish, Edinburgh, father of Peter born on 14 Jan.

1768.[Edinburgh OPR]

MCDIARMID, ANGUS, born in 1727, a farmer from Breadalbane, Perthshire, with his wife Katherine McMartin and daughter Betty, via Greenock to NY on the Commerce in Feb. 1775. [PRO.T47.12]

MCDIARMID, DUNCAN, born in 1753, a smith from Breadalbane, Perthshire, son of Angus McDiarmid and Katherine McMartin, via Greenock to NY on the Commerce in Feb. 1775. [PRO.T47.12]

MCDIARMID, ELIZA, born in 1758, a servant from Breadalbane, Perthshire, via Greenock to NY on the Commerce in Feb. 1775. [PRO.T47.12]

MCDIARMID, HUGH, born 1750, tailor/indentured servant, absconded from James Moore in Schnectady, Albany, NY, 15 Feb.1775. [NYGaz-Merc.6.3.1775]

MCDIARMID, JEAN, born in 1772, from Breadalbane, Perthshire, via Greenock to NY on the Commerce in Feb. 1775. [PRO.T47.12]

MCDIARMID, JOHN, born in 1772, from Breadalbane, Perthshire, via Greenock to NY on the Commerce in Feb. 1775. [PRO.T47.12]

MCDIARMID, KATHERINE, born in 1761, from Breadalbane, Perthshire, via Greenock to NY on the Commerce in Feb. 1775. [PRO.T47.12]

MCDIARMID, MARY, born in 1754, a servant from Breadalbane, Perthshire, via Greenock to NY on the Commerce in Feb. 1775. [PRO.T47.12]

MCDONALD, ALEXANDER, born 1725, officer during the French and Indian Wars, settled in NY, Loyalist in 1776. [PRO.AO.12.24.48][NAS.CS17.1.2/272]

MCDONALD, ALEXANDER, born in 1751, a servant from Duffus, Morayshire, via Stornaway to Philadelphia on the Clementina in July 1775. [PRO.T47.12]

MCDONALD, ALEXANDER, born in 1754, a servant from, Strathpeffer, via Stornaway to Philadelphia on the Clementina in July 1775. [PRO.T47.12]

MACDONALD, ALEXANDER, born in 1762, son of Alexander MacDonald and Helen McNab, to NY in 1773, a Loyalist and an officer of Butler's Rangers, married Anne Smith, father of Allan, James, Angus, Alexander, Samuel, Helen Anne and Henrietta, died on 18 Mar. 1842.[CD#3.59]

MACDONALD, ALLAN, of Cullachie, son of Alexander MacDonald, a Jacobite in 1745, then an officer in the French Army, to America in 1773, settled in Sohoharie, Tryon County, NY, a Loyalist in 1776, Captain of the 84th [RHE] Regiment, married Catherine McNab, father of Angus, Alexander, James, Henrietta and Catherine, died Quebec 1792, buried at St Foy. [CD#3.356]

MCDONALD, ARCHIBALD, born 1757, a servant from Beauly, Inverness-shire, via Stornaway to Philadelphia on the Clementina in July 1775. [PRO.T47.12]

MCDONALD, BATHIA, born in 1760, a servant from Beauly, Inverness-shire, via Stornaway to Philadelphia on the Clementina in July 1775. [PRO.T47.12]

MCDONALD, CATHERINE, born in 1757, a servant from Inverness, via

Stornaway to Philadelphia on the <u>Clementina</u> in July 1775.
[PRO.T47.12]

MCDONALD, CHRISTIAN, born in 1757, a servant from Beauly,
Inverness-shire, via Stornaway to Philadelphia on the <u>Clementina</u> in
July 1775. [PRO.T47.12]

MCDONALD, COLIN, born in the Highlands in 1736, tailor/indentured
servant, via Londonderry to Philadelphia on the <u>Wolfe</u> absconded in
Nov. 1772. [Pa.Gaz.#2292]

MACDONALD, DANIEL, born around 1730, a Highland indentured
servant who absconded from Huntingdon County, NJ, in 1749.
[Pa.Gaz.,8.6.1749]

MCDONALD, DONALD, indentured servant, to East NJ in 1684.
[NJSA.EJD.A184]

MCDONALD, DONALD, a Scottish indentured servant, who absconded
from Huntingdon County, West NJ, during 1753.[NY. Gaz.,
14.1.1754]

MCDONALD, DONALD, emigrated in 1773, settled in Tryon County,
NY, Loyalist. [PRO.AO.12.29.74]

MCDONALD, DONALD, born in 1717, a laborer from Kinmily, via
Stornaway to Philadelphia on the <u>Clementina</u> in July 1775.
[PRO.T47.12]

MCDONALD, DONALD, born in 1758, a weaver from Paisley, via
Greenock to NY on the <u>Commerce</u> in Feb. 1774. [PRO.T47.12]

MCDONALD, DONALD, born in 1763, a servant from Stornaway, Isle of
Lewis, via Stornaway to Philadelphia on the <u>Friendship</u> in May 1774.
[PRO.T47.12]

MCDONALD, DUNCAN, born 1725, a farmer from Beauly, Inverness-
shire with his wife Christian, via Stornaway to Philadelphia on the
<u>Clementina</u> in July 1775. [PRO.T47.12]

MCDONALD, ELIZABETH, born in 1754, a servant from Loch Broom,
Wester Ross, via Stornaway to Philadelphia on the <u>Clementina</u> in
July 1775. [PRO.T47.12]

MCDONALD, ESPIA, born in 1759, a servant from Kinmily, via
Stornaway to Philadelphia on the <u>Clementina</u> in July 1775.
[PRO.T47.12]

MCDONALD, HENRY, born in 1719, a cooper, enlisted in the PA
Regiment on 10 May 1759. [Pa.Archives#5/1/299]

MCDONALD, HUGH, an indentured servant, to Philadelphia on the <u>Anne</u>
<u>galley</u>, assigned to Philip White in Bucks Co., PA, for six years 20
Sep.1745. [EP#64]

MCDONALD, HUGH, born in 1750, a servant from Loch Broom, Wester
Ross, via Stornaway to Philadelphia on the <u>Clementina</u> in July 1775.
[PRO.T47.12]

MCDONALD, ISOBEL, born in 1760, a servant from Inverness, via
Stornaway to Philadelphia on the <u>Clementina</u> in July 1775.
[PRO.T47.12]

MCDONALD, JAMES, settled in Albany, NY, before 1776, Loyalist.
[PRO.AO.12.112.3]

MCDONALD, JAMES, born in 1765, a servant from Beauly, Inverness-

shire, via Stornaway to Philadelphia on the Clementina in July 1775.
[PRO.T47.12]

MCDONALD, JANET, born in 1757, a servant from Beauly, Inverness-
shire, via Stornaway to Philadelphia on the Clementina in July 1775.
[PRO.T47.12]

MCDONALD, JOHN, from Islay, Argyll, in June 1739 aboard the Happy
Return bound for NY and Wood Creek on the Hudson River.[HSBC]

MCDONALD, JOHN, settled in Dutchess County, NY, by 1764, Loyalist
soldier of the 84th Regiment. [PRO.AO.12.25.156]

MCDONALD, JOHN, born in 1737, a farmer from Stirling, with his wife
Margaret Grieve via Greenock to NY on the Monimia in May
1775.[PRO.T47.12]

MCDONALD, JOHN, born in 1752, a farmer from Strathspey, with his
wife Margery, via Greenock to NY on the George in May 1774.
[PRO.T47.12]

MCDONALD, JOHN, born in 1762, a servant from Stornaway, Isle of
Lewis, via Stornaway to Philadelphia on the Friendship in May 1774.
[PRO.T47.12]

MCDONALD, JOSEPH, born in 1748, a laborer from Wigtown, via
Greenock to NY on the Christy in May 1775. [PRO.T47.12]

MCDONALD, KATHERINE, born in 1744, a servant from Coriby, via
Stornaway to Philadelphia on the Friendship in May 1774.
[PRO.T47.12]

MCDONALD, MARTHA, born in 1757, a servant from Beauly, Inverness-
shire, via Stornaway to Philadelphia on the Clementina in July 1775.
[PRO.T47.12]

MCDONALD, MARY, born in 1745, a servant from Kinmily, via
Stornaway to Philadelphia on the Clementina in July 1775.
[PRO.T47.12]

MCDONALD, MARY, born in 1757, a servant from Beauly, Inverness-
shire, via Stornaway to Philadelphia on the Clementina in July 1775.
[PRO.T47.12]

MCDONALD, MARY, born in 1758, a servant from Perth, via Leith to
Philadelphia on the Friendship in May 1775. [PRO.T47.12]

MCDONALD, MARY, born in 1760, a servant from Perth, via Leith to
Philadelphia on the Friendship in May 1775. [PRO.T47.12]

MCDONALD, NEIL, with his wife Anna McDuffie, and their children
Donald, Archibald, and Catherine, from Islay, Argyll, aboard the
Happy Return bound for NY in July 1738 to have settled at Wood
Creek on the Hudson River, in 1763 he, his wife and six children
were granted 400 acres on the Argyle Patent,
NY.[HSPC][NY.Col.MS#72/170]

MCDONALD, NEAL, in NY, probate 31 Mar. 1779 NY

MCDONALD, PETER, born in 1725, a smith, enlisted in Captain William
Trent's Company of the PA Regiment on 29 June 1746.
[PaArch#5/1/8]

MCDONALD, RANDALL, settled on the Mohawk River, Tryon County,
NY, by 1776, Loyalist. [PRO.AO.12.28.23]

MCDONALD, WILLIAM, born in 1759, a servant from Beauly, Inverness-

shire, via Stornaway to Philadelphia on the <u>Clementina</u> in July 1775.
[PRO.T47.12]

MCDONELL, ALEXANDER, born in Boleskine, Stratherick, to America
in 1773, settled on the Kingsborough Patent, NY, a Loyalist and
soldier of the Royal Regiment of NY from 1776 to 1783, settled at
River Raison, Ontario. [DF.pp][PRO.AO.12.31.192]

MCDONELL, ALEXANDER, born in Knoydart, Inverness-shire, to
America in 1773, settled on the Kingsborough Patent, NY, a Loyalist
and soldier of the 84th Regiment, later settled in Cornwall, Ontario.
[DF.pp][PRO.AO.13.14.93]

MCDONELL, ALEXANDER, born in Aberchalder, Inverness-shire, a
Jacobite in 1745, from Fort William, Inverness-shire, to NY in 1773
aboard the <u>Pearl</u>, a Loyalist and Captain of the Royal Regiment of
NY and of the 84th Regiment, married .... McDonell, later settled in
Glengarry,Ontario. [DF.pp][PRO.AO.13.80.289]

MCDONELL, ALEXANDER, born Fort Augustus, Inverness,1762, son of
Allan McDonell and Helen Chisholm, to NY on the <u>Pearl</u> in 1773, a
Loyalist soldier of the 84th Regiment and Butler's Rangers, died in
Toronto 1842. [DF.pp]

MCDONELL, ALLAN, born in Collachie, Loch Oich, Inverness-shire,
during 1712, a Jacobite in 1745, from Fort William to NY on the
<u>Pearl</u> in 1773, settled on the Kingsborough Patent, NY, a Loyalist and
Captain of the 84th Regiment, later settled in Quebec in 1779,
married Helen McNab, died at Cap Rouge, Quebec, during 1792.
[DF.pp][PRO.AO12.27.396]

MCDONELL, ALLEN, to America in 1773, settled on the Kingsborough
Patent, NY, a Loyalist and soldier of the Royal Regiment of NY from
1776 to 1783, later settled in Charlottenburg, Ontario. [DF.pp]

MCDONELL, ANGUS, to America in 1773, settled on the Kingsborough
Patent, NY, a Loyalist and soldier of the 84th Regiment, later settled
in Cornwall, Ontario. [DF.pp][PRO.AO13.8.228]

MCDONELL, ARCHIBALD, settled on the Kingsborough Patent, NY, by
1780, Loyalist, Lieutenant of the 84th Regiment. [DF.pp]

MCDONELL, DONALD, born in Kilmorack, Inverness-shire, to America
in 1773, a Loyalist and Corporal of the 84th Regiment, later settled in
Charlottenburg, Ontario. [DF.pp]

MCDONELL, DONALD, born in Glenmoriston, Inverness-shire, to
America in 1773, settled on the Kingsborough Patent, NY, a Loyalist
and soldier of the 2nd Battalion of Royal Regiment of NY from 1780
to 1783, later settled in Cornwall, Ontario. [DF.pp]

MCDONELL, DUNCAN, to America 1773, settled Tryon County, NY,
Loyalist in 1776. [PRO.AO.12.31.147]

MCDONELL, HUGH, Tryon County, NY, Loyalist in 1776.
[PRO.AO12.29.103]

MCDONELL, JOHN, born in Inveroucht, Inverness-shire, to America in
1773, settled on the Kingsborough Patent, NY, a Loyalist and soldier
of the 2nd Battalion of Royal Regiment of NY from 1780 to 1783,
later settled at River Raison, Ontario. [DF.pp][PRO.AO12.31.179]

MCDONELL, JOHN, born in Dalchreggan, Inverness-shire, to America in

1774, settled on the Kingsborough Patent, NY, a Loyalist and soldier of the 1st Battalion of the Royal Regiment of NY, later settled in Canada. [DF.pp]

MCDONELL, JOHN, born in Collachie, Inverness-shire, to America in 1773, settled on the Kingsborough Patent, NY, a Loyalist and soldier of the 84th Regiment from 1776 to 1783, later settled in Ontario. [DF.pp][PRO.AO12.28.401]

MCDONELL, JOHN, born in Leek, Loch Oich, Inverness-shire, a Jacobite in 1745, an Officer of the 78th Regiment during the French and Indian Wars, later from Fort William to NY on the _Pearl_ in 1773, settled as a farmer on the Kingsborough Patent, NY, married Jean Magdalena Chisholm, a Loyalist and Captain of the 84th Regiment, later settled in Canada, died in Montreal on 11 Nov. 1782. [DF.pp][PCCol.5.597][PRO.AO13.80.288]

MCDONELL, JOHN, born in Baldron, Inverness-shire, to America in 1774, settled on the Kingsborough Patent, NY, a Loyalist and soldier of the Royal Regiment of NY in 1782, later settled in Charlottenburg, Ontario. [DF.pp]

MCDONELL, JOHN, born in Fort Augustus, Inverness-shire, to America in 1773, settled on the Kingsborough Patent, NY, soldier of the Royal Regiment of NY, died 1786. [DF.pp]

MCDONELL, JOHN, born in Aughengleen, Inverness-shire, to America in 1773, settled on the Kingsborough Patent, NY, a Loyalist and soldier of the 84th Regiment from 1776 to 1783, later settled New Johnstown, Ontario. [DF.pp][PRO.AO12.29.242]

MCDONELL, JOHN, from North Uist, to America in 1768, settled Fort Ann, Argyle Patent, NY, Loyalist. [PRO.AO12.29.244]

MCDONELL, JOHN ROY, to America in 1773, settled on the Kingsborough Patent, NY, a soldier of the 84th Regiment from 1776 to 1783, settled in Glengarry, Canada. [DF.pp]

MCDONELL, KENNETH, to America in 1773, settled on the Kingsborough Patent, NY, a Loyalist and soldier of the 84th Regiment from 1776 to 1783, later in Cornwall, Ontario. [DF.pp][PRO.AO.12.31.49]

MCDONELL, MILES, born in Inverness during 1767, settled Tryon County, NY, a Loyalist in 1776, later an officer of Royal Canadian Volunteers, in Hudson Bay Company Service from 1811 to 1820, died at Port Fortune on the Ottawa River on 28 June 1828. [HBRS#2.232]

MCDONELL, PETER, 5'4", a tinker, enlisted in the PA Regiment in Philadelphia on 25 May 1758. [Pa.Archives#5/1/363]

MCDONELL of ARDNABEE, RANOLD, a soldier during the French and Indian Wars, from Fort William, Inverness-shire, to NY on the _Pearl_ in 1773, settled Kingsborough Patent, NY, Loyalist, settled Cornwall, Ontario, 1783. [DF.pp]

MCDONELL, RODERICK, born in Glen Moriston, Inverness-shire, to America in 1774, settled on the Kingsborough Patent, NY, a Loyalist, soldier of the Royal Regiment of NY from 1776 to1783, later in Charlottenburg, Ontario. [DF.pp][PRO.AO12.28.390]

MCDOUGALL, ALEXANDER, born in Torodale, Kildalton, Islay, Argyll, during 1732, with his parents to NY on the Happy Return, married (1) Nancy MacDougall in 1751, who died in 1763, (2) Hannah Bostwick, commander of a privateer from 1756 to 1763, Major General in Washington's Army, died in NY during 1786.[Day Book of Daniel Campbell of Shawfield, 1767, AUP]

MCDOUGALL, ALEXANDER, born in 1753, a gardener from Galloway, via Stranraer to NY on the Galein May 1774. [PRO.T47.12]

MCDOUGALL, ALLAN, with his wife Elizabeth Graham, and their daughters Margaret, Anna and Hannah, from Islay, Argyll, aboard the Happy Return bound for NY in July 1738 to have settled at Wood Creek on the Hudson River, by 1763 Allan was dead but his widow, a son and four daughters were granted 300 acres on the Argyle Patent, NY. [HSPC][NY.Col.MS#72/170]

MCDOUGALL, ANGUS, from Islay, Argyll, aboard the Happy Return in June 1739 bound for NY and Wood Creek on the Hudson River, by 1763 he was married and living in the Highlands of NY when he was granted 200 acres on the Argyle Patent, NY. [HSBC][NY.Col.MS#72/170]

MCDOUGALL, ARCHIBALD, and his wife Christian McIntyre, with their sons John and Alexander, from Islay, Argyll, aboard the Happy Return bound for NY in July 1738 to have settled at Wood Creek on the Hudson River, in 1763 he, his wife, and five children were granted 350 acres on the Argyle Patent, NY. [HSPC][NY.Col.MS#72/170]

MCDOUGALL, DUNCAN, with his wife Janet Calder, and children John, Alexander, Ronald, Dugald and Margaret, from Islay, Argyll, aboard the Happy Return in June 1739 bound for NY and Wood Creek on the Hudson River, granted 400 acres on the Argyle Patent, NY, in 1763. [HSBC][NY.Col.MS#72/170]

MCDOUGALL, HUGH, from Islay, Argyll, aboard the Happy Return bound for NY in July 1738 to have settled at Wood Creek on the Hudson River, by 1763 he was resident on the Livingston Manor, NY, and was granted 200 acres on the Argyle Patent, NY. [HSPC][NY.Col.MS#72/170]

MCDOUGAL, JOHN, to America in 1773, settled in Argyle, Charlotte County, NY, Loyalist. [PRO.AO.12.29.230]

MCDOUGALL, JOHN, from Islay, Argyll, on the Happy Return to NY in 1739, during the French and Indian War of 1756-1763 he had fought and died as a privateer, in 1763 his brother Dugald McDougall in NY claimed his right to a grant on the Argyle Patent, NY. [NY.Col.MS#72/171]

MCDOUGALL, PETER, born in Inveraray, Argyll, a merchant in NY from 1782 onwards, married Helen Robertson in 1791, died on 19 Sep. 1798. [ANY#1.175] [NAS.CS17.1.6/51]

MCDOUGALL, RONALD, and his wife Bettie McDougall, and their sons John and Alexander, from Islay, Argyll, aboard the Happy Return bound for NY in July 1738 to have settled at Wood Creek on the Hudson River, in 1763 Ronald, his wife, Alexander a son, were

granted 300 acres on the Argyle Patent, NY.
[HSPC][NY.Col.MS#72/170]

MCDOWALL, ALEXANDER, born in 1749, a laborer from Galloway, via
Stranraer to NY on the Gale in May 1774. [PRO.T47.12]

MCDRUMMONT, MARY, born in 1759, a servant from Glen Coe, Argyll,
via Greenock to NY on the Commerce in Feb. 1775. [PRO.T47.12]

MCDUFFIE, ALEXANDER, (died on the voyage), and his wife Anna
Campbell, with their children Archibald, Duncan, James, Mary and
Isabel, from Islay, Argyll, in June 1739 aboard the Happy Return
bound for NY and Wood Creek on the Hudson River, in 1763 his
family was granted 250 acres on the Argyle Patent, NY.
[HSBC][NY.Col.MS#72/170]

MCDUFFIE, ARCHIBALD, with his wife Catherine Campbell, and sons
John and Duncan, from Islay, Argyll, in June 1739 aboard the Happy
Return bound for NY and Wood Creek on the Hudson River, dead by
1763 when his son Duncan and children were granted 150 acres on
the Argyle Patent, NY. [HSBC][NY.Col.MS#72/170]

MCDUFFIE, DUDLEY, with his wife Margaret Campbell, and son
Archibald, from Islay, Argyll, aboard the Happy Return bound for
NY in July 1738 to have settled at Wood Creek on the Hudson River,
dead by 1763 but his son and daughter were granted 150 acres on the
Argyle Patent, NY. [HSPC][NY.Col.MS#72/170]

MCDUFFIE, DUDLEY, with his wife Margaret McDougall, and their
children Dugald and Mary, from Islay, Argyll, in Nov. 1740 aboard
the Happy Return bound for NY and Wood Creek on the Hudson
River, in 1763 his widow, two sons and two daughters were granted
250 acres on the Argyle Patent, NY. [HSBC][NY.Col.MS#72/170]

MCDUFFIE, MALCOLM, with his wife Rose Docherty, and daughters
Margaret and Janet, from Islay, Argyll, aboard the Happy Return
bound for NY in July 1738 to have settled at Wood Creek on the
Hudson River, they, three sons and four daughters were granted 450
acres on the Argyle Patent, NY, in 1763.
[HSPC][NY.Col.MS#72/170]

MCECHERN, ARCHIBALD, with his wife Jean McDonald, and their
daughter Catherine, from Islay, Argyll, aboard the Happy Return
bound for NY in July 1738 to have settled at Wood Creek on the
Hudson River, by 1763 in their absence his cousin Finlay McEachern
offered to take their grant on their behalf.
[HSPC][NY.Col.MS#72/171]

MCEACHERN, DONALD, with his wife Anna McDonald, and daughter
Catherine, from Islay, Argyll, aboard the Happy Return bound for
NY in July 1738 to have settled at Wood Creek on the Hudson River,
he was dead by 1763 but his widow, three sons and three daughters
were granted 350 acres on the Argyle Patent,
NewYork.[HSPC][NY.Col.MS#72/170]

MCEACHERN, PATRICK, with Mary McQuarrie his wife, from Islay,
Argyll, in June 1739 aboard the Happy Return bound for NY and
Wood Creek on the Hudson River, in 1763 his widow was granted
100 acres on the Argyle Patent, NY. [HSBC][NY.Col.MS#72/170]

MCEUAN, ARCHIBALD, with his wife Janet McDougall, from Islay, Argyll, in June 1739 aboard the Happy Return bound for NY and Wood Creek on the Hudson River, he was dead by 1763 and a son and a daughter were granted 150 acres on the Argyle Patent, NY. [HSBC][NY.Col.MS#72/170]

MCEWAN, DUNCAN, a Covenanter who was transported from Leith to East NJ in July 1685. [RPCS#11.131]

MCEUAN, DUNCAN, son of Hugh McEuan, from Islay, Argyll, aboard the Happy Return bound for NY in July 1738 to have settled at Wood Creek on the Hudson River, by 1763 he had settled in NJ.[HSPC][NY.Col.MS#72/170]

MCEUAN, JAMES, from Islay, Argyll, in Nov. 1740 aboard the Happy Return bound for NY and Wood Creek on the Hudson River, believed to have settled in Boston by 1763. [HSPC][NY.Col.MS#72/170]

MCEWAN, JAMES, born in 1756, a nailer from Stirling, via Greenock to NY on the Lilly in Apr. 1775. [PRO.T47.12]

MCEUAN, JANET, daughter of Hugh McEuan, from Islay, Argyll, aboard the Happy Return bound for to NY in July 1738 to have settled at Wood Creek on the Hudson River, by 1763 she had settled in NJ. [HSPC][NY.Col.MS#72/170]

MCEWAN, JOHN, a Covenanter who was transported from Leith to East NJ on the Henry and Francis in Aug. 1685. [RPCS#11.154]

MCEUAN, JOHN, with Anna Johnston his wife, and son Malcolm, from Islay, Argyll, in June 1739 aboard the Happy Return bound for NY and Wood Creek on the Hudson River, in 1763 he, his wife and five sons were granted 400 acres on the Argyle Patent, NY. [NY.Col.MS#72/170] [HSBC]

MCEUAN, JOHN, from Islay, Argyll, in Nov. 1740 aboard the Happy Return bound for NY and Wood Creek on the Hudson River. [HSBC]

MCEUAN, MALCOLM, from Islay, Argyll, in June 1739 aboard the Happy Return bound for NY and Wood Creek on the Hudson River, dead by 1763 when his three children who had settled in NY were granted 200 acres on the Argyle Patent, NY. [HSBC][NY.Col.MS#72/170]

MCEUAN, MARY, from Islay, Argyll, aboard the Happy Return bound for NY in July 1738 to have settled at Wood Creek on the Hudson River, by 1763 she had settled in NJ. [HSPC][NY.Col.MS#72/170]

MCEUAN, MARY, daughter of John McEuan, from Islay, Argyll, aboard the Happy Return bound for NY in July 1738 to have settled at Wood Creek on the Hudson River, dead by 1763. [HSPC][NY.Col.MS#72/170]

MCEUAN, MERRAN, and her daughter, from Islay, Argyll, in June 1739 aboard the Happy Return bound for NY and Wood Creek on the Hudson River. [HSBC]

MCEWAN, ROBERT, from Leith to East NJ 1685. [NWI.I.423]

MCEWAN, WALTER, from Leith to East NJ 1685. [NWI.I.423]

MCEWER, KENNETH, born in 1751, a laborer from Loch Broom, Wester Ross, via Stornaway to Philadelphia on the Clementina in July 1775.

[PRO.T47/12]

MCFADYEN, DANIEL, a lorimer from Glasgow, settled in NY, husband
of Elizabeth ....., probate 1781 PCC

MCFAIDEN, DONALD, born in 1733, a farmer from Perthshire, via
Greenock to NY on the Monimia in May 1775. [PRO.T47.12]

MCFAIL, JAMES, probate 13 Nov. 1719 NY

MCFARLANE, ANDREW, a merchant from Blairnairns, Dunbartonshire,
settled in NY before 1752; son of Walter McFarlane in Stickentibert,
Arrochar.   [NAS.RS10.8.276; NAS.RD2.171.233/259]

MCFARLAN, ANN, born in 1757, a servant from Stornaway via Stornaway
to Philadelphia on the Friendship in May 1774. [PRO.T47.12]

MCFARLANE, JANET, born in 1756, a spinner from Glasgow, via
Greenock to NY on the Lilly in May 1775. [PRO.T47.12]

MCFARLANE, JOHN, born in 1755, a ropemaker from Glasgow, via
Greenock to NY on the Commerce in Feb. 1774. [PRO.T47.12]

MCFARLANE, JOHN, born in 1757, a hatter from Glasgow, from
Greenock to NY on the Commerce in Feb. 1774. [PRO.T47.12]

MCFARLAN, JOHN, born in 1758, a servant from Lochs, Isle of Lewis,
from Stornaway to Philadelphia on the Friendship in May 1774.
[PRO.T47.12]

MCFARLAN, KATHERINE, born in 1758, a servant from Edinburgh,
from Leith to Philadelphia on the Friendship in May 1775.
[PRO.T47.12]

MCFARLAN, PETER, born in 1755, a servant from Galson, Isle of Lewis,
from Stornaway to Philadelphia on the Friendship in May 1774.
[PRO.T47.12]

MCFARLANE, ROBERT, born in 1730, a farmer from Caithness, from
Greenock to NY or GA on the Christy in May 1775. [PRO.T47.12]

MCFARLANE, WALTER, son of Andrew McFarlane in Glenfruin, sought
in NY during 1773. [NY Gaz. & Wkly. Merc. 16.8.1773]

MCFEE, ARCHIBALD, born in 1745, a shoemaker from Banff, from
Greenock to Philadelphia on the Magdalene in Aug. 1774.
[PRO.T47.12]

MCGIBBON, JOHN, from Islay, Argyll, in Nov. 1740 aboard the Happy
Return bound for NY and Wood Creek on the Hudson River.
[HSBC]

MCGIBBON, PETER, born in 1748, a tailor from Paisley, from Greenock
to NY or GA on the Christy in May 1775. [PRO.T47.12]

MCGIE, JEAN, a Covenanter who was transported from Leith to East NJ
on the Henry and Francis on 5 Sep. 1685. [RPCS#11.166]

MCGIE, JOHN, a Covenanter who was transported from Leith to East NJ
on the Henry and Francis on 5 Sep. 1685. [RPCS#11.154]

MCGIE, WILLIAM, from Islay, Argyll, aboard the Happy Return bound
for NY in July 1738 to have settled at Wood Creek on the Hudson
River.[HSPC]

MCGILLIS, DONALD, born in Muneraghie, Inverness-shire, from Fort
William, Inverness-shire, on the Pearl bound for NY in 1773, settled
on the Kingsborough Patent, NY, a Loyalist and Sergeant of the
Royal Regiment of NY from 1777 to 1783, later settled in

Williamstown, Charlottenburg, Ontario. [DF.pp]

MCGILLVRAY, JOHN, indented in Chester County, PA, Sep.1695.
[Sgen.29.1.11]

MCGILVRAY, JOHN, with his wife Catherine McDonald, and their
children Hugh, Donald, Bridget, and Mary, from Islay, Argyll, in
Nov. 1740 aboard the Happy Return bound for NY and Wood Creek
on the Hudson River, by 1763 he was dead but a son then living in NJ
was granted 100 acres on the Argyle Patent, NY.
[HSBC][NY.Col.MS#72/170]

MCGILVRAY, EFFIE, from Islay, Argyll on the Happy Return to NY in
1739, by 1763 she was living in NY. [NY.Col.MS#72/171]

MCGLASHAN, ROBERT, born in 1736, a farmer from Stranraer,
Wigtownshire, with his daughters Jean and Catherine from Greenock
to NY or GA on the Christy in May 1775. [PRO.T47.12]

MCGLON, ANDREW, grocer in Philadelphia, Loyalist in 1776.
[PRO.AO13.71A.155]

MCGOUGHTRY, JOHN, born in 1734, a farmer from Gatehouse,
Kirkcudbrightshire, with his children James, John, Agnes,
Alexander, and William, from Stranraer to NY on the Galeof
Whitehaven in May 1774. [PRO.T47.12]

MCGOUGHTRY, MARGARET, born in 1753, from Girthon,
Kirkcudbrightshire, with daughter Jane, from Stranraer to NY on the
Galeof Whitehaven in May 1774. [PRO.T47.12]

MCGOUGHTRY, RICHARD, born in 1706, a farmer from Gatehouse,
from Stranraer to NY on the Galeof Whitehaven in May 1774.
[PRO.T47.12]

MCGOWAN, ARCHIBALD, and his three children, Duncan, John and
Margaret, from Islay, Argyll, in June 1739 aboard the Happy Return
bound for NY and Wood Creek on the Hudson River, dead by 1763
when his grandson Archibald and a daughter with four sons were
granted 200 acres on the Argyle Patent, NY.
[HSBC][NY.Col.MS#72/170]

MCGOWAN, JAMES, born in Glasgow during 1735, a laborer and a
soldier of Captain John Haslet's Company of the PA Regiment who
enlisted on 7 May 1759.[Pa.Archives#5/1/285]

MCGOWN, JOHN, with his wife Anna McCuarg, and sons Malcolm and
Angus, from Islay, Argyll, aboard the Happy Return in June 1739
bound for NY and Wood Creek on the Hudson River, in 1763 John
and his wife were granted 200 acres on the Argyle Patent, NY.
[HSBC][NY.Col.MS#72/170]

MCGOWN, MALCOLM, with his children Patrick and Hector, from Islay,
Argyll, in June 1739 aboard the Happy Return bound for NY and
Wood Creek on the Hudson River, in 1763 a son was granted 200
acres on the Argyle Patent, NY. [HSBC][NY.Col.MS#72/170]

MCGOWAN, MARGARET, born in 1754, from Stirling, from Greenock
to NY on the Matty in May 1774. [PRO.T47.12]

MCGREGOR, ALEXANDER, a soldier, married Mary Swan, in NY on 19
Jan. 1763. [PCR]

MCGREGOR, DONALD, a thief, transported from Leith to East NJ in

1684, settled in Perth-Amboy. [Insh#245][RPCS#8.514]

MCGREGOR, DONALD, to America in 1764, settled Johnstown, Tryon County, NY, Loyalist. [PRO.AO12.28.364]

MCGREGOR, DUNCAN, a horsethief from Perthshire, transported from Greenock to NJ in Nov. 1764. [NAS.B59.26.11.6.39]

MCGREGOR, DUNCAN, a soldier, married Mary Christie, in NY on 5 Mar. 1760. [PCR]

MCGREGOR, HUGH, born in 1733, a farmer from Breadalbane, Perthshire, with his wife Jean McNaughton and children Donald and Katherine, from Greenock to NY on the Commerce in June 1775. [PRO.T47.12]; possibly settled in Tryon County, NY, Loyalist. [PRO.AO.12.3.61]

MCGREGOR, Captain PATRICK, from Perthshire, to East NJ in 1684. [Insh#236]

MCGREGOR, PETER, indentured servant, to East NJ 1684. [NJSA.EJD.A184]

MCGRIGOR, DUNCAN, born in 1736, a piper from Glen Coe, Argyllshire, with his wife Katherine Duncan and children Mary and Hugh, from Greenock to NY on the Commerce in Feb. 1775. [PRO.T47.12]

MCGRUER, DONALD, to America in 1773, a farmer at Johnson's Bush, Kingsborough Patent, NY, a Loyalist and a soldier of the 84th Regiment, died at Sorel 1781 [DF.pp][PRO.AO12.29.252]

MCGRUER, JOHN, born in Boleskine, Abertarff, Inverness-shire, from Fort William, Inverness-shire, to America on the Pearl in 1773, settled on the Kingsborough Patent, NY, by 1775, a Loyalist and Corporal of the Royal Regiment of NY, later settled in Charlottenburg, Ontario. [DF.pp] [PRO.AO12.29.49]

MCGUIRE, LAUCHLANE MCQUARY, a shipmaster from Campbeltown, Argyll, settled in NY, husband of Katherine ...., died in Jan. 1783, cnf 1785. [NAS.CC8.8.126]

MCGUMRI, ANGUS, born in 1755, from Branahuie, Isle of Lewis, from Stornaway to Philadelphia on the Friendship in May 1774. [PRO.T47.12]

MCHAIG, JOHN, born in 1738, a farmer from Galloway, with his wife Grizzel and daughters Margaret and Ann, from Stranraer to NY on the Gale of Whitehaven in May 1774. [PRO.T47.12]

MCHARG, THOMAS, born in 1723, a tailor, enlisted in the PA Regiment on 6 May 1759. [Pa.Archives#5/1/299]

MCILPHEDER, ARCHIBALD, who had settled in the Highlands of NY, was granted 200 acres on the Argyle Patent, NY, in 1763. [NY.Col.MS#72/170]

MCILPHEDER, CATHERINE, from Islay, Argyll, in June 1739 aboard the Happy Return bound for NY and Wood Creek on the Hudson River, by 1763 she was married with children and living in the Highlands of New York when she was granted 150 acres on the Argyle Patent, NY. [HSBC][NY.Col.MS#72/170]

MCILVAINE, WILLIAM, born in Ayr, to Philadelphia around 1740, a merchant resident in Fairview near Bristol, PA, died 1770.

[AP#244][NAS.CS16.1.130]

MCILVREY, EFFIE, from Islay, Argyll, in Nov. 1740 aboard the Happy Return bound for NY and Wood Creek on the Hudson River.[HSBC]

MCINDEORA, MERRAN, from Islay, Argyll, in Nov. 1740 aboard the Happy Return bound for NY and Wood Creek on the Hudson River. [HSBC]

MACINNISH, MURDO, with his wife Merran McDonald, and children Catherine, Archibald, Neil, Anna and Florence, from Islay, Argyll, in June 1739 aboard the Happy Return bound for NY and Wood Creek on the Hudson River, in 1763 his six grandchildren were granted 200 acres on the Argyle Patent, NY. [NY.Col.MS#72/170][HSBC]

MCINNISH, NEIL, with his wife Catherine McDonald, from Islay, Argyll, in June 1739 aboard the Happy Return bound for NY and Wood Creek on the Hudson River. [HSBC]

MCINNISH, NEIL, son of Murdoch McInnish, had deceased and his widow, now married to Allen McDonald, was granted 100 acres on the Argyle Patent, NY.[NY.Col.MS#72/170]

MCINTAGGART, JOHN, from Islay, Argyll, aboard the Happy Return bound for NY in July 1738 to have settled at Wood Creek on the Hudson River.[HSPC]

MCINTAYLOR, DONALD, from Islay, Argyll, aboard the Happy Return bound for NY in July 1738 to have settled at Wood Creek on the Hudson River.[HSPC]

MCINTAYLOR, JOHN, born 1717, a tailor, settled in NY as an indentured servant to Lt. Gov. George Clark in 1738, ran away in 1739. [NY Gaz., 29.10.1739]

MCINTAYLOR, JOHN, from Islay, Argyll, aboard the Happy Return bound for NY in July 1738 to have settled at Wood Creek on the Hudson River, by 1763 he was dead when his cousin Donald Smith, a mariner in NY, claimed a right to his grant on the Argyle Estate, NY.[HSPC][NY.Col.MS#72/171]

MCINTOSH, ALEXANDER, born in 1754, a servant from Balnacoter, from Stornaway to Philadelphia on the Clementina in July 1775. [PRO.T47.12]

MCINTOSH, ALEXANDER, to America 1773, Loyalist soldier 1778. [PRO.AO12.29.318]

MCINTOSH, ANDREW, born in 1748, a laborer from Elgin, Moray, from Stornaway to Philadelphia on the Clementina in July 1775. [PRO.T47.12]

MACINTOSH, ANGUS, from Islay, Argyll, in June 1739 aboard the Happy Return bound for NY and Wood Creek on the Hudson River.[HSBC]

MCINTOSH, DAVID, born in 1752, a farmer from Perth, from Greenock to NY on the Lilly in May 1775. [PRO.T47.12]

MCINTOSH, DONALD, a thief from Stirling, was transported from Leith to East NJ in 1684. [RPCS#8.514]

MCINTOSH, DONALD, indented in Chester County, PA, 5 Aug.1697. [Sgen.29.1.13]

MCINTOSH, GEORGE, a laborer who was killed in NY during 1764.
[NY Merc., 21.5.1764]

MCINTOSH, HUGH, born in Perth during 1723, a laborer, enlisted in the
PA Regiment on 8 May 1758. [PaArch#5/1/143]

MCINTOSH, HUGH, settled in NY 1763, Loyalist in 1776.
[PRO.AO12.102.176]

MCINTOSH, JAMES, soldier in the French and Indian Wars, settled at
Ticonderoga, NY, Loyalist, died 1785. [PRO.AO12.26.308]

MCINTOSH, JAMES, born in Strathdearn during 1754, son of William
Roy McIntosh of Dell and Marjory McIntosh, to NY in 1776, a
merchant in NY, died 4 Nov. 1811. [ANY#1.176]

MCINTOSH, JOHN, born Inverness 1737, a silversmith who deserted the
17th Foot at Ticonderoga, NY, 1760. [NY.Merc., 3.3.1760]

MCINTOSH, JOHN, 5'3", a goldsmith, enlisted in the PA Regiment on
May 1758 in Bucks County, PA. [Pa.Archives:#5/1/358]

MCINTOSH, JOHN, to America in 1773, settled on the Kingsborough
Patent, NY, soldier of the 84th Regiment from 1776 to 1783, later
settled at River aux Raisins, Ontario. [DF.pp]

MCINTOSH, MARY, born in 1767, a spinster from Baluinch, Daviot,
Inverness-shire, to NY on the George on 12 Aug. 1807.
[PRO.PC1.3790]

MCINTOSH, PETER, born in 1747, a wright from Glasgow, from
Greenock to NY on the Monimia in May 1775. [PRO.T47.12]

MCINTYRE, ARCHIBALD, born in Ayr during 1739, a laborer and a
soldier of Captain John Haslet's Company of the PA Regiment who
enlisted on 5 May 1759. [Pa.Archives#5/1/285]

MCINTYRE, CHARLES, born in 1761, a servant from Kilsyth, from
Leith to Philadelphia on the Friendship in May 1775. [PRO.T47.12]

MCINTYRE, DONALD, from Islay, Argyll, aboard the Happy Return
bound for NY in July 1738 to have settled at Wood Creek on the
Hudson River, by 1763 he was living in NY with his son and wife
when he was granted 250 acres on the Argyle Patent, NY.
[HSPC][NY.Col.MS#72/170]

MCINTYRE, DONALD, born in 1732, a schoolmaster from Breadalbane,
Perthshire, with his wife Ann Walker and children Katherine, Ann,
and Archibald, from Greenock to NY on the Commerce in June
1775.[PRO.T47.12]

MCINTYRE, DUNCAN, born in 1733, a mason from Perthshire, from
Greenock to NY on the Monimia in May 1775. [PRO.T47.12]

MCINTYRE, JOHN, from Islay, Argyll, in Nov. 1740 aboard the Happy
Return bound for NY and Wood Creek on the Hudson River, by 1763
he was a clergyman in PA, and was granted 200 acres on the Argyle
Patent, NY, and a further 500 acres for a place of worship and a
schoolhouse. [HSBC][NY.Col.MS#72/170]

MCINTYRE, NICHOLAS, with his wife Margaret Paterson, and children
John and Catherine, from Islay, Argyll, in June 1739 aboard the
Happy Return bound for NY and Wood Creek on the Hudson River,
in 1763 his widow, two sons and two daughters were granted 250
acres on the Argyle Patent, New York. [HSBC][NY.Col.MS#72/170]

MCINTIRE, PETER, born in 1744, a laborer, deserted from Captain Richard Rea's NY troops at Schenectady, NY, in 1764. [NY.Merc., 5.4.1764]

MCISAAC, MALCOLM, born in 1746 son of Archibald McIsaac, a smith from Breadalbane, Perthshire, from Greenock to NY on the Commerce in June 1775, died in NY, probate 1781 PCC [PRO.T47.12]

MCIVER, ALEXANDER, born in 1753, a merchant from Glasgow, from Greenock to NY on the Matty in May 1774. [PRO.T47.12]

MCIVER, ANGUS, born in 1757, a servant from Back, Isle of Lewis, from Stornaway to Philadelphia on the Friendship in May 1774. [PRO.T47.12]

MCIVER, ANGUS, born in 1761, a servant from Uig, Isle of Lewis, from Stornaway to Philadelphia on the Friendship in May 1774. [PRO.T47.12]

MCIVER, ANGUS, born in 1746, a servant from Stornaway, Isle of Lewis, from Stornaway to Philadelphia on the Friendship in May 1774. [PRO.T47.12]

MACIVER, DONALD, born at Lochalsh, Wester Ross, on 1 Nov. 1778, son of Reverend Murdoch MacIver and Mary McKenzie, later a merchant in NY, died in Bermuda. [F#7.155]

MCIVER, DUNCAN, born 1746, a farmer from Coll, Lewis, with Margaret his wife from Stornaway to Philadelphia on the Friendship in May 1774. [PRO.T47.12]

MCIVER, JAMES, in NY, 1769. [NAS.CS16.1.138]

MCIVER, JOHN, born in 1765, from Sheshader, Isle of Lewis, from Stornaway to Philadelphia on the Friendship in May 1774. [PRO.T47.12]

MCIVER, KATHERINE, born in 1761, a servant from Sheshader, Isle of Lewis, from Stornaway to Philadelphia on the Friendship in May 1774. [PRO.T47.12]

MCIVER, MARY, born in 1769, from Sheshader, Isle of Lewis, from Stornaway to Philadelphia on the Friendship in May 1774. [PRO.T47.12]

MCIVER, PETER, born in 1759, a servant from Bragar, Isle of Lewis, from Stornaway to Philadelphia on the Friendship in May 1774. [PRO.T47.12]

MCKACKEY, JOHN, born in 1749, a smith from Galloway, from Stranraer to NY on the Galein May 1774. [PRO.T47.12]

MCKAIRICK, JAMES, born in 1740, a farmer from Morayshire, with Mary his wife and children John, Alexander, William and Elizabeth, from Stornaway to Philadelphia on the Clementina, in July 1775. [PRO.T47.12]

MCKAY, AENEAS, former army officer, settled in NY, Loyalist. [PRO.AO13.56.95]

MCKAY, ALEXANDER, born in 1748, a laborer fron Beauly, Inverness-shire, with his wife Anne and daughter Jean, from Stornaway to Philadelphia on the Clementina in July 1775. [PRO.T47.12]

MCKAY, ANGUS, to America in 1772, settled on the Kingsborough

Patent, NY. 25 Sep. 1773, a Loyalist who moved to Canada in 1776, then a soldier of the Royal Regiment of NY, later in Lancaster, Glengarry, Ontario.[PRO.AO12.31.87]

MCKAY, DONALD, to America in 1773, settled on the Kingsborough Patent, NY, a Loyalist and soldier of the Royal Regiment of NY, married Elspeth Kennedy settled at River aux Raisins, Ontario. [DF.pp][PRO.AO12.29.150]

MCKAY, DUNCAN, from Islay, Argyll, in Nov. 1740 aboard the Happy Return bound for NY and Wood Creek on the Hudson River. [HSBC]

MCKAY, ISOBEL, born in 1752, a servant from Ross-shire, from Leith to Philadelphia on the Friendship in May 1775. [PRO.T47.12]

MCKAY, JAMES, born in 1759, from Edinburgh, from Leith to Philadelphia on the Friendship in May 1775. [PRO.T47.12]

MCKAY, JANET, spouse of ......McGeachy a merchant in NY, edict of Executry, 1781. [NAS.CC2.8.83, 6/7]

MCKAY, JOHN, born in 1756, a farmer from Strathspey, from Greenock to NY on the George May 1774. [PRO.T47.12]

MACKAY, JOHN, born in 1759, a husbandman from Inverness, from London to Philadelphia on the Amelia in Jan. 1774. [PRO.T47.9/11]

MCKAY, JOHN, born in 1759, a servant from Beauly, Inverness-shire, from Stornaway to Philadelphia on the Clementina in July 1775. [PRO.T47.12]

MCKAY, JOHN, born in 1760, a ballad singer from Rogart, Sutherlandshire, from Leith to Philadelphia on the Friendship in May 1775.[PRO.T47.12]

MCKAY, WILLIAM, born in 1751, a farmer from Inverness, from Greenock to NY on the George, May 1774. [PRO.T47.12]

MCKAY, WILLIAM, born in 1751, a servant from Duffus, Morayshire, from Stornaway to Philadelphia on the Clementina in July 1775. [PRO.T47.12]

MCKELLAR, ARCHIBALD, with his wife Janet Reid, from Islay, Argyll, aboard the Happy Return bound for NY in July 1738 to have settled at Wood Creek on the Hudson River, in 1763 he was dead and his widow and eight children were granted 450 acres on the Argyle Patent, NY.[HSPC][NY.Col.MS#72/170]

MCKELLAR, CHARLES, and his wife Florence McEachern, with their daughters Margaret, Catherine and Mary, from Islay, Argyll, to NY in July 1738 to have settled at Wood Creek on the Hudson River, in 1763 his widow and seven children were granted 400 acres on the Argyle Patent, NY. [HSPC]

MCKELSON, JOHN, with wife Margaret Sturrock, indentured servants, to East NJ 1684. [NJSA.EJD.A187]

MACKEMIE, ANDREW, indentured servant, to East NJ 1684. [NJSA.EJD.A196]

MCKENNA, JOHN, settled in NY, Loyalist in 1776. [PRO.AO12.24.243]

MCKENNOT, JAMES, born in 1756, a coppersmith from Glasgow, from Greenock to NY on the Commerce in Feb. 1774. [PRO.T47.12]

MCKENNY, DANIEL, born in 1716, a laborer, enlisted in Captain John Deimer's Company of the PA Regiment in 1746. [PaArch#5/1/6]

MACKENNY, JAMES, born in 1714, from Atholl, Perthshire, from
    London to PA in Sep. 1733. [CLRO/AIA]

MACKENNY, JOHN, probate 6 Dec. 1690 Newcastle County, Del.

MCKENNY, JOHN, a tailor in NY, probate 2 May 1777 NY.

MACKENZIE, AENEAS, born in 1675, a minister educated at Aberdeen
    and Edinburgh universities around 1692, by 1705 in NJ and in NY.
    [EMA#42]

MCKENZIE, ALEXANDER, born 1681, indented in Chester County, PA,
    5 Aug.1697. [Sgen.29.1.13]

MCKENZIE, ALEXANDER, born in 1733, a weaver from Inverness, with
    his wife Isabel and children Anne, Catherine, Alexander and Isobel,
    from Stornaway to Philadelphia on the Clementina in July 1775.
    [PRO.T47.12]

MCKENZIE, ALEXANDER, born in 1755, a servant from Fairburn, Ross-
    shire, from Stornaway to Philadelphia on the Clementina in July
    1775. [PRO.T47.12]

MCKENZIE, ALEXANDER, born in 1762, from Stornaway, Isle of Lewis,
    from Stornaway to NY on the Peace and Plenty in Nov. 1774.
    [PRO.T47.12]

MCKENZIE, ALEXANDER, sometime Ensign of the 2nd Battalion of the
    King's Royal Regiment of NY, afterwards tacksman of Elgin in
    Assynt, deceased, and his relict Isabella, 1799. [NAS.CS17.1.18/194]

MCKENZIE, ANGUS, born in 1757, a spinner from Paisley, from
    Greenock to NY on the Commerce in Feb. 1774. [PRO.T47.12]

MCKENZIE, ANN, born in 1756, a servant from Coigach, Ross-shire,
    from Stornaway to NY on the Peace and Plenty in Nov. 1774.
    [PRO.T47.12]

MCKENZIE, ANNE, born in 1750, a servant from Beauly, Inverness-shire,
    from Stornaway to Philadelphia on the Clementina, in July 1775.
    [PRO.T47.12]

MCKENZIE, CATHERINE, born in 1746, a servant from Beauly,
    Inverness-shire, from Stornaway to Philadelphia on the Clementina
    in July 1775. [PRO.T47.12]

MCKENZIE, CHRISTINE, born in 1763, a servant from Wester Leys, Isle
    of Lewis, from Stornaway to Philadelphia on the Clementina in July
    1775. [PRO.T47.12]

MCKENZIE, CHRISTINE, born in 1771, a servant from Stornaway, Isle
    of Lewis, from Stornaway to Philadelphia on the Friendship in July
    1774. [PRO.T47.12]

MCKENZIE, DAVID, from Auldearn, Nairnshire, from London to NY in
    Aug. 1754. [CLRO/AIA]

MCKENZIE, DONALD, born in 1762, a servant from Wester Leys, Isle of
    Lewis, from Stornaway to Philadelphia on the Clementina in July
    1775. [PRO.T47.12]

MCKENZIE, DONALD, son of William McKenzie born 1748
    schoolmaster at Leys died 7 July 1838 and Janet Chisholm born 1754
    died 1815, settled in Caledonia, Livingstone County, NY. [Dunlichty
    g/s, Inverness-shire]

MACKENZIE, DUNCAN, born in 1752, a farmer from Strathspey, via

Greenock to NY on the <u>George</u> in May 1774. [PRO.T47.12]

MACKENZIE, DUNCAN, born in 1758, a servant from Coll, Isle of Lewis, from Stornaway to Philadelphia on the <u>Friendship</u>, in May 1774. [PRO.T47.12]

MCKENZIE, ELIZABETH, born in 1763, a servant from Wester Lys, Isle of Lewis, from Stornaway to Philadelphia on the <u>Clementina</u> in July 1775.[PRO.T47.12]

MACKENZIE, FINLAY born 1702, a cooper from Stornaway, Isle of Lewis, with his wife Mary and sons John and Donald from Stornaway to Philadelphia on the <u>Friendship</u> in May 1774. [PRO.T47.12]

MACKENZIE, FINLAY, born in 1729, a cooper from Stornaway, Isle of Lewis, with his wife Mary and son John from Stornaway to Philadelphia on the <u>Friendship</u> in May 1774. [PRO.T47.12]

MCKENZIE, FRANCIS, born in 1746, a laborer from Islay, Argyll, from Greenock to NY on the <u>Lilly</u> in Apr. 1775. [PRO.T47.12]

MCKENZIE, GEORGE, a merchant from Edinburgh, son of Sir John MacKenzie, to East NJ 1684, in Elizabethtown, NJ. [Insh#237], in NY 1689. [NYD.3/614][SPAWI.1689.352/360]

MCKENZIE, GEORGE, with his wife Catherine McNiven, and sons Donald and Colin, from Islay, Argyll, to NY in July 1738 to have settled at Wood Creek on the Hudson River, by 1763 they had moved to NJ but were granted 300 acres on the Argyle Patent, NY. [HSPC]

MCKENZIE, ISOBEL, born in 1735, from Inverness, with her children Anne and John from Stornaway to Philadelphia on the <u>Clementina</u> in July 1775.[PRO.T47.12]

MCKENZIE, ISABEL, born in 1747, a servant from Braen, from Stornaway to Philadelphia on the <u>Clementina</u> in July 1775. [PRO.T47.12]

MCKENZIE, ISABEL, born in 1756, a servant from Stornaway, Isle of Lewis, from Stornaway to NY on the <u>Peace and Plenty</u> in Nov. 1774. [PRO.T47.12]

MCKENZIE, ISABEL, born in 1757 a servant from Coigach, Ross-shire, from Stornaway to NY on the <u>Peace and Plenty</u> in Nov. 1774. [PRO.T47.12]

MCKENZIE, ISABEL, born in 1758, a servant from Ross-shire, from Leith to Philadelphia on the <u>Friendship</u> in May 1775. [PRO.T47.12]

MCKENZIE, JEAN, born in 1754, a servant from Stornaway, Isle of Lewis, from Stornaway to Philadelphia on the <u>Friendship</u> in May 1774.[PRO.T47.12]

MCKENZIE, JOHN, indentured servant in Middlesex County, NJ, 1693. [NJSA.EJD.D]

MCKENZIE, JOHN, born in 1736, a laborer from Beauly, Inverness-shire, with his wife Anne and sons James and Donald from Stornaway to Philadelphia on the <u>Clementina</u> in July 1774. [PRO.T47.12]

MCKENZIE, JOHN, born in 1744, a tailor from Loch Broom, Wester Ross, from Stornaway to NY on the <u>Peace and Plenty</u> in Nov. 1774. [PRO.T47.12]

MCKENZIE, JOHN, born in 1749, a farmer from Strathspey, from

Greenock to NY on the George, May 1774. [PRO.T47.12]

MCKENZIE, JOHN, born in 1754, a servant from Stornaway, Isle of
Lewis, from Stornaway to Philadelphia on the Peace and Plenty in
Nov. 1774.[PRO.T47.12]

MCKENZIE, JOHN, born in 1756, a servant from Ness, Isle of Lewis,
from Stornaway to Philadelphia on the Friendship in May
1774.[PRO.T47.12]

MCKENZIE, JOHN, born in 1757, a servant from Poolewe, Wester Ross,
from Stornaway to Philadelphia on the Peace and Plenty in Nov.
1774. [PRO.T47.12]

MCKENZIE, JOHN, born in 1757, a servant from Inverness, from
Stornaway to Philadelphia on the Clementina in July 1775.
[PRO.T47.12]

MCKENZIE, JOHN, born in 1764, a servant from Beauly, Inverness-shire,
from Stornaway to Philadelphia on the Clementina in July 1775.
[PRO.T47.12]

MACKENZIE, JOHN, born in 1777, a farmer from Baluich, Daviot,
Inverness-shire, to NY on the George 12 Aug.1807. [PRO.PC1.3790]

MCKENZIE, KATHERINE, born in 1765, from Stornaway, Isle of Lewis,
from Stornaway to Philadelphia on the Friendship in May 1774.
[PRO.T47.12]

MCKENZIE, KENNETH, the younger, from Kildin, Isle of Lewis, to East
NJ in 1684. [Insh#236]

MCKENZIE, KENNETH, born in 1737,a farmer from Fairburn, Ross-
shire, from Stornaway to Philadelphia with his children John and
Mary on the Clementina in July 1775. [PRO.T47.12]

MCKENZIE, KENNETH, born in 1750, a gardener from Edinburgh, from
Leith to Philadelphia on the Friendship in May 1775. [PRO.T47.12]

MCKENZIE, KENNETH, born in 1761, a servant from Beauly, Inverness-
shire, from Stornaway to Philadelphia on the Clementina in July
1775. [PRO.T47.12]

MCKENZIE, JOHN, and his wife Mary McVurrich, and their children
Archibald and Florence, from Islay, Argyll, to NY in July 1738 to
have settled at Wood Creek on the Hudson River, in 1763 a surviving
daughter was granted 100 acres on the Argyle Patent, NY. [HSPC]

MCKENZIE, MALCOM FORBES, born in 1752, a barber from
Edinburgh, from Greenock to NY on the Lilly in 1775. [PRO.T47.12]

MCKENZIE, MARGARET, born in 1752, a servant from Culduthel,
Inverness-shire, from Stornaway to Philadelphia on the Clementina in
July 1775.[PRO.T47.12]

MCKENZIE, MARGARET, born in 1753, a servant from Inverness, from
Stornaway to Philadelphia on the Clementina in July 1775.
[PRO.T47.12]

MCKENZIE, MARJORY, born in 1755, a servant from Wester Leys, Isle
of Lewis, from Stornaway to Philadelphia on the Clementina in July
1775. [PRO.T47.12]

MCKENZIE, MARY, born in 1749, a servant from Stornaway, Isle of
Lewis, from Stornaway to Philadelphia on the Peace and Plenty in
Nov. 1774. [PRO.T47.12]

MCKENZIE, MARY, born in 1763, a servant from Stornaway, Isle of Lewis, from Stornaway to Philadelphia on the Friendship in May 1774. [PRO.T47.12]

MCKENZIE, MURDO, born in 1734, a farmer from Bayble, Isle of Lewis, with Annabella McIver his wife and their children Mary, Katherine, and Christian from Stornaway to Philadelphia on the Friendship in May 1774. [PRO.T47.12]

MCKENZIE, MURDO, born in 1744, a farmer from Bayble, Isle of Lewis, with Donald his son from Stornaway to Philadelphia on the Friendship in May 1774. [PRO.T47.12]

MCKENZIE, MURDOCH, born in 1738, a servant from Leys, Isle of Lewis, from Stornaway to Philadelphia on the Clementina in July 1775. [PRO.T47.12]

MCKENZIE, MURDOCH, born in 1747, a servant from Blysary, Inverness-shire, from Stornaway to Philadelphia on the Peace and Plenty, in Nov. 1774. [PRO.T47.12]

MCKENZIE, MURDOCH, born in 1757, a servant from Stornaway, Isle of Lewis, from Stornaway to Philadelphia on the Peace and Plenty in Nov. 1774. [PRO.T47.12]

MCKENZIE, NORMAN, indentured servant, to East NJ 1684. [NJSA.EJD.A184]

MCKENZIE, RORY, born in 1760, a servant from Stornaway, Isle of Lewis, from Stornaway to Philadelphia on the Friendship in May 1774. [PRO.T47.12]

MCKENZIE, SIMON, son of William McKenzie born 1748 schoolmaster at Leys died 7 July 1838 and Janet Chisholm born 1754 died 1815, settled in Caledonia, Livingstone County, NY. [Dunlichty g/s, Inverness-shire]

MCKENZIE, THOMAS, born in 1757, a servant from Fairburn, Ross-shire, from Stornaway to Philadelphia on the Clementina in July 1775. [PRO.T47.12]

MCKENZIE, WILLIAM, born in 1729, a farmer from Auchall, Ross-shire, with Mary his wife and their children Catherine, Barbara, Molly, Ann, Florence, Thomas, Murdoch, Belle, and Nelly C. from Stornaway to NY on the Peace and Plenty in Nov.1774. [PRO.T47.12]

MCKENZIE, WILLIAM, born in 1757, a farmer from Strathspey, via Greenock to NY on the George in May 1774. [PRO.T47.12]

MCKENZIE, WILLIAM, born in 1759, a servant from Poolewe, Wester Ross, from Stornaway to NY on the Peace and Plenty in Nov. 1774. [PRO.T47.12]

MCKIE, GEORGE, born in 1727, a farmer from Inch, Wigtownshire, with Jean McMiken his wife and their children Peter, Thomas, Janet, David, Jean and Alexander, from Stranraer to NY aboard the Jackie of Glasgow on 31 May 1775. [PRO.T47.12]

MCKIE, JANET, a prisoner from the Tolbooth of Edinburgh, transported from Greenock to NY on 21 Oct. 1682. [NAS.HH11#221]

MCKIE, JEAN, born in 1772, from Galloway, from Stranraer to NY on the Gale of Whitehaven in May 1774. [PRO.T47.12]

MCKIE, JOHN, born in 1757, a laborer from Water of Orr, Colvend, Kirkcudbrightshire, from Kirkcudbright to NY on the Adventure of Liverpool in May 1774.[PRO.T47.12]

MCKIE, MARGARET, born in 1748, from Galloway, from Stranraer to NY on the Gale of Whitehaven, in May 1774. [PRO.T47.12]

MCKIE, SAMUEL, born in 1748, a weaver from Galloway, from Stranraer to NY on the Gale, in May 1774. [PRO.T47.12]

MCKIE, WILLIAM, a Covenanter who was transported from Leith to East NJ in July 1685. [RPCS#11.95]

MCKINLY, JEAN, born in 1748, from Galloway, from Stranraer to NY on the Gale of Whitehaven in May 1774. [PRO.T47.12]

MCKINLAY, JOHN, born in 1754, a weaver from Paisley, from Greenock to NY on the Lilly in May 1775. [PRO.T47.12]

MCKINLY, MICHAEL, born in 1734, a farmer from Galloway,from Stranraer to NY on the Gale in May 1774. [PRO.T47.12]

MCKINLAY, PETER, born in 1751, a wright from Glasgow, from Greenock to NY on the Monimia, in May 1775. [PRO.T47.12]

MCKINNELL, JOHN, in NY, shipmaster of the Fame of New York cnf 16 July 1784. [NAS.CC8.8.126]

MCKINNEL, MARY, born in 1750, from Kirkmichael, from Stranraer to NY aboard the Gale on 31 May 1775. [PRO.T47.12]

MCKINNEY, ALEXANDER, indented in Chester County, PA, 3 Oct.1693. [Sgen.29.1.11]

MCKINVEN, DUNCAN, with his wife Marian McCollum, and their children Donald and Mary, from Islay, Argyll, in Nov. 1740 bound for NY and Wood Creek on the Hudson River, in 1763 he, a son and three daughters were granted 250 acres on the Argyle Patent, NY. [HSBC][NY.Col.MS#72/170]

MCKIRCHEN, JOHN, born in 1726, a farmer from Glen Coe, Argyll, with Ann McGreig his wife and their children Donald, Margaret, Donald and Eliza, from Greenock to NY on the Commerce in Feb. 1775. [PRO.T47.12]

MCKISSACK, JANET, born in 1718, from Galloway, from Stranraer to NY on the Gale of Whitehaven in May 1774. [PRO.T47.12]

MCKISSACK, THOMAS, born in 1748, a farmer from Galloway, from Stranraer to NY on the Gale in May 1774. [PRO.T47.12]

MCKNIGHT, HUGH, born in Argyllshire during 1729, 5'4", a laborer who enlisted in the PA Regiment on 4 May 1758. [Pa.Archives#5/1/158]

MCKOREST, MARY, born in 1757, a servant from Breadalbane, Perthshire, from Greenock to NY on the Commerce in June 1775. [PRO.T47.12]

MACKY, ALEXANDER, a petitioner in NY 1701. [DNY.IV.934]

MCLAINE, HECTOR, in NY 1776. [NAS.GD174.1303]

MCLAINE, JOHN, in NY, 1784. [NAS.GD174.1361]

MCLAINE, PETER, a petitioner in NY 1701. [DNY.IV.934]

MCLAREN, DUNCAN, son of Donald McLaren and Margaret McGregor, settled in NY during 1783, died there on 17 Aug. 1825, buried in Greenwood Cemetery. [Comrie g/s, Perthshire]

MCLAREN, HUGH, born 1741, farmer from Breadalbane, Perthshire, from

Greenock to NY on the Commerce in June 1775. [PRO.T47.12]

MCLAREN, JOHN, born in 1754, a wright from Edinburgh, from
Greenock to NY on the Lilly in Apr. 1775. [PRO.T47.12]

MCLAURENCE, DAVID, born in 1752, a barber from Edinburgh, from
Greenock to NY on the Lilly in Apr. 1775. [PRO.T47.12]

MCLEA, WILLIAM, born in 1746, a laborer from Islay, Argyll, from
Greenock to NY on the Lilly in Apr. 1775. [PRO.T47.12]

MCLEAN, ALEXANDER, indented in Chester County, PA, by 1696,
settled in Del. [Sgen.29.1.12]

MCLEAN, ALEXANDER, from Islay, Argyll, to NY in July 1738 to have
settled at Wood Creek on the Hudson River, died in Cuba.[HSPC]

MCLEAN, ALLAN, 5'3", a laborer, 'strong, well made', enlisted in the PA
Regiment in York, PA, on 9 May 1758. [Pa.Arch.#5/1/133]

MCLEAN, ARCHIBALD, born in Mull, Argyll, a surgeon and physician in
the parish of Trelawney, Jamaica, then in NY City during 1772.
[NAS.GD174.159]; probate 29 Apr. 1772 NY

MCLEAN, DONALD, son of Charles McLean of Drimmin, Morvern,
Argyll, and Isobel Cameron, surgeon of the 77th [Montgomery's
Highlanders] Regiment in America from 1757 to 1763, settled in
Cairo, Greene County, NY, by 1768, a Loyalist, died in NY city on
10 Jan. 1782. [ANY#1.106][NY.Gaz.&Wkly.Merc.,14.1.1782]
[NAS.GD174.159]

MCLEAN, DONALD, born in 1749, a tailor from Stirling, from Greenock
to Philadelphia on the Sally Oct. 1774. [PRO.T47.12]

MCLEAN, DUNCAN, to America in 1773, settled on the Kingsborough
Patent, NY, on 25 Sep. 1773, a Loyalist and soldier of the Royal
Regiment of NY from 1776 to 1783, later settled in Charlottenburg,
Ontario. [DF.pp]

MCLEAN, DUNCAN, born in 1744, a laborer from Lochaber, Inverness-
shire, from Greenock to NY or GA on the Christy, in May 1775.
[PRO.T47.12]

MCLEAN, JAMES, {"Jeems McLeain"}, and Mary McDonnell, {"Marie
Mektonel"}, both natives of Scotland, were married in the Dutch
Reformed Church of Kingston, Ulster County, NY, during 1778.
[Kingston Old Dutch Church Records]

MCLEAN, JOHN, {"Jan Macklin"}, born in Scotland, married Marritje de
Wit, both residents of Kingston, Ulster County, NY, in the Dutch
Reformed Church there in 1702. [Kingston Old Dutch Church
Records]

MCLEAN, JOHN, died in Orange County, NY, during 1770. [SM#32/630]

MCLEAN, JOHN, from Islay, Argyll, to NY in July 1738 to have settled at
Wood Creek on the Hudson River, by 1763 he was dead and his
cousin Alexander McLean in Albany claimed his grant of lands on
the Argyle Patent, NY. [HSPC][NY.Col.MS#72/171]

MCLEAN, JOHN, born in 1740, a laborer from Lochaber, Inverness-shire,
from Greenock to NY or GA on the Christy in May 1775.
[PRO.T47.12]

MCLEAN, JOHN, born in 1754, a servant from Loch Broom, Wester Ross,
from Stornaway to NY on the Peace and Plenty in Nov. 1774.

[PRO.T47.12]

MCLEAN, LAUCHLIN, from Islay, Argyll, in Nov. 1740 bound for NY
and Wood Creek on the Hudson River, married Mary Ross after their
arrival in NY, their daughter Catherine move to Albany, and was
granted 200 acres on the Argyle Patent, NY.
[HSBC][NY.Col.MS#72/170]

MCLEAN, MALCOLM, born in 1750, a farmer from Barvas, Isle of
Lewis, from Stornaway to Philadelphia on the Friendship, in May
1774. [PRO.T47.12]

MCLEAN, MALCOLM, former soldier, settled in NJ 1763, Loyalist in
1776. [PRO.AO13.26.294]

MCLEAN, MARY, born in 1734, an indentured servant who absconded
from Jacob Eage, Campbell Hall, Ulster County, NY, in 1759.
[NY.Merc., 17.12.1759]

MCLEAN, MURDOCH, to America in 1773, settled on the Kingsborough
Patent, NY, a Loyalist and Sergeant of the Royal Regiment of NY
from 1776 to 1783, later settled in Charlottenburg, Ontario.
[DF.pp][PRO.AO12.27.194]

MCLEAN, NEIL, born 13 May 1736, son of Rev. Archibald McLean and
Susanna Campbell, Commissary at Niagara. [F#4.113]

MCLEAN, PEGGY, born in 1756, from Edinburgh, from Greenock to NY
on the Lilly in Apr. 1775. [PRO.T47.12]

MCLEAN, WILLIAM, born in 1744, a farmer from Bayble, Isle of Lewis,
with Hendrea Murray his wife and their children Donald and John,
from Stornaway to Philadelphia on the Friendship in May 1774.
[PRO.T47.12]

MCLEAN, ..., and his wife, possibly from Paisley, settled 50 miles
north of Albany, NY, in 1774. [Hugh Simm papers, Princeton
University]

MCLEANAN, ALEXANDER, born in 1735, a servant from Beauly,
Inverness-shire, from Stornaway to Philadelphia on the Clementina,
in July 1775.[PRO.T47.12]

MCLEANAN, ANNE, born in 1755, a servant from Ferintosh, Ross and
Cromarty, from Stornaway to Philadelphia on the Clementina in July
1775.[PRO.T47.12]

MCLEANAN, ANNE, born in 1762, a servant from Beauly, Inverness-
shire, from Stornaway to Philadelphia on the Clementina in July
1775.[PRO.T47.12]

MCLEANAN, MARION, born in 1757, a servant from Inverness,
from Stornaway to Philadelphia on the Clementina in July
1775.[PRO.T47.12]

MCLELAN, MARGARET, a Covenanter who was transported from Leith
to East NJ on the Henry and Francis in Sep. 1685. [RPCS#11/154]

MCLELLAN, HUGH, born in 1757, a weaver from Paisley, from Greenock
to NY on the Commerce in Feb. 1774. [PRO.T47/12]

MCLELLAN, JOHN, born St Ninians, Stirlingshire, 1722, settled
Cambridge, Albany, NY, by 1775, Loyalist. [PRO.AO13.56.107]

MCLELLAN, JOHN, born in 1748, a laborer from Glasgow, from
Greenock to NY on the Lilly in Apr. 1775. [PRO.T47.12]

MCLELLAN, ROBERT, from Leith to East NJ 5 Sep.1685. [NWI.I.423]

MCLENNAN, JOHN, born in 1743, a servant from Isle of Skye,
    from Stornaway to Philadelphia on the Clementina in July 1775.
    [PRO.T47.12]

MCLENNAN, KENNETH, born in 1753, a servant from Contin, Ross-
    shire, from Stornaway to NY on the Peace and Plenty in
    Nov. 1774. [PRO.T47.12]

MCLENNAN, MURDOCH, born in 1765, a servant from Beauly,
    Inverness-shire, from Stornaway to Philadelphia on the Clementina in
    July 1775.[PRO.T47.12]

MCLEOD, ANGUS, born in 1744, a weaver from Stornaway, Isle of Lewis,
    with his wife Ann McDonald and daughter Ann from Stornaway to
    Philadelphia on the Friendship, in May 1774. [PRO.T47.12]

MCLEOD, ANGUS, born in 1759, a servant from Brenish, Isle of Lewis,
    from Stornaway to Philadelphia on the Friendship in May 1774.
    [PRO.T47.12]

MCLEOD, ANN, born in 1752, a servant from Barvas, Isle of Lewis,
    from Stornaway to Philadelphia on the Friendship in May 1774.
    [PRO.T47.12]

MCLEOD, DONALD, indentured servant, to East NJ 1684.
    [NJSA.EJD.A184]

MCLEOD, DONALD, with his wife Catherine Graham, and sons John and
    Duncan, from Islay, Argyll, to NY in July 1738 to have settled at
    Wood Creek on the Hudson River, by 1763 he was dead but a
    surviving daughter was granted 150 acres on the Argyle Patent, NY.
    [HSPC]

MCLEOD, FERGUSON, a petitioner in NY 1701. [DNY.IV.934]

MCLEOD, JANET, indentured servant, to East NJ 1684.
    [NJSA.EJD.A184]

MCLEOD, JEAN, born in 1758, from Bayble, Isle of Lewis, from
    Stornaway to Philadelphia on the Friendship in May 1774.
    [PRO.T47.12]

MCLEOD, JOHN, born in 1741, a farmer from Carlaway, Isle of Lewis,
    with his wife Catherine McIver and their children Margaret, Ann,
    John and Malcolm from Stornaway to Philadelphia on the Friendship
    in May 1774. [PRO.T47.12]

MCLEOD, JOHN, born in 1759, a servant from Galson, Isle of Lewis, from
    Stornaway to Philadelphia on the Friendship in May 1774.
    [PRO.T47.12]

MCLEOD, JOHN, born in 1739, a tailor from Glasgow, from
    Greenock to NY on the Commerce in Feb. 1774. [PRO.T47.12]

MCLEOD, JOHN, jr., born in 1760, a tailor from Glasgow, from
    Greenock to NY on the Commerce in Feb. 1774. [PRO.T47.12]

MCLEOD, MALCOLM, a soldier in the French and Indian Wars, settled
    on the Kingsborough Patent, NY, a Loyalist in 1776, died in 1778,
    his wife Isobel and their six children moved to Cornwall, Ontario, in
    1783. [DF.pp]

MCLEOD, MALCOLM, born in 1756, a servant from Stornaway, Isle of
    Lewis, from Stornaway to Philadelphia on the Friendship in May

1774.[PRO.T47.12]

MCLEOD, MALCOLM, born in 1760, a servant from Contin, Ross-shire, from Stornaway to NY on the <u>Clementina</u> in July 1775. [PRO.T47.12]

MCLEOD, MARY, born in 1746, from Paisley, from Greenock to NY on the <u>Lilly</u> in Apr. 1775. [PRO.T47.12]

MCLEOD, MARY, born in 1754, a servant, from Stornaway to Philadelphia on the <u>Friendship</u> in May 1774. [PRO.T47.12]

MCLEOD, MURDOCH, born 1742, a farmer from Coigach, Ross-shire, with his wife Christian and their daughters Mary and Isabel from Stornaway to NY on the <u>Peace and Plenty</u> in Nov. 1774. [PRO.T47.12]

MCLEOD, MURDOCH, born in 1757, a servant from Contin, Ross-shire, from Stornaway to Philadelphia on the <u>Clementina</u> in July 1775. [PRO.T47.12]

MCLEOD, NEIL, born in 1744, a farmer from Melbost, Isle of Lewis, with Margaret Murray his wife and their children Christian, Normand and Margaret from Stornaway to Philadelphia on the <u>Friendship</u> in May 1774. [PRO.T47.12]

MCLEOD, NEILL, born in 1740, a merchant from Stornaway, Isle of Lewis, with Margaret his wife and their children John, Janet and Allan from Stornaway to NY on the <u>Peace and Plenty</u> in Nov. 1774. [PRO.T47.12]

MCLEOD, NORMAND, officer during the French and Indian War, then Commisary of Indian Trade at Caughnawaga, Mohawk River, Loyalist soldier in 1776. [PRO.AO12.24.171]

MCLEOD, NORMAN, born in 1760, a servant from Bayble, Isle of Lewis, from Stornaway to Philadelphia on the <u>Friendship</u> in May 1774. [PRO.T47.12]

MCLEOD, PEGGY, born in 1754, a servant from Stornaway, Isle of Lewis, from Stornaway to Philadelphia on the <u>Friendship</u> in May 1774. [PRO.T47.12]

MCLEOD, RANALD, born in 1724, a farmer from Coigach, Ross-shire, from Stornaway to NY on the <u>Peace and Plenty</u> in Nov. 1774. [PRO.T47.12]

MCLEOD, WILLIAM, soldier in the French and Indian Wars, settled in Elizabethtown, NJ, Loyalist in 1776. [PRO.AO13.91.282]

MCLEOD, WILLIAM, to America in 1773, settled on the Kingsborough Patent, NY, a Loyalist and Lieutenant of the Royal Regiment of NY from 1776 to 1783, later settled in Charlottenburg, Ontario. [DF.pp]

MCMARTIN, DUNCAN, born in 1728, a farmer from Glen Coe or Breadalbane, with Isobel Robertson his wife and their children Eliza, Katherine, Janet, John, Isobel and Mary, from Greenock to NY on the <u>Commerce</u> in Feb. 1775; settled on the Kingsborough Patent, NY, before 1780.[PRO.T47.12] [DF.pp]

MCMARTINE, DUNCAN, born in 1755, son of Duncan McMartine and Isobel McGregor, a wright from Breadalbane, Perthshire,   from Greenock to NY on the <u>Commerce</u> in June 1775. [PRO.T47.12]

MCMARTINE, DUNCAN, born in 1712, a farmer from Breadalbane,

Perthshire, with his wife Isobel McGregor from Greenock to NY on the Commerce in June 1775. [PRO.T47.12]

MCMARTINE, HUGH, born in 1754, son of Duncan McMartine and Isobel McGregor, a servant from Breadalbane, Perthshire, from Greenock to NY on the Commerce in June 1775. [PRO.T47.12]

MCMARTINE, JOHN, born in 1750, a tailor from Glasgow, from Greenock to NY on the Lilly in Apr. 1775. [PRO.T47.12]; settled in Tryon County, NY, Loyalist in 1776. [PRO.AO12.31.121]

MCMARTINE, MALCOLM, born in 1746, a cooper from Glasgow, from Greenock to NY on the Lilly in Apr. 1775. [PRO.T47.12]; settled Tryon County, NY, Loyalist in 1776. [PRO.AO12.31.115]

MCMARTINE, MARGARET, born in 1751, daughter of Duncan McMartine and Isobel McGregor, a servant from Breadalbane, Perthshire, from Greenock to NY on the Commerce in June 1775. [PRO.T47.12]

MCMARTINE, MARY, born in 1752, a brushmaker from Glasgow, from Greenock to NY on the Lilly in Apr. 1775. [PRO.T47.12]

MCMARTINE, PETER, born in 1754, a smith from Breadalbane, Perthshire, from Greenock to NY on the Commerce in June 1775. [PRO.T47.12]

MCMASTER, ELIZABETH, born in 1753, from Galloway, from Stranraer, to NY on the Gale, in May 1774.[PRO.T47.12]

MCMASTER, JOHN, born in 1754, a wright from Galloway, from Stranraer to NY on the Gale in May 1774.[PRO.T47.12]

MCMASTER, ROBERT, born in 1750, a merchant from Galloway, from Stranraer, to NY on the Gale in May 1774.[PRO.T47.12]

MCMIKEN, ALEXANDER, born in 1755, a laborer from Inch, from Stranraer to NY on the Jackie in May 1775. [PRO.T47.12]

MCMICKEN, ELEANORA, born in 1749, from Galloway, from Stranraer, to NY on the Gale in May 1774.[PRO.T47.12]

MCMIKEN, GILBERT, born in 1735, a laborer from Inch, Wigtownshire, with his wife Jean McKinnel from Stranraer to NY on the Jackie of Glasgow in May 1775. [PRO.T47.12]

MCMIKING, JAMES, a farmer from Galloway, from Stranraer to New York on the Gale of Whitehaven in May 1774.]PRO.T47.12]

MCMICKEN, JAMES, born in 1770, from Galloway, from Stranraer to NY on the Gale of Whitehaven in May 1774. [PRO.T47.12]

MCMIKEN, JANET, born in 1739, from New Luce, Wigtownshire, from Stranraer to NY on the Jackie in May 1775. [PRO.T47.12]

MCMICKEN, JANET, born in 1753, from Galloway, from Stranraer to NY on the Gale in May 1774.[PRO.T47.12]

MCMIKINE, JOHN, born in 1734, a joiner from Galloway, with wife Rosina and their children Rosina, Agnes, May, Jean and Nanny, from Stranraer to NY on the Gale in May 1774. [PRO.T47.12]

MCMIKEN, SARAH, born in 1754, from New Luce, from Stranraer to NY on the Jackie of Glasgow in May 1775. [PRO.T47.12]

MCMICKEN, WILLIAM, born in 1749, a laborer from Dailly, from Stranraer to NY on the Gale in May 1774. [PRO.T47.12]

MCMICKEN, WILLIAM, born in 1772, from Galloway, from

Stranraer to NY on the Gale in May 1774. [PRO.T47.12]

MCMICKING, JOHN, born in 1753, a farmer from Galloway, from Stranraer to NY on the Gale in May 1774. [PRO.T47.12]

MCMICKING, THOMAS, born in 1750, a farmer from Galloway, from Stranraer to NY on the Gale in May 1774. [PRO.T47.12]

MCMILLAN, DONALD, with his wife Mary McEachern, from Islay, Argyll, to NY in July 1738 to have settled at Wood Creek on the Hudson River, they and their five children were granted 400 acres on the Argyle Patent, NY, in 1763, his kinsman Allan McDonald, an innkeeper in NY, claimed his share. [HSPC][NY.Col.MS#72/171]

MCMILLAN, DONALD, with his wife Janet Gillies, and son Alexander, from Islay, Argyll, in June 1739 bound for NY and Wood Creek on the Hudson River, in 1763 he, his two sons and three daughters were granted 350 acres on the Argyle Patent, NY. [HSBC][NY.Col.MS#72/170]

MCMULLEN, DONALD, to America in 1773, settled on the Kingsborough Patent, NY, a Loyalist, later settled at River aux Raisins, Ontario. [DF.pp]

MCMILLAN, JOHN, born in 1738, from Balmaghie, Kirkcudbrightshire, with his wife Elizabeth Carson and their children James, James, Janet, Agnes and Elizabeth, from Kirkcudbright to NY on the Gale, May 1774.[PRO.T47.12]

MCMILLAN, JOHN, born in 1750, a laborer from Wigtown, from Greenock to NY on the Lilly in Apr. 1775. [PRO.T47.12]

MCMILLAN, JOHN, born in 1755, a servant from Poolewe, Wester Ross, from Stornaway to Philadelphia on the Friendship in May 1774. [PRO.T47.12]

MCMILLAN, MARGARET, born in 1749, from Galloway, from Stranraer to NY on the Galein May 1774. [PRO.T47.12]

MCMILLAN, WILLIAM, a minister educated at Glasgow University in 1720, to Philadelphia in 1724. [AP#193][F#7/664]

MCMORRAN, EDWARD, born in 1749, a merchant from Dumfries, from Dumfries to NY on the Adventure in May 1774. [PRO.T47.12]

MCMURRAY, ALEXANDER, born in 1748, a husbandman from Queenshill, from Stranraer to NY on the Galein May 1774. [PRO.T47.12]

MCMURPHY, ARCHIBALD, born in 1731, a laborer who enlisted in the PA Regiment on 22 Apr. 1758. [Pa.Archives#5/1/187]

MCNAB, DONALD, a soldier, married Mary McDougall, in NY on 4 Apr. 1759.[PCR]

MCNAUGHT, DANIEL, born in 1751, a husbandman from Largs of Twynholm, Kirkcudbrightshire, from Stranraer to NY on the Gale of Whitehaven in May 1774. [PRO.T47.12]

MCNAUGHT, JOHN, born in 1754, a husbandman from Largs of Twynholm, Kirkcudbrightshire, from Stranraer to NY on the Gale of Whitehaven in May 1774. [PRO.T47.12]

MCNAUGHTON, ALEXANDER, with his wife Mary McDonald, and their children John, Moses, Janet, and Eleanor, from Islay, Argyll, to NY in July 1738 to have settled at Wood Creek on the Hudson River,

in 1763 they were granted 500 acres on the Argyle Patent, NY.
[HSPC]

MCNAUGHTON, ANGUS, born in 1746, a farmer from Breadalbane,
Perthshire, with his wife Katherine Robertson and their children
John and Jean, from Greenock to NY on the Commerce in June
1775. [PRO.T47.12]

MCNAUGHTON, CHRISTIAN, born in 1755, a servant from
Breadalbane, Perthshire, from Greenock to NY on the Commerce in
June 1775. [PRO.T47.12]

MCNAUGHTON, DONALD, born in 1745, a farmer from Breadalbane,
Perthshire, from Greenock to NY on the Lilly in May 1775.
[PRO.T47.12]

MCNAUGHTON, DONALD, born in 1756, a servant from Breadalbane,
Perthshire, from Greenock to NY on the Commerce in June 1775.
[PRO.T47.12]

MCNAUGHTON, JAMES, to NY in 1740, dead by 1763 when
his brother John then living in Tappan claimed his proportion on 10
May 1763. [NY.Col.MS#72/171]

MCNAUGHTON, JANET, born in 1742, from Breadalbane, Perthshire,
from Greenock to NY on the Commerce in June 1775. [PRO.T47.12]

MCNAUGHTON, JOHN, born in 1737, a farmer from Breadalbane,
Perthshire, with his wife Janet Anderson and their children Christian,
Katherine, Duncan, Katherine, John, Elizabeth, Daniel, Jane,
Christian and Kat., from Greenock to NY on the Commerce in June
1775. [PRO.T47.12]; settled in New Jerseyfield, Tryon County, NY,
Loyalist in 1776. [PRO.AO12.29.138]

MCNAUGHTON, JOHN, born in 1751, a farmer from Breadalbane,
Perthshire, from Greenock to NY on the Commerce in June 1775.
[PRO.T47.12]

MCNEELAGE, DONALD, born in Argyll during 1736, a housecarpenter
who deserted from the 1st Highland Regiment in America during
1759. [NY.Merc.,4.6.1759]

MCNEIL, ANNE, widow of Hugh McEuan, with their children Alexander
McEuan and Mary McEuan, from Islay, Argyll, in Nov. 1740 bound
for NY and Wood Creek on the Hudson River, by 1763 they were
living at Basking Ridge, NJ. [HSBC][NY.Col.MS#72/170]

MCNEIL, ARCHIBALD, born in 1751, a weaver from Paisley, from
Greenock to NY on the Commerce in Feb. 1774.[PRO.T47.12]

MCNEIL, CHRISTIAN, born in 1754, a spinner from Paisley, from
Greenock to NY on the Commerce in Feb. 1774.[PRO.T47.12]

MCNEIL, DANIEL, a cordiner and indentured servant who absconded
from Randal McKenzie of the London Coffee House in Philadelphia
in 1771.[Pa.Chron: 6.5.1771]

MCNEIL, GILBERT, born in 1753, a merchant from Kilmarnock from
Greenock to NY on the George May 1774. [PRO.T47.12]

MCNEIL, JOHN, with his wife Elizabeth Campbell, and their children
Barbara, Peggie, Catherine, Betty, and Neil, from Islay, Argyll, to
NY in July 1738 to have settled at Wood Creek on the Hudson River,
by 1763 he was dead, four daughters were granted 200 acres on the

Argyle Patent, NY.[HSPC]

MCNEIL, MARGARET, from Islay, Argyll, to NY in July 1738
     to have settled at Wood Creek on the Hudson River.[HSPC]

MCNEIL, ROGER, from Islay, Argyll, in Nov. 1740 bound for NY
     and Wood Creek on the Hudson River, by 1763 he was living on
     Long Island when he was granted 200 acres on the Argyle Patent,
     NY. [HSBC][NY.Col.MS#72/170]

MCNEIL, WILLIAM, born in 1757, a weaver from Paisley, from
     Greenock to NY on the Commerce in Feb. 1774.[PRO.T47.12]

MCNISH, Rev. GEORGE, born in Glasgow 1684, educated at Glasgow
     University, to Philadelphia in 1705, settled in Jamaica, NY, died on
     10 Mar. 1722 in NY. [F#7/664][AP#140]

MCNIVEN, JOHN, with his wife Mary McArthur, and daughters Elizabeth
     and Mary, from Islay, Argyll, to NY in July 1738 to have settled at
     Wood Creek on the Hudson River, he was dead by 1763 but his son
     and four daughters were granted 250 acres on the Argyle Patent, NY.
     [HSPC]

MCNIVEN, MERRAN, from Islay, Argyll, to NY in July 1738 to have
     settled at Wood Creek on the Hudson River, by 1763 was living in
     NY and was granted 200 acres on the Argyle Patent,
     NY.[HSPC][NY.Col.MS#72/170]

MCNIVEN, RACHEL, from Islay, Argyll, to NY in July 1738 to have
     settled at Wood Creek on the Hudson River, by 1763 she was living
     in NY when she was granted 200 acres on the Argyle Patent, NY.
     [HSPC][NY.Col.MS#72/170]

MCOWEN, AGNES, born in 1751, from Glen Luce, Wigtownshire, from
     Stranraer to NY on the Galein May 1774. [PRO.T47.12]

MCPHADEN, DONALD, from Islay, Argyll, in June 1739 bound for NY
     and Wood Creek on the Hudson River. [HSBC]

MCPHADEN, DUNCAN, with his wife Flory McCollum, and their children
     John & Duncan, from Islay, Argyll, in Nov. 1740 bound for NY and
     Wood Creek on the Hudson River, by 1763 Duncan sr. and his son
     John were dead, when son Duncan was granted land on the Argyle
     Patent, NY. [HSBC][NY.Col.MS#72/170]

MCPHADEN, LACHLIN, a mariner in NY, pro. 10 Nov. 1772 NY

MCPHADEN, NEIL, and his wife Mary McDearmid, and daughters
     Dirvorgill and Margaret, from Islay, Argyll, in June 1739 bound for
     NY and Wood Creek on the Hudson River, granted 200 acres in
     1763. [HSBC]

MCPHAIL, ALEXANDER, born in 1763, a servant from Wester Leys, Isle
     of Lewis, from Stornaway to Philadelphia on the Clementina, in July
     1775. [PRO.T47.12]

MCPHAIL, DONALD, born in 1766, from Leys, Isle of Lewis, from
     Stornaway to Philadelphia on the Clementina in July 1775.
     [PRO.T47.12]

MCPHAIL, JEAN, born in 1739, from Inverness, with her children
     Duncan and Jean from Stornaway to Philadelphia on the Clementina
     in July 1775. [PRO.T47.12]

MCPHAIL, JOHN, and his wife Christy, from Islay, Argyll, in June 1739

bound for NY and Wood Creek on the Hudson River, dead by 1763 when his widow and daughter were granted 200 acres on the Argyle Patent, New York. [HSBC][NY.Col.MS#72/170]

MCPHAIL, JOHN, born in 1739, a servant from Wester Leys, Isle of Lewis, from Stornaway to Philadelphia on the <u>Clementina</u>, in July 1775. [PRO.T47.12]

MCPHAIL, JOHN, born in 1760, a servant from Wester Leys, Isle of Lewis, from Stornaway to Philadelphia on the <u>Clementina</u> in July 1775. [PRO.T47.12]

MCPHAIL, WILLIAM, born in 1758, a servant from Wester Leys, Lewis, from Stornaway to Philadelphia on the <u>Clementina</u> in July 1775. [PRO.T47.12]

MCPHERSON, ALEXANDER, to America in 1773, settled on the Kingsborough Patent, NY, a Loyalist and soldier of the Royal Regiment of NY from 1776 to 1783, later settled in Edwardsburgh, Grenville County, Ontario. [DF.pp]

MCPHERSON, ALEXANDER, born in 1717, a farmer from Inverness, from Stornaway to Philadelphia on the <u>Clementina</u> in July 1775. [PRO.T47.12]

MCPHERSON, CHARLES, born in 1753, from Perthshire, settled in Kingsbridge, NY, in 1776, a Loyalist who moved to New Brunswick in 1783, died there in July 1823. [NBr. Royal Gazette]

MCPHERSON, DONALD, soldier of the 42nd Regiment, married Elletta Marsh, in New York on 3 May 1763. [PCR]

MCPHERSON, DONALD, born in 1728, a farmer from Perthshire, with Mary McFee his wife from Greenock to NY on the <u>Monimia</u> in May 1775. [PRO.T47.12]; Loyalist. [PRO.AO12.109.220]

MCPHERSON, DONALD, born in 1743, a farmer from Perthshire, with Janet McTaggart his wife from Greenock to NY on the <u>Monimia</u> in May 1775. [PRO.T47.12]

MCPHERSON, DUNCAN, born in 1743, a farmer from Stirling, with Jane McBride his wife from Greenock to NY on the <u>Monimia</u> in May 1775.[PRO.T47.12]

MCPHERSON, ISOBEL, born in 1754, a servant from Inverness, from Stornaway to NY on the <u>Clementina</u> in July 1775. [PRO.T47.12]

MCPHERSON, JAMES, settled in Scotch Bush, Johnson's Patent, Tryon County, NY, before 1776, a Loyalist who moved to Canada after 1783. [PRO.AO13.14.226]

MCPHERSON, JANET, born in 1757, a servant from Inverness, from Stornaway to Philadelphia on the <u>Clementina</u> in July 1775. [PRO.T47.12]

MCPHERSON, JANET, born in 1763, a servant from Inverness, from Stornaway to Philadelphia on the <u>Clementina</u> in July 1775. [PRO.T47.12]

MCPHERSON, JEAN, born in 1755, a servant from Wester Leys, Isle of Lewis, from Stornaway to Philadelphia on the <u>Clementina</u>, in July 1775. [PRO.T47.12]

MCPHERSON, JOHN, born in Edinburgh during 1726, fourth son of William McPherson a writer and Jean Adamson, later a skipper and privateer based in Philadelphia by 1751, admitted as a burgess and guild brother of Edinburgh on 15 Aug. 1764, died in Philadelphia on 6 Sep.1792. [CF#5.364][AP#259][EBR]

MCPHERSON, JOHN, born in 1732, a shipmaster from Greenock, from Greenock to NY on the George in May 1774. [PRO.T47.12]

MCPHERSON, JOHN, born in 1754, a servant from Inverness, from Stornaway to Philadelphia on the Clementina, in July 1775. [PRO.T47.12]

MCPHERSON, KATHERINE, born in 1753, a servant from Inverness, from Leith to Philadelphia on the Friendship, in May 1775. [PRO.T47.12]

MCPHERSON, LAUCHLAN, to America in 1773, settled on the Kingsborough Patent, NY, a Loyalist and soldier of the Royal Regiment of NY. [DF.pp]

MCPHERSON, MARGARET, born in 1754, a servant from Inverness, from Stornaway to Philadelphia on the Clementina, in July 1775. [PRO.T47.12]

MCPHERSON, MURDOCH, to America on the Pearl in 1773, a soldier of the 22nd Regiment who settled on the Kingsborough Patent, NY, a Loyalist and soldier of the Royal Regiment of NY from 1776 to 1783, later settled in Charlottenburg, Ontario. [DF.pp][PRO.AO12.29.179]

MCPHERSON, PEGGY, born in 1758, from Aberdeen, via Leith to Philadelphia on the Friendship in May 1775. [PRO.T47.12]

MCPHERSON, WILLIAM, to America on the Pearl in 1773, settled on the Kingsborough Patent, NY. [DF.pp]

MCQUARRIE, DUNCAN, alias Brown, and his wife Effie McIlpheder, and their children Donald, John, Gilbert, and Christian, from Islay, Argyll, in June 1739 bound for NY and Wood Creek on the Hudson River, in 1763 he, his wife, four sons and one daughter were granted 400 acres on the Argyle Patent, NY.[HSBC][NY.Col.MS#72/170]

MCQUARY, JOHN, with Anna Quary his wife, from Islay, Argyll, in June 1739 bound for NY and Wood Creek on the Hudson River, by 1763 he was married and living in the Highlands of NY when he petitioned Governor Tryon and was granted 300 acres on the Argyle Patent, NY, in 1763. [HSBC][NY.Col.MS#72/171]

MCQUEEN, DUNCAN, born in 1761, from Braen, Isle of Lewis, from Stornaway to Philadelphia on the Clementina, in July 1775. [PRO.T47.12]

MCQUEEN, JOHN, from Leith to East NJ on the Henry and Francis in 1685. [NWI.I.423]

MCQUEEN, ISOBEL, born in 1765, from Braen, Isle of Lewis, from Stornaway to Philadelphia on the Clementina, in July 1775. [PRO.T47.12]

MCQUEEN, MARGARET, born in 1756, a spinner from Paisley, , from Greenock to NY on the Commerce in Feb. 1774. [PRO.T47.12]

MCQUEEN, MARGARET, born in 1759, a servant from Braen, Isle of Lewis, from Stornaway to Philadelphia on the Clementina in July 1775. [PRO.T47.12]

MCQUEEN, ROBERT, a Covenanter from Nithsdale, Dumfriesshire, was transported   from Leith to East NJ on the <u>Henry and Francis</u>, 5 Sep. 1685. [RPCS#11.154]

MCQUEEN, WALTER, was transported from Leith to East NJ on the <u>Henry and Francis</u> 5 Sep. 1685. [RPCS#11.154]

MCQUEEN, WILLIAM, born in 1749, a husbandman from Glen Luce, Wigtownshire, from Stranraer to NY on the <u>Gale of Whitehaven</u> in May 1774. [PRO.T47.12]

MCQUEESTON, ANTHONY, born in 1756, a baker from Galloway, from Stranraer to NY on the <u>Gale,</u> in May 1774. [PRO.T47.12]

MCQUIRE, ANNE, born in 1763, a servant from Braen, Isle of Lewis, from Stornaway to Philadelphia on the <u>Clementina,</u> in July 1775. [PRO.T47.12]

MCQUIRRICH, DONALD, in Orange Co., NY, later by 1685 in East NJ. [NJSA.EJD.A299/B8/15]

MCRAE, MARGARET, born in 1756, a servant from Edinburgh, from Leith to Philadelphia on the <u>Friendship</u> in May 1775. [PRO.T47.12]

MCROBERT, PETER, born in 1736, a farmer from Drumlanrig, Dumfries-shire, from Kirkcudbright to NY on the <u>Adventure</u> of Liverpool in May 1774.[PRO.T47.12]

MCTAGGART, JAMES, born in 1754, a laborer from Galloway, from Stranraer to NY on the <u>Gale of Whitehaven</u> in May 1774. [PRO.T47.12]; Loyalist in 1776. [PRO.AO12.28.243]

MCVIAN, DONALD, born in 1736, a farmer from Breadalbane, Perthshire, with his son Duncan, from Greenock to NY on the <u>Commerce</u> in June 1775. [PRO.T47.12]

MCVIAN, JOHN, born in 1754, a wright from Breadalbane, from Greenock to NY on the <u>Commerce,</u> in June 1775. [PRO.T47.12]

MCVIAN, MARY, born in 1754, a servant from Breadalbane, from Greenock to NY on the <u>Commerce,</u> in June 1775.[PRO.T47.12]

MCVIAN, SARAH, born in 1758, a servant from Breadalbane, from Greenock to NY on the <u>Commerce,</u> in June 1775. [PRO.T47.12]

MCVICAR, ARCHIBALD, born in 1752, a sailor who absconded from the transport ship Christie in the North River, NY, during 1777.[NY.Gaz.&Merc., 26.5.1777]

MCVICAR, ARCHIBALD, born in 1747, a farmer from Stirling, from Greenock to NY on the <u>Lilly</u> in May 1775. [PRO.T47.12]

MCVICKER, PETER, born in 1725, enlisted in the PA Regiment on 18 May 1759. [Pa.Archives#5/1/299]

MCVURICH, ARCHIBALD, with his wife Merran Shaw, from Islay, Argyll, in June 1739 bound for NY and Wood Creek on the Hudson River, dead by 1763. [HSBC]

MCVURICH, FLORENCE, from Islay, Argyll, in June 1739 bound for NY and Wood Creek on the Hudson River, by 1763 she was married and living with her children on the Livingston Manor, NY, and was granted 200 acres on the Argyle Patent, NY. [HSBC][NY.Col.MS#72/170]

MCVUIRICH, LAUCHLAN, from Islay, Argyll, to NY in July 1738 to have settled at Wood Creek on the Hudson River.[HSPC]

MCVURICH, LAUCHLIN, from Islay, Argyll, in June 1739 bound for
New York and Wood Creek on the Hudson River. [HSBC]

MCVORICH, MALCOLM, a thief who was transported from Leith to
East NJ in 1684. [RPCS#8.514]

MCVURAH, PETER, born in 1756, a founder from Breadalbane,
Perthshire, from Greenock to NY on the Commerce in June 1775.
[PRO.T47.12]

MCWHAE, ROBERT, born in 1745, a millwright from Genoch,
Balmaghie,Kirkcudbrightshire, from Kirkcudbright to NY on the
Adventure of Liverpool in May 1775. [PRO.T47.12]

MCWILLIAM, GEORGE, born in 1749, a husbandman from Galloway,
from Stranraer to NY on the Gale of Whitehaven in May 1774.
[PRO.T47.12]

MCWILLIAM, JAMES, born in 1750, a mason from Galloway, from
Stranraer to NY on the Gale in May 1774. [PRO.T47.12]

MCWILLIAM, JAMES, born in 1751, a farmer from Galloway, from
Stranraer to NY on the Gale in May 1774. [PRO.T47.12]

MCWILLIAM, JANET, born in 1715, from Kirkmichael, from Stranraer
to NY on the Jackie in May 1775. [PRO.T47.12]

MCWILLIAM, JANET, born in 1747, from Galloway, from
Stranraer to NY on the Gale in May 1774. [PRO.T47.12]

MCWILLIAM, JOHN, born in 1749, a farmer from Galloway, from
Stranraer to NY on the Gale in May 1774. [PRO.T47.12]; settled in
Tryon County, NY, Loyalist in 1776. [PRO.AO13.8.282]

MCWILLIAM, THOMAS, a farmer in NY, husband of Margaret Russell,
1773. [NAS.CS116.1.168]

MAIDEN, WILLIAM, born on 8 July 1733 in Mains son of John Maiden
and Elspet Pattullo, died Philadelphia, pro.1756 PCC

MAIN, JOHN, born in 1739, a laborer from Glen Luce, Wigtownshire,
with Margaret Thornton his wife and their children Anne and John,
from Stranraer to NY on the Jackie of Glasgow in May 1775.
[PRO.T47.12]

MAIN, WILLIAM, an indentured servant from Glasgow, to NY on the
Commerce, absconded 22 June 1774.[NYGaz-Merc.27.6.1774]

MAIR, DANIEL, born in 1739, a weaver from Glasgow, from Greenock to
NY on the Commerce in Feb. 1774. [PRO.T47.12]

MAIR, WILLIAM, prisoner transported to East NJ on the Henry and
Francis in 1685. [RPCS.II ..]

MAITLAND, RICHARD, born 1724, Deputy Adjutant General in North
America, died on 13 July 1772, buried in Trinity Church, NY,
probate 7 Sep. 1772 NY.

MALCOLM, ALEXANDER, a schoolteacher in NY around 1738.
[EUL:LaingMS/II/91]

MALCOLM, ISOBEL, born in 1754, from Greenock to NY on the Lilly in
Apr. 1775. [PRO.T47.12]

MALCOLM, WILLIAM, in NY, 1769. [NAS.CS16.1.138]

MAN, ROBERT, an indentured servant, from Scotland to Philadelphia on
the Anne galley, assigned to Mahlon Kirkbride for four years from 20
Sep. 1745.[EP#65]

MANSON, JAMES, born in 1738, from Gatehouse, Kirkcudbrightshire, from Stranraer to NY on the Gale in May 1774.[PRO.T47.12]

MANSON, WILLIAM, born in 1744, a laborer from Ferrytown, Wigtownshire, from Stranraer to NY on the Gale of Whitehaven in May 1774. [PRO.T47.12]

MARJORYBANKS, THOMAS, born in 1749, a baker from Glasgow, from Greenock to Philadelphia on the Sally in Oct. 1774. [PRO.T47.12]

MARSHALL, AGNES, indentured servant, to East NJ 1685. [NJSA.EJD.A225]

MARSHALL, EDWARD, a petitioner in NY 1701. [DNY.IV.934]

MARSHALL, JOHN, quit rent in Delaware, 1 Oct. 1669. [NY.Hist.MS.Dutch,XX/XXI, pr28]

MARSHALL, JOHN, transported from Leith to East NJ on the Henry and Francis of Newcastle on 5 Sep. 1685.[RPCS#11.167]

MARSHALL, MICHAEL, from Strathaven, Lanarkshire, transported from Leith to East NJ on the Henry and Francis on 5 Sep. 1685. [RPCS#11.159][NJSA.EJD.A225]

MARSHALL, ROBERT, born in 1746, a wright from Glasgow, from Greenock to NY on the Lilly in Apr. 1775. [PRO.T47.12]

MARSHALL, WILLIAM, born in Fife around 1740, licensed as a minister of the Associate Church in Edinburgh during 1762, to Philadelphia, minister in Deep Run, Bucks County, and by 1769 in Philadelphia, died there on 17 Nov. 1802. [UPCNA#484]

MARSHALL, WILLIAM, born in 1748, a laborer from Renfrew, from Greenock to NY on the Lilly, in Apr. 1775. [PRO.T47.12]

MARTIN, DAVID, son of Hugh Martin in Banchory, Kincardineshire, by 1750, a sheriff and schoolmaster in Philadelphia. [APB#3.175]

MARTIN, GRIZEL, from Mill of Aries, Glasgow, settled in Janefield, NY(?), married William McCandlish, parents of Patrick, John and Grizel, died in 1770, cnf 1777 Edinburgh. [NAS.CC8.8.124]

MARTIN, JOHN, Kirkmichael, Kintyre, a Covenanter, transported from Leith to East NJ on the Henry and Francis in 1685. [RPCS.II.114][NWI.I.423]

MARTIN, JOHN, born 1686, indented in Chester Co., PA, 14 July 1697. [Sgen.29.1.2]

MARTIN, JOHN, born in Glasgow during 1747, a barber and indentured servant who absconded from Frederick Baker in Philadelphia on 9 May 1769.   [Pa.Chron: 15.5.1769]

MARTIN, JOHN, born in 1732, a farm servant from Achall, Ross-shire, from Stornaway to NY on the Peace and Plenty in Nov.1774. [PRO.T47.12]

MARTIN, JOHN, born in Aberdeen during 1748, a journeyman printer who died in NY on 12 Dec. 1778. [NYGaz-Mercury, 14.12.1778]

MARTIN, MALCOLM, and his wife Florence Anderson, from Islay, Argyll, to NY in July 1738 to have settled at Wood Creek on the Hudson River, dead by 1763.[HSPC]

MARTIN, MARY, born in 1759, a servant from Edinburgh, via Leith to Philadelphia on the Friendship in May 1775. [PRO.T47.12]

MARTIN, MURDOCH, born in 1734, a sheriff's officer in Stornaway, Isle of Lewis, with his son John from Stornaway to NY on the Peace and Plenty in Nov. 1774.[PRO.T47.12]

MASON, JOHN, from Craigmailen, to NY by 1756, minister of the Associate Congregation, Cedar Street, NY.[UPC#654]

MASTERTON, JAMES, born 1683, indented in Chester Co., PA, 14 July 1697. [Sgen.29.1.12]

MATHESON, ALEXANDER, born in 1747, a husbandman, from London to Friendship on the Sally in May 1774. [PRO.T47.12]

MATHEW, ISABEL, indentured servant, to East NJ 1684. [NJSA.EJD.A195]

MATHEW, SAMUEL, indentured servant, to East NJ 1684. [NJSA.EJD.A195]

MATHIESON, E., born in 1758, from Edinburgh, from Greenock to NY on the Lilly in Apr. 1775. [PRO.T47.12]

MATHIESON, ROBERT, born in 1752, a laborer from Elgin, Morayshire, from Greenock to NY on the Lilly in Apr. 1775. [PRO.T47.12]

MATHISON, JANET, born in 1763, a servant from Ness, Isle of Lewis, from Stornaway to Philadelphia on the Friendship, in May 1775. [PRO.T47.12]

MATLOCK, ISOBEL, born in 1757, a servant from Breadalbane, Perthshire, from Greenock to NY on the Commerce in June 1775.[PRO.T47.12]

MATTHEW, JOHN, born in 1750, a shoemaker from Ayr, from Greenock to NY on the Matty in May 1774. [PRO.T47.12]

MATTHEW, WILLIAM, born in 1749, a shoemaker from Ayr, from Greenock to NY on the Matty in May 1774. [PRO.T47.12]

MAXLIE, CATHERINE, indentured servant, to East NJ 1684. [NJSA.EJD.A196]

MAXWELL, DAVID, born in 1740, a tailor from Galloway, with Jean McGarvin his wife and daughter Marion, from Stranraer to NY on the Gale of Whitehaven in May 1774. [PRO.T47.12]

MAXWELL, GEORGE, born in Glasgow around 1735, a laborer, deserted from the 22nd Regt in 1757. [N.Y.Postboy, 5 Dec. 1757]

MAXWELL, JEAN, born in 1742, from Galloway, with her son John from Stranraer to NY on the Gale in May 1774. [PRO.T47.12]

MAXWELL, JOHN, of Blastcombe, (?), Scotland, died 12 May 1682 on the Rebecca, mr James Duncan, on the voyage from Scotland, inventory 1682 NY [Liber 19B#66]

MAXWELL, ROBERT, born in 1725, a weaver from Inch, Wigtownshire, with his wife Martha Carnochan and their children Margaret, Janet, Sarah and Martha, from Stranraer to NY on the Jackie of Glasgow 31 May 1775. [PRO.T47.12]

MEAN, WILLIAM, born in 1753, a tailor from Ayr, from Stranraer to NY on the Gale of Whitehaven in May 1774.[PRO.T47.12]

MEARSON, JOHN, born in 1744, a wright from Stirling, from Greenock to NY on the Christy in May 1775. [PRO.T47.12]

MEIKLE, ALEXANDER, indentured servant, to East NJ 1684. [NJSA.EJD.A195]

MEIN, AGNES, an indentured servant from Scotland who arrived in

Philadelphia on the <u>Anne galley</u> assigned to William Miller, Chester County, PA, 20 Sep. 1745.[EP#59]

MELDRUM, JAMES, soldier during the French and Indian Wars, settled in Otter Creek, NY, 1767, Loyalist in 1776. [PRO.AO12.102.170]

MELVIN, JAMES, indentured servant, to East NJ 1684. [NJSA.EJD/A]

MENTEITH, ALEXANDER, indentured servant, to East NJ 1684. [NJSA.EJD.A18][RPCS.8.709]

MENZIES, JOHN, a bookseller in Port Glasgow then in NY, 1778. [NAS.CS16.1.174]

MERCER, General HUGH, born in New Pitsligo, Aberdeenshire, on 17 Jan. 1726, son of Reverend William Mercer and Anne Munro, educated at King's College, Aberdeen, graduated MD in 1744, possibly a Jacobite, from Leith to Philadelphia during 1746, settled in Mercerburg, Franklin County, PA, and Fredericksburg, King George County, VA, a planter and physician, married Isabella Gordon, parents of William, John and Ann Gordon,   Revolutionary Army officer, died at Princeton, NJ, on 12 Jan. 1777. [AP#275][KCA#2.315][OD#43][SA#188]

MERCER, Colonel JAMES FRANCIS, son of the Reverend Laurence Mercer and Jean Lindsay in Gask, Perthshire, died at Fort Oswego on 13 Aug. 1756. Probate 1760 PCC. [F#4.274]

MERCER, ROBERT, indented in Chester Co., PA, 14 July 1697. [Sgen.29.1.13]

MERCER, ROBERT, a merchant from Pittendreich, to NY before 1770, a merchant in NY. [NAS.GD1.787.36-38; RD4.261.1068]

MESTON, JOHN, indented in Chester Co., PA, 14 Dec.1698. [Sgen.29.1.13]

MIDDLETON, JOHN, born in 1760, from Edinburgh, from Leith to Philadelphia on the <u>Friendship</u> in May 1775. [PRO.T47.12]

MIDDLETON, PETER, son of Rev. John Middleton, a physician educated at Edinburgh and St Andrews Universities by 1750, died in NY in 9 Jan.1781. [NAS.RD2.235.730][NAS.RS27.202/203] [SA#181][NYGaz-Merc.29.1.1781][NAS.NRAS.OO54, 11] [NAS.CS16.1.141/151/318]

MILL, ANNA, daughter of Robert Mill a master mason in Edinburgh, in NJ by 1687. [NJSA.EJD.B139]

MILLER, ANDREW, transported from Greenock to NY on 21 Oct. 1682. [NAS.HH11#221]

MILLER, ELIZABETH, born 1752, a servant from Perth, via Leith to Philadelphia on the <u>Friendship</u> in May 1775. [PRO.T47.12]

MILLER, GAVIN, born in 1738, a farmer, from Greenock to NY on the <u>Lilly</u> in Apr. 1775. [PRO.T47.12]

MILLER, JAMES, from Carshorne, later a merchant in Perth Amboy, NJ by 1685. [NJSA.EJD.A282; B175]

MILLER, JAMES, born in 1753, a weaver from Paisley, from Greenock to NY on the <u>Commerce</u> in Feb. 1774. [PRO.T47.12]

MILLER, JOHN, born in 1710, from Edinburgh, from London to NY or PA in July 1728. [CLRO/AIA]

MILLER, JOHN, born in Edinburgh on 27 July 1760, son of Professor John

Miller of Glasgow University, educated at Glasgow University in
 1774, an advocate in 1783, died in PA during 1796.
 [MAGU#107][CM#11736;19.11.1796]

MILLER, MARGARET, a Covenanter, transported from Leith to East NJ
 on the Henry and Francis 5 Sep. 1685. [RPCS#11.154]

MILLER, THOMAS, born in 1748, a farmer from Kilbarchan, from
 Greenock to NY on the Lilly in Apr. 1775. [PRO.T47.12]

MILLER, WILLIAM, born in 1751, a weaver from Paisley,from Greenock
 to NY on the Commerce in Feb.1774. [PRO.T47.12]

MILLIGAN, AGNES, born in 1743, from Gatehouse, Kirkcudbright,
 from Stranraer to NY on the Galein May 1774. [PRO.T47.12]

MILLIGAN, DAVID, a merchant in NY, 1781. [NAS.CS16.1.183]

MILLIGAN, JAMES, a merchant, son of Quintin Milligan, St John's
 Clachan, Dalry, Kirkcudbrightshire, to Philadelphia by 1772.
 [NAS.RS23.20.461]

MILLIGAN, MARY, born in 1740, from Gatehouse, from Stranraer to NY
 on the Gale of Whitehaven in May 1774. [PRO.T47.12]

MILROY, ANTHONY, a laborer from Galloway, from Stranraer to
 NY on the Gale of Whitehaven in May 1774. [PRO.T47.12]

MILLROY, JOHN, born in 1734, a farmer from Galloway, with his wife
 Eliza and their children Mary, Janet, Eliza, Anthony, John, and
 Agnes, from Stranraer to NY on the Gale of Whitehaven
 in May 1774. [PRO.T47.12]

MILLROY, JOHN, born in 1744, a shoemaker from Galloway, with
 Sarah his wife from Stranraer to NY on the Gale of Whitehaven,
 in May 1774. [PRO.T47.12]

MILWAIN, JANET, born in 1717, from New Luce, Wigtownshire, from
 Stranraer to NY on the Jackie 31 May 1775. [PRO.T47.12]

MILLWANE, MARY, born in 1748, from Galloway, from Stranraer to NY
 on the Gale of Whitehaven in May 1774. [PRO.T47.12]

MILLWANE, THOMAS, born in 1757, a farmer from Galloway, from
 Stranraer to NY on the Gale, in May 1774. [PRO.T47.12]

MILNE, DAVID, transported from Greenock to NY on 21 Oct.
 1682.[NAS.HH11#221]

MILNE, WILLIAM, born in 1755, a laborer from Sutherland, from
 Greenock to Philadelphia on the Sally in Oct. 1774.[PRO.T47.12]

MITCHELL, GEORGE, born 1747, a joiner from Glasgow, via Leith to
 Philadelphia on the Friendship in May 1775. [PRO.T47.12]

MITCHELL, GILBERT, born in 1753, a ropemaker from Glasgow, from
 Greenock to NY on the Matty in May 1774. [PRO.T47.12]

MITCHELL, HENRY, a merchant in NY then in Glasgow 1783.
 [NAS.CS17.1.2/294]

MITCHELL, JAMES, born in 1751, a weaver from Paisley, via
 Greenock to Philadelphia on the Sally in Oct. 1774. [PRO.T47.12]

MITCHELL, JAMES, born in 1752, a farmer from Strathspey, with his
 wife Mary and son John, from Greenock to NY on the George in May
 1774. [PRO.T47.12]

MITCHELL, JOHN, born in 1749, a farmer from Glasgow, from
 Greenock to New York on the Matty in May 1774. [PRO.T47.12]

MITCHELL, JOHN, born in 1751, a servant from Rothiemay, Banffshire, from Stornaway to Philadelphia on the <u>Clementina</u> in July 1775. [PRO.T47.12]

MITCHELL, MARY, to East NJ by 1683. [NJSA.EJD]

MITCHELL, WILLIAM, born in 1742, from Fife, via Stornaway to Philadelphia on the <u>Clementina</u> in July 1775. [PRO.T47.12]

MITCHELL, WILLIAM, born in 1743, a laborer from Paisley, via Greenock to NY on the <u>Lilly</u> in Apr. 1775. [PRO.T47.12]

MITCHELSON, DAVID, born in Kirriemuir, Angus, on 26 Jan. 1732, admitted as a member of the Scots Charitable Society of Boston, Massachusetts, in 1767, "late of NY", died at Fyfe Place, Leith Walk, Edinburgh, 24 Oct. 1802. [SCS/NEHGS][Canongate g/s] [NAS.GD5.416][NAS.RD2.250.950]

MOFFAT GEORGE,, a merchant, to NY in 1699. [DP#143]

MOFFAT, JEAN, a Covenanter transported from Leith to East NJ on the <u>Henry and Francis</u> on 5 Sep. 1685. [RPCS#11.154]

MOFFAT, JOHN, a minister/teacher, emigrated 1751, settled in Wallkill, Orange Co., died in Little Britain on 22 Apr. 1788. [F#7.664]

MOLLESON, GILBERT, in Perth Amboy, NJ, 1699. [SPAWI#1699.95]

MOLLISON, JOHN, indentured servant, to East NJ by 1688. [NJSA.EJD.B403]

MONRO, GEORGE, born in 1717, an indentured servant who absconded in June 1752. [NYGaz#XIX/165]

MONRO, HENRY, a Society for the Propagation of the Gospel minister at Albany, NY, on 25 Jan. 1765. [FPA#21/280,3]

MONTEITH, ALEXANDER, transported from Leith to NY in May 1684.[RPCS#8.709]

MONTEATH, WILLIAM, born in 1747, a farmer from Caithness, from Greenock to NY on the <u>Lilly</u> in May 1775. [PRO.T47.12]

MONTGOMERY, ALEXANDER, and his wife Anna Sutherland, from Islay, Argyll, to NY in July 1738 to have settled at Wood Creek on the Hudson River, allocated 200 acres on the Argyle Patent, NY, in 1763.[HSPC]

MONTGOMERY, HUGH, from Islay, Argyll, to NY in July 1738 to have settled at Wood Creek on the Hudson River, by 1763 he had settledwith two children in NY and was granted 200 acres on the Argyle Patent,NY.[HSPC][NY.Col.MS#72/170]

MONTGOMERIE, JOHN, soldier and administrator, Governor of NY from 1728 to 1731.

MONTGOMERY, MARY, born in 1756, a servant from Inverness, from Stornaway to Philadelphia on the <u>Clementina,</u> in July 1775. [PRO.T47.12]

MOODY, DAVID, settled in NY by 1689. [SPAWI.1689.350]

MOODIE, JOHN, born in 1757, a servant from Perth, from Leith to Philadelphia on the <u>Friendship</u> in May 1775. [PRO.T47.12]

MOORE, ALEXANDER, indented in Chester Co., PA, 14 July 1697. [Sgen.29.1.13]

MOOR, BENJAMIN, son of William Moor, a joiner in Piscataqua, Ranton River,Middlesex County, NJ, 1762. [NAS.CS16.1.114]

MOORE, DONALD, a Covenanter who was transported from Leith to East NJ in July 1685. [RPCS#11.136]

MOORE, GEORGE, a Covenanter who was transported from Leith to East NJ on the Henry and Francis 5 Sep. 1685. [RPCS#11.154]

MOORE, JOHN, indentured servant, to East NJ 1684. [NJSA.EJD.A195]

MOORE, ROBERT, indentured servant, to East NJ 1684. [NJSA.EJD.A195]

MORE, PETER, born in 1744, a mason from Perthshire, from Greenock to NY on the Monimia in May 1775. [PRO.T47.12]

MORGAN, CHARLES, carpenter, settled Burlington, NJ, 1758, Loyalist. [PRO.AO12.100.155]

MORGAN, WILLIAM, indentured servant, to East NJ 1684. [NJSA.EJD.A196]

MORISON, ALEXANDER, born in 1742, a mason from Aberdeen, with Mary his wife from Greenock to NY on the George in May 1774. [PRO.T47.12]

MORISON, ANNE, born in 1762, a servant from Ness, Isle of Lewis, from Stornaway to Philadelphia on the Friendship, in May 1774. [PRO.T47.12]

MORISON, CHRISTIAN, born in 1750, from Stirling, from Greenock to NY on the Lilly in May 1775. [PRO.T47.12]

MORISON, DAVID, born in 1749, a wright from Glasgow, from Greenock to NY on the Matty in May 1774. [PRO.T47.12]

MORISON, DONALD, born in 1749, a cooper from Stornaway, Isle of Lewis, from Greenock to NY on the George in May 1774. [PRO.T47.12]

MORISON, DUGAL, 5'6", 'well made', a laborer, enlisted in the PA Regiment in York, PA, on 19 May 1758. [Pa.Arch#5/1/150]

MORISON, DUNCAN, born in 1747, a farmer from Stirling, via Greenock to NY on the Lilly in May 1775. [PRO.T47.12]

MORISON, GEORGE, born in 1760, a servant from Beauly, Inverness-shire, from Stornaway to Philadelphia on the Clementina in July 1775. [PRO.T47.12]

MORRISON, HUGH. soldier in the French and Indian Wars, settled in Charlotte Co.,NY, 1763, Loyalist soldier in 1776. [PRO.AO12.10.12]

MORISON, HUGH, born 1762, servant from Beauly, Inverness-shire, from Stornaway to Philadelphia on the Clementina, in July 1775. [PRO.T47.12]

MORRISON, JAMES, absconded from Stephen Leach a tailor in NY city 1758. [NYMerc.17.7.1758]

MORRISON, JAMES, born in 1760, an apprentice blacksmith from Stornaway, Isle of Lewis, from Stornaway to NY on the Peace and Plenty in Nov. 1774. [PRO,T47.12]

MORRISON, JANET, transported from Greenock to NY on 21 Oct. 1682.[NAS.HH11#221]

MORRISON, JEAN, indentured servant, to East NJ by 1686. [NJSA.EJD.A260]

MORISON, JOHN, born 1749, servant from Beauly, Inverness-shire, with Isobel Fraser his wife and son Alexander, from Stornaway to

Philadelphia on the Clementina, July 1775. [PRO.T47.12]

MORRISON, JOHN, born 1758, servant from Beauly, Inverness-shire, via Stornaway to Philadelphia on the Clementina in July 1775. [PRO,T47.12]

MORRISON, MALCOLM, settled in Fredericksburg, Dutchess Co., NY, as a merchant in 1762, Loyalist in 1776. [PRO.AO12.22.1]

MORISON, MARY, born in 1753, a servant from Inverness, from Stornaway to Philadelphia on the Clementina in July 1775. [PRO.T47.12]

MORISON, MURDO, born in 1757, a servant from Uig, Isle of Lewis, via Stornaway to Philadelphia on the Friendship in May 1774. [PRO.T47.12]

MORISON, NORMAN, born in 1724, a farmer from Bragar, Isle of Lewis, via Stornaway to Philadelphia on the Friendship in May 1774. [PRO.T47.12]

MORISON, PETER, born in 1728, a fisherman from Beauly, Inverness-shire, with his wife Anne and daughter Betty from Stornaway to Philadelphia on the Clementina in July 1775. [PRO.T47.12]

MORRISON, ROBERT, 5'7", 'well made', a laborer, enlisted in the PA Regiment in York, PA, on 18 May 1858. [Pa.Arch#5/1/150]

MORRISON, Mr ..., recently arrived in NY city, drowned off Staten Island 17 Aug.1763, buried at Constable Point, NJ. [NYGaz-Merc.29.8.1763]

MOUNCEY, MARGARET, born 1686, indented in Chester Co., PA, 5 Aug.1697. [Sgen.29.1.13]

MOUNT, WILLIAM, indentured servant, to East NJ 1685. [NJSA.EJD.A226]

MOWAT, JANET, a spinner from Sutherland, from Greenock to Philadelphia on the Sally in Oct. 1774. [PRO.T47.12]

MOWAT, JOHN, born in Montrose, Angus, on 11 Aug. 1740, son of Alexander Mowat and Anne Walker, a cabinetmaker and ironmonger in NY from 1777 to 1829, died there on 15 Mar. 1829. [ANY#1.265]

MUDIE, DAVID, from Montrose, Angus, in 1684, settled in New Perth, East NJ. [Insh#240][NJSA.EJD.A196/A223/A240/A423]

MUDIE, JAMES, from Montrose, Angus, in 1684, settled in New Perth, East NJ. [Insh#260]

MUDIE, MARGARET, indentured servant, to East NJ 1684. [NJSA.EJD.A196]

MUIR, ANN, born in 1755, a servant from Edinburgh, from Leith to Philadelphia on the Friendship in May 1775. [PRO.T47.12]

MUIR, DAVID, born in 1755, a farmer from Kilsyth from Greenock to NY on the George of Greenock in May 1774, arrived in NY on 18 July 1774. [PRO.T47.12][SM.36/446]

MUIR, JAMES, a Covenanter from Lesmahagow, Lanarkshire, was transported from Leith to NY in May 1684. [RPCS#8.516]

MUIR, JANET, born in 1746, a servant from Edinburgh, from Leith to Philadelphia on the Friendship in May 1775. [PRO.T47.12]

MUIR, JOHN, born in 1757, a weaver from Paisley, from Greenock to NY on the Commerce in Feb. 1774. [PRO.T47.12]

MUIR, ROBERT, Covenanter in Argyll, from Leith to East NJ on the
　　Henry and Francis 1685. [RPCS.11.129][NJSA.EJD.A226]

MUIR, ROBERT, born in 1744, a weaver from Paisley, with his wife Jane
　　... and their children Margaret, Ann and James, from
　　Greenock to NY on the Commerce in Feb. 1774. [PRO.T47.12]

MUIR, ROBERT, born in 1753, a weaver from Paisley, via Greenock to
　　NY on the Commerce in Feb. 1774. [PRO.T47.12]

MUIR, WILLIAM, from Stirling, was transported from Leith to East NJ on
　　the Henry and Francis on 5 Sep. 1685. [RPCS#10.206]

MUIR, WILLIAM, born in 1754, from Kirkcudbright to America during
　　1774, settled in NY, married Mary Ritchie, died on 9 Feb. 1809.
　　[BLG#2937]

MUIR, WILLIAM, born in 1757, a weaver from Paisley, from Greenock to
　　NY on the Commerce in Feb. 1774. [PRO.T47.12]

MUIRHEAD, GAVIN, a Covenanter from Cambusnethan, Lanarkshire,
　　was transported from Leith to NY in May 1684. [RPCS#8.516]

MUIRHEAD, JAMES, Covenanter, transported from leith to East NJ on the
　　Henry and Francis in 1685. [RPCS.II.155][NWI.I.423]

MUIRHEAD, JOHN, a Covenanter imprisoned in Edinburgh Tolbooth who
　　was transported from Leith to East NJ on the Henry and Francis, 5
　　Sep. 1685. [NAS.HH11#376][RPCS#11.159]

MUIRHEAD, JOHN, a merchant who settled in Philadelphia before 1699.
　　[SPC.1699.248]

MUNDILL, JOHN, a Covenanter imprisoned in Edinburgh Tolbooth who
　　was transported from Leith to East NJ on the Henry and Francis 5
　　Sep. 1685. [NAS.HH11#369][RPCS#11#330]

MUNN, ALEXANDER, merchant in NY, 1784. [NAS.CS17.1.3/324]

MUNRO, ANNE, born in 1757, a servant from Balconie, Ross and
　　Cromarty, from Stornaway to Philadelphia on the Clementina, in July
　　1775.[PRO.T47.12]

MUNRO, DANIEL, soldier of the French and Indian War, settled
　　Elizabethtown, NJ. Loyalist. [PRO.AO13.26.324]

MUNRO, DUNCAN, born in 1732, a tailor from Perthshire, with his wife
　　Janet Brown, from Greenock to NY on the Monimia in May
　　1775.[PRO.T47.12]

MUNRO, FLORENCE. born in 1754, a spinner from Glasgow,
　　from Greenock to NY on the Commerce in Feb. 1774. [PRO.T47.12]

MUNRO, GEORGE, born in 1745, a wright from Glasgow, via
　　Greenock to NY on the Monimia in May 1775. [PRO.T47.12]

MUNRO, Reverend HENRY, minister in Albany, NY, 25 Jan. 1765,
　　father of Peter and Elizabeth, Loyalist in 1776, died in Edinburgh
　　during 1797.[PRO.AO12.24.36][FPA#304] [NAS.RD3.289.289;
　　RD3.289.717]

MUNRO, HUGH, soldier in the French and Indian Wars, settled in St
　　Haick, and later Queensborough, Albany County, NY, Loyalist
　　soldier in 1776. [PRO.AO12.31.99]

MUNROE, HUGH, to America in 1774, settled on the Kingsborough
　　Patent, NY, a Loyalist and soldier of the Royal Regiment of NY 1776
　　to 1783, later settled at River aux Raisons, Ontario. [DF.pp]

MUNRO, JOHN, settled in NY as a trader in 1756, Loyalist soldier in 1776. [PRO.AO12.12.1]

MUNRO, MARGARET, born in 1754, a servant from Inverness, from Stornaway to Philadelphia on the Clementina in July 1775. [PRO.T47.12]

MURCHIE, WILLIAM, born in 1737, a weaver from Paisley with his wife Agnes ...... and their children William, James, John, and Gavin, from Greenock to NY on the Commerce in Feb. 1774.[PRO.T47.12]

MURCHIE, WILLIAM, jr., born in 1756, a weaver from Paisley, via Greenock to NY on the Commerce in Feb. 1774.[PRO.T47.12]

MURCHISON, DUNCAN, to America in 1773, settled on the Kingsborough Patent, NY, a Loyalist and soldier of the Royal Regiment of NY from 1776 to 1783, later in Ontario. [DF.pp]; Loyalist in 1776. [PRO.AO13.14.411]

MURCHISON, JOHN, to America in 1773, settled on the Kingsborough Patent, NY, a Loyalist and soldier of the Royal Regiment of NY from 1776 to 1783, later settled in Charlottenburg, Ontario. [DF.pp]; Loyalist in 1776, [PRO.AO13.14.412]

MURDOCH, ANDREW, possibly from Morayshire, in Philadelphia, 1785.[NAS.GD248.box 354, bundle 4]

MURDOCH, ARCHIBALD, born in 1757, a weaver from Paisley, , from Greenock to NY on the Commerce in Feb. 1774. [PRO.T47.12]

MURDOCH, DAVID, and his wife Mary, settled in NY, pro. 1687 PCC

MURDOCH, JAMES, born in 1743, a gardener from Glasgow, from Greenock to NY on the Commerce in Feb. 1774.[PRO.T47.12]

MURDOCH, JOHN, married Elizabeth Dishington, in the Dutch Reformed Church of NY on 11 Sep. 1715. [DRC]

MURDOCH, JOHN, born in 1749, a farmer from Stirling, from Greenock to NY on the Matty in May 1774. [PRO.T47.12]

MURDOCH, PATRICK, son of William Murdoch and Mary McDouall in Cumloden, Minnigaff, Galloway, with his wife Nicola Gibson and their children John, William, Samuel and Thomas, to America in May 1774, he died in NY during 1775. [G#21.6.104]

MURDOFF, GEORGE, to America in 1773, settled on the Kingsborough Patent, NY, a Loyalist and soldier of the Royal Regiment of NY from 1776 to 1783, later settled in Fredericksburg, Ontario. [DF.pp]

MURISON, GEORGE, born in 1675, educated at King's College, Aberdeen, in 1701, a schoolmaster in Albany, NY, in 1703, then a minister in NY and CT from 1705 to 1708, died in Rye, Westchester County, NY, on 12 Oct. 1708. [CCMC]; probate 13 Nov. 1708 NY

MURPHY, ANTHONY, from Islay, Argyll, in Nov. 1740 bound for NY and Wood Creek on the Hudson River. [HSBC]

MURRAY, Reverend ALEXANDER, born in New Deer, Aberdeenshire, 1727, educated at King's College, Aberdeen, around 1746, a minister and schoolmaster in Glenlivet, Banffshire, to America in 1762, settled in Reading, PA, Loyalist 1776, died on 14 Sep. 1793, buried in Christ Church, Philadelphia. Pro 1795 PCC. [PRO.AO12.42.1] [AP#297][F#6.341/664][EMA#47][FAB#209][SNQ#2.10]

MURRAY, ANDREW, born in 1749, a tailor from Paisley, via Greenock to
     Philadelphia on the Sally in Oct. 1774.[PRO.T47.12]
MURRAY, JAMES, a Covenanter from Argyll, transported from Leith to
     East NJ on the Henry and Francis 5 Sep. 1685. [RPCS#11.330]
MURRAY, JAMES, born in 1754, a laborer from Gatehouse,
     Kirkcudbrightshire, from Stranraer to NY on the Galeof Whitehaven
     in May 1774. [PRO.T47.12]
MURRAY, JAMES, a druggist, son of George Murray in Edinburgh, died
     in NY during Sep. 1767. [SM#29.557]
MURRAY, JOHN, born in 1734, a laborer who enlisted in the PA Regiment
     on 8 May 1758. [Pa.Archives#5/1/186]
MURRAY, JOHN, a merchant in NY, 1786. [NAS.RD3.245.1215;
     CS17.1.6, 251]
MURRAY, KATHERINE, born in 1753, a servant from Stornaway, Isle of
     Lewis, from Stornaway to Philadelphia on the Friendship in May
     1774. [PRO.T47.12]
MURRAY or MCLEOD, MARGARET, born in 1749, a sailor's wife from
     Stornaway, Isle of Lewis, with her children George, Malcolm and
     Janet, from Stornaway to Philadelphia on the Friendship in May
     1774. [PRO.T47.12]
MURRAY, PATRICK, in Albany, NY, 1679. [CMA405]
MURRAY, ROBERT, a merchant in NY, 1786. [NAS.RD3.245.1215;
     CS17.1.6]
MURRAY, WALTER, born in 1752, a tailor from Banff, from Greenock to
     Philadelphia on the Magdalene in Aug. 1774. [PRO.T47.12]
MURRAY, WILLIAM, indented in Chester Co., PA, 5 Aug.1697.
     [Sgen.29.1.13]
MURRAY, WILLIAM, from Darien to NY on the Caledonia in Aug.
     1699.[SPC#1699.478]
MURRAY, WILLIAM, born in 1731, a farmer from Breadalbane,
     Perthshire, with his wife Margaret McDougald and children John,
     Alexander, Archibald, Christian, Kathrine and James, from Greenock
     to NY on the Commerce in June 1775. [PRO.T47.12]
MURRAY, WILLIAM, skipper and merchant in NY, 1764.
     [NAS.CS16.1.117]
MURT, ALEXANDER, indentured servant, to East NJ 1684.
     [NJSA.EJD.A]
MUSHET, DAVID, born in 1737, a farmer from Stirling, from Greenock to
     NY on the Lilly in Apr. 1775. [PRO.T47.12]
NAIRN, JAMES, born in 1755, a smith from Paisley, via Greenock to NY
     on the Commerce in Feb.1774. [PRO.T47.12]
NAPIER, ALEXANDER, to East NJ in 1684. [NJSA.EJD.A183]
NAPIER, THOMAS, a farmer from Monkland, Lanarkshire, from
     Greenock to Philadelphia on the Sally in Oct. 1774. [PRO.T47.12]
NAYSMITH, JOHN, indentured servant, to East NJ 1684.
     [NJSA.EJD.A/B403]
NEIL, HENRY, born in 1756, a spinner from Paisley, from
     Greenock to NY on the Commerce in Feb. 1774. [PRO.T47.12]
NEILSON, WILLIAM, born in 1754, a weaver from Paisley, via Greenock

to NY on the Commerce in Feb. 1774. [PRO.T47.12]

NELSON, JOHN, born in 1728, 5'3", a shoemaker who enlisted in
   Philadelphia into the PA Regiment on 19 May 1758.
   [Pa.Archives#5/1/198]

NEWLANDS, JAMES, born around 1702, an indentured servant from
   Glasgow in 1732, sought by brother Alexander a skinner in
   Edinburgh in 1737. [Zenger's NY Wkly Jl.24.10.1737]

NICHOLL, JOHN, from Livingston, West Lothian, a physician educated at
   Edinburgh University, settled in NY before 1712.
   [NAS.CH1.2.49.52]

NICHOLS, ALEXANDER born 1686, indented in Chester Co., PA, 14 July
   1697. [Sgen.29.1.13]

NICHOLS, HENRY, indented in Chester Co., PA, Sept. 1695.
   [Sgen.29.1.11]

NICOL, ANDREW, from Aberdeen, died in NY during 1742. [APB.3.112]

NICOL, JAMES, born around 1756, a sailor who deserted from the
   transport ship Christie in the North River, NY, May 1777. [NYGaz-
   Merc.26.5.1777]

NICOLL, JOHN, born in Livingston, educated in West Calder and at
   Edinburgh University, a physician and surgeon settled in Long
   Island, New York, 1712, Presbyterian in NY 1724.
   [NAS.CH1.2.49.44]

NICOLL, W., took the Oath of Association in NY on 26 May 1696.
   [PRO.C213: OR469/1]; a petitioner in NY 1701. [DNY.IV.934]

NICOLSON, FINLOW, born in 1758, a servant from Bayble, Isle of Lewis,
   from Stornaway to Philadelphia on the Friendship in May 1774.
   [PRO.T47.12]

NICHOLSON, GEORGE, born in Leith during 1746, an apprentice ship's
   carpenter who absconded from George McAlin, a ship's carpenter in
   Philadelphia on 19 July 1765. [NY.Merc., 12.8.1765]

NICOLSON, JOHN, an adulterer from Bridgend, Liberton, Edinburgh, was
   transported from Leith to East NJ in 1684.
   [NAS.HH11#257][Liberton KSR][NJSA.EJD.B351]

NICOLSON, KATHERINE, born in 1756, a servant from Stornaway, Isle
   of Lewis, from Stornaway to Philadelphia on the Friendship in May
   1774. [PRO.T47.12]

NISBET, ARCHIBALD, born in 1747, a farmer from Stirling, from
   Greenock to NY on the Matty in May 1774.[PRO.T47.12]

NISBET, ROBERT, a petitioner in NY 1701. [DNY.IV.934]

NIVEN, DANIEL, born in Islay, Argyll, during 1742, son of Duncan Niven,
   to NY in 1765, an engineer and architect, died in Newburgh, NY, on
   20 Nov 1809 [ANY#1.180]

NIVEN, WILLIAM, a farmer and a Covenanter, transported from Leith to
   East NJ on the Henry and Francis on 5 Sep. 1685. [RPCS#11.155]

NUTT, JAMES, with his wife Rebecca Creightoun, and children Robert,
   John, and Elizabeth, from Islay, Argyll, in June 1739 bound for NY
   and Wood Creek on the Hudson River, he and a son were granted 200
   acres on the Argyle Patent, NY, in 1763. [HSBC]

OCHTERLONY, ALEXANDER, born in the 1690s, son of Reverend John

Ochterlony and Margaret Graham in Aberlemno, Angus, a merchant
in Montrose, Angus, then in Philadelphia. [F#5.277]

OCHTERLONY, DAVID, from Montrose, Angus, a mariner in Boston,
husband of Catherine, probate 1 July 1767 NY

OCKMAN, MARY, born in 1739, a spinner from Stirling, with her
children Lisa, Nelly, and Margaret, from Greenock to NY on the
Monimia in May 1775. [PRO.T47.12]

OGILVIE, JAMES, born around 1729, deserted the 35th Regiment between
Stillwater and Albany 17 Aug.1761. [NYGaz-Merc.17.8.1761]

OGILVIE, Reverend JOHN, born around 1723, assistant minister of
Trinity Church, NY, died 26 Nov. 1774, probate 3 Mar. 1775 NY

OGILVIE, JOHN, born in 1745, a wright from Stirling, from Greenock to
NY on the Monimia, in May 1775.[PRO.T47.12]

OLIPHANT, JOHN, wife Janet Gilchrist, and daughters Margaret and
Janet, from Pencaitland, indentured servants, to East NJ 1685.
[NJSA.EJD.A252]

OLIPHANT, WILLIAM, a Covenanter, from Leith to East NJ on the
Henry and Francis on 5 Sep. 1685. [RPCS#11.154]

OMAN, DANIEL, born in 1760, a servant from Leith, Midlothian, from
Leith to Philadelphia on the Friendship in May 1775. [PRO.T47.12]

OMAN, MARY, born 1754, a milliner from Edinburgh, via Leith to
Philadelphia on the Friendship in May 1775. [PRO.T47.12]

ORMISTON, JOSEPH, in East NJ 1699. [SPAWI.1699/164]

ORMOND, JOHN, born in 1759, a laborer from Angus, from
Leith to Philadelphia on the Friendship in May 1775. [PRO.T47.12]

ORR, ANN, born in 1756, a spinner from Paisley, from
Greenock to NY on the Commerce in Feb. 1774. [PRO.T47.12]

ORR, ISABELLA, born in 1754, a spinner from Paisley from
Greenock to NY on the Commerce in Feb. 1774. [PRO.T47.12]

ORR, JEAN, born 1747, a spinner from Paisley, with son John, from
Greenock to NY on the Commerce in Feb. 1774. [PRO.T47.12]

ORR, WILLIAM, a minister educated at Glasgow University around 1712,
to Philadelphia in 1730. [APC#237]

OSBURNE, WILLIAM, son of Rev. William Osburne and Ann Caddell, in
Fintry, Aberdeenshire, a sailor in Philadelphia 17... [F#6.57]

PADER, JANET, born 1754, a spinner from Paisley, via Greenock to NY
on the Commerce in Feb. 1774. [PRO.T47.12]

PANTON, DAVID, born in 1756, a tailor from Rattray, Perthshire, from
Leith to Philadelphia on the Friendship in May 1775. [PRO.T47.12]

PANTON, GEORGE, from Jedburgh, Roxburghshire, a minister and
schoolmaster, educated at Marischal College, Aberdeen, to America
in 1772, settled in Trenton, NJ, Loyalist in 1776.
[SA#107][PRO.AO12.15.8]

PARKER, JAMES, born in 1729, a laborer who enlisted in Captain Robert
Boyd's Company of the PA Regiment on 8 May 1759.
[Pa.Archives#5/1/292]

PATERSON, ANDREW, from Hamilton, Lanarkshire, transported from
Leith to East NJ on the Henry and Francis on 5 Sep. 1685.
[RPCS#11.154]

PATERSON, ANDREW, born in 1744, a sawyer from Glasgow, with
     Elizabeth his wife and their son John, from Greenock to NY on the
     Commerce in Feb. 1774. [PRO.T47.12]

PATERSON, CHRISTIAN, from Islay, Argyll, to NY in July 1738 to have
     settled at Wood Creek on the Hudson River.[HSPC]

PATERSON, GEORGE, born in 1753, a farmer from Kilsyth, from
     Greenock to NY on the George in May 1774. [PRO.T47.12]

PATTERSON, JOHN, born 1730, deserted from the transport Mary in
     1756. [NYMerc.6.9.1756]

PATERSON, JOHN, with wife Janet, to Philadelphia in 1771, merchant in
     Front Street, Loyalist, died NY. [PRO.AO12.40.40]

PATERSON, JOHN, born in 1744, a blacksmith from Stornaway, with his
     wife Margaret and son John, from Stornaway to Philadelphia to NY
     on the Peace and Plenty in Nov. 1774. [PRO.T47.12]

PATERSON, KATHERINE, a servant from Stornaway, from Stornaway to
     Philadelphia on the Friendship, in May 1774. [PRO.T47.12]

PATTERSON, NINIAN, transported from Glasgow to East NJ on 21
     Feb.1684. [RPCS#8.379]

PATTERSON, THOMAS, minister of Borthwick, to East NJ 1685.
     [Insh#176]

PATERSON, Mr WILLIAM, in Albany, NY, 1669/1679. [CMA@415]

PATERSON, WILLIAM, born in 1746, a coppersmith from Glasgow,
     from Greenock to NY on the Lilly in Apr. 1775. [PRO.T47.12]

PATON, JOSEPH, born in 1745, a farmer from Glasgow, from Greenock
     to NY on the Commerce in Feb. 1774. [PRO.T47.12]

PATON, THOMAS, born in 1746, a shoemaker from Edinburgh, from
     Greenock to NY or GA on the Christy in May 1775. [PRO.T47.12]

PATON, WILLIAM, born in 1742, a weaver from Paisley, with Mary his
     wife and their children Janet, Margaret and Catherine, from Greenock
     to NY on the Commerce in Feb. 1774. [PRO.T47.12]

PAUL, JAMES, indentured servant, to East NJ, 1684. [NJSA.EJD.A]

PAUL, JAMES, born in 1748, a laborer from Ayr, from Greenock to NY
     on the Lilly in Apr. 1775. [PRO.T47.12]

PAUL, JOHN, born 1745, a farmer from Glasgow, with daughter Margaret,
     from Greenock to NY on the Matty in May 1774. [PRO.T47.12]

PAUL, RICHARD, in Woodbridge, East NJ, 1685. [NJSA.EJD.A265]

PEDDIE, WILLIAM, indentured servant, to East NJ, 1684.
     [NJSA.EJD.A302]

PENNY, WILLIAM, an indentured servant, to East NJ 1684.
     [NJSA.EJD.A196]

PETTIGREW, ROBERT, soldier during the French and Indian War,
     settled in NY, Loyalist soldier in 1776. [PRO.AO13.81.330]

PHILIP, MARGARET, born in 1757, a servant from Edinburgh, from
     Leith to Philadelphia on the Friendship in May 1775. [PRO.T47.12]

PITTERKIN, THOMAS, born in 1755, from Fort Augustus, Inverness-
     shire, from Leith to Philadelphia on the Friendship in May 1775.
     [PRO.T47.12]

POLLOCK, BESSIE, indentured servant to East NJ 1685.
     [NJSA.EJD.A225]

POLLOCK, JOHN, a Covenanter who was transported from Leith to East NJ on the Henry and Francis 5 Sep. 1685. [RPCS#11.154]

PORTERFIELD, JOHN, a merchant in Trenton, Hunterdon County, NJ, probate 16 June 1738 NJ. [NJSA:Liber 4/136]

PRESTON, WILLIAM, born in Edinburgh during 1718, son of George Preston, educated at Balliol College, Oxford, from 1735 to 1739, an Episcopal minister in NJ from 1767 to 1777, died in Shrewsbury, NJ, on 7 Mar. 1781. [CCMC]

PRIDE, DAVID, born in 1757, a shoemaker from Fife, from Leith to Philadelphia on the Friendship in May 1775. [PRO.T47.12]

PRINGLE, Reverend FRANCIS, born in Fife during 1747, died in NY on 2 Nov. 1833. [AJ#44990]

PRINGLE, ROBERT, son of John Pringle of Haining, a physician who settled in Jamaica, died in Philadelphia on 13 Oct. 1775. [SM#38.53]

PRINGLE, WILLIAM, born on 22 Jan. 1745, settled in America during the 1760s, married Mary Wetz in Lancaster County, PA, died in Frankstown, Huntingdon County, PA, on 22 June 1829. [SG#3.2.201]

PROUDFOOT, JAMES, born in Perth during 1732, to Boston in 1754, an Associate Presbyterian minister in PA and in NY from 1757 to 1799, died in Salem, NY, on 22 Oct. 1802. [CCMC]

PROVOST, JOHN, born 1732, farmer from Siddy, with wife Isobel and sons John and Alexander, from Stornaway, Isle of Lewis, to Philadelphia on the Clementina in July 1775. [PRO.T47.12]

PROVOST, PAUL, born in 1760, a servant from Balmaduthy, Ross and Cromarty, from Stornaway, Isle of Lewis, to Philadelphia on the Clementina in July 1775.[PRO.T47.12]

PROVOST, RORY, born in 1757, a servant from Balmaduthy, Ross and Cromarty, from Stornaway, Isle of Lewis, to Philadelphia on the Clementina in July 1775.[PRO.T47.12]

PURDY, ALEXANDER, born in 1731, a carpenter, enlisted in Captain John Haslet's Co. of the PA Regt. 8 May 1758.[Pa.Arch#5/1/149]

RAIN, JOHN, born in 1738, a laborer from Kirkcudbright, with his wife Elizabeth McWhinnie and son Thomas, from Kirkcudbright to NY on the Adventure in May 1774. [PRO.T47.12]

RALSTON, MARION, born in 1756, a spinner from Paisley, via Greenock to NY on the Commerce in Feb.1774. [PRO.T47.12]

RAMSAY, FANNY, born in 1752, from Edinburgh, from Greenock to NY on the Lilly in Apr. 1775.[PRO.T47.12]

RAMSAY, JOHN, born in Perthshire during 1731, son of James Ramsay, to NY in 1752, an import merchant, died 1 Dec. 1816. [NAS.GD1.787.40] [ANY]

RAMSAY, PETER, born in 1716, a laborer, enlisted in Captain John Shannon's Co. of the PA Regt. 9 July 1746. [PaArch#5/1/11]

RAMSAY, SAMUEL, born in 1727, a joiner from Gatehouse, Kirkcudbrightshire, with his children Jane, John, William, George, Jane, Elizabeth, and Margaret, from Stranraer to NY on the Gale of Whitehaven, in May 1774. [PRO.T47.12]

RANKIN, DANIEL, born in 1756, a laborer from Paisley, via Greenock to NY on the Commerce in Feb. 1774. [PRO.T47.12]

RANKIN, HUGH, born 1752, a barber from Saltcoats, via Greenock to
   Philadelphia on the Magdalene in Aug. 1774. [PRO.T47.12]
RARITY, JOHN, born in 1752, a weaver from Paisley, , from Greenock to
   NY on the Commerce, in Feb. 1774. [PRO.T47.12]
RAY, FRANCIS, born 1723, a runaway from the snow Elizabeth of
   Aberdeen in NY (?) 1741. [Zenger's NY Wkly Jl.29.6.1741]
REDFORD, SAMUEL, a yeoman in Freehold, NJ, probate 7 June 1711
   Monmouth Wills
REDFORD, THOMAS, to East New Jersey 1684. [NJSA.EJD/A]
REDFORD, WILLIAM, born in Friershaw, Teviotdale, 1642, to East NJ
   1682, settled in Essex Co., died 1 March 1725. [NJSA.EJD.A114]
REID, ALEXANDER, born in 1729, a farmer from Brodie, Morayshire,
   with Katherine Hutchison his wife and their children Alexander,
   Mary, Isobel, James, George, David, Katherine, Henry and John,
   from Stornaway to Philadelphia on the Friendship, in May 1774.
   [PRO.T47.12]
REID, ANDREW, son of John Reid, to East NJ on the Exchange of
   Stockton in 1683. [MNJ]
REID, DUNCAN, and his wife Mary Semple, with their children Alexander,
   Nicholas, Angus and Jennie, from Islay, Argyll, in June 1739 bound
   for NY and Wood Creek on the Hudson River, by 1763 his wife and
   eight children had died and Duncan was granted 500 acres on the
   Argyle Patent, NY, Loyalist in 1776.
   [HSBC][NY.Col.MS#72/170][PRO.AO13.15.214]
REID, GEORGE, to East NJ 1684. [NJSA.EJD/A]
REID, JAMES, to East NJ on the Exchange 1683, settled in Perth Amboy
   and later in Freehold, died 1711. [NJSA.EJD.B326]
REID, JOHN, born on 13 Feb. 1655 in Kirkliston, West Lothian, a
   gardener, with his wife Margaret Miller, from Leith to East NJ on the
   Henry and Francis, in Sep. 1685, settled in Perth Amboy. [Insh#240];
   in Hortencie, NJ, Administration 27 Feb. 1724 NJ. [NJ Archives,
   Liber A/281]
REID, JOHN, and his wife Margaret Hymen, with their son Donald, from
   Islay, Argyll, in June 1739 bound for NY and Wood Creek on the
   Hudson River, in 1763 he, his wife and five children were granted
   350 acres on the Argyle Patent, NY. [HSBC][NY.Col.MS#72/170]
REID, JOHN, former soldier, settled on Montgomery's Patent, Charlotte
   Co., NY, 1763, Loyalist in 1776. [PRO.AO13.26.254]
REID, JOHN, former soldier, settled Charlotte County, NY, 1764, Loyalist
   soldier 1776. [PRO.AO12.42.392]
REID, JOHN, born in 1749, a farmer from Stirling, from Greenock to New
   York on the Matty in May 1774. [PRO.T47.12]
REID, JOHN, born in 1749, a cooper from Glasgow, from Greenock to
   New York on the Matty in May 1774. [PRO.T47.12]
REID, MARY, born in 1758, a servant from Edinburgh, from Leith to
   Philadelphia on the Friendship, in May 1775. [PRO.T47.12]
REID, ROGER, from Islay, Argyll, in June 1739 bound for NY and Wood
   Creek on the Hudson River, by 1763 he was married with three
   children and living in the Highlands of NY, when he was granted 200

acres on the Argyle Patent, NY. [HSBC][NY.Col.MS#72/170]

REID, WALTER, born in 1759, a wright from Dundee, via Greenock to Philadelphia on the <u>Magdalene</u>, in Aug. 1774. [PRO.T47.12]

REID, WILLIAM, born in 1746, a barber from Paisley, via Greenock to NY or GA on the <u>Christy</u> in May 1775. [PRO.T47.12]

RENFREW, JANET, born in 1757, a spinner from Paisley, via Greenock to NY on the <u>Commerce</u>, in Feb. 1774. [PRO.T47.12]

RENNIE, JOHN, a Covenanter, transported from Leith to East NJ on the <u>Henry and Francis</u>, on 5 Sep. 1685. [RPCS#11.154]

RENNIE, MARION, a Covenanter, transported from Leith to East NJ on the <u>Henry and Francis</u>, on 5 Sep. 1685. [RPCS#11.154]

RENTA, JAMES, born in 1747, a laborer from Glasgow, from Greenock to NY on the <u>Commerce</u> in Feb.1774. [PRO.T47.12]

RESTON, JAMES, a Covenanter, transported from Leith to East NJ on the <u>Henry and Francis</u>, on 5 Sep. 1685. [RPCS#11.166]

RHEA, ROBERT, a carpenter, to East NJ 1685, settled in Monmouth. [NJSA.EJD.B164]

RHIND, WILLIAM, born 1713, from Prestonpans, via London to PA as an indentured servant in July 1731. [CLRO/AIA]

RICHARDSON, BESSIE, indentured servant, to East NJ 1685. [NJSA.EJD.A225]

RICHARDSON, WILLIAM, a petitioner in NY 1701. [DNY.IV.934]

RIDDELL, ARCHIBALD, born in 1635 son of Sir Walter Riddell and Janet Rigg, a minister educated at Edinburgh University in 1656, a Covenanter from Kippen, husband of Helen Aitkenhead, transported from Leith to East NJ on the <u>Henry and Francis</u>, settled in Woodbridge, NJ, died in Scotland on 17 Feb. 1708. [F.7.665][RPCS#10.79][NAS.RH15]

RIDDELL, HUGH, a Covenanter who was transported from Leith to NY in 1683.[RPCS#8.253]

RIDDELL, WALTER, son of Reverend Archibald Riddell, a witness in NY on 31 May 1687. [NAS.RD4.67.97]

RIDDOCH, JOHN, born in 1748, a laborer from Kilmacolm, via Greenock to NY on the <u>Lilly</u> in Apr. 1775. [PRO.T47.12]

RIG, WILLIAM, son of Thomas Rig of Athorney, died on the <u>Henry and Francis</u> bound for NJ, probate 9 Jan. 1686 NJ. [NJ Archives: East Jersey Deeds, Liber B/475]

RITCHIE, ALEXANDER, indented in Edinburgh for 4 years in East NJ in 1685. [NJSA.EJD.A252]

RITCHIE, WILLIAM, a shipmaster, Peck's Slip, NY, husband of Elizabeth, probate 2 Aug. 1781 NY

RISH, JOHN, born in 1736, a gardener from Glasgow, via London to Philadelphia on the <u>Sally</u> in May 1774. [PRO.T47.9/11]

ROBB, HUGH, born in 1735, a tailor from Glasgow, via Greenock to NY on the <u>Commerce</u> in Feb. 1774. [PRO.T47.12]

ROBB, JOHN, born in 1748, a servant from Duffus, Morayshire, from Stornaway to Philadelphia on the <u>Clementina</u> in July 1775. [PRO.T47.12]

ROBERTS, MARGARET, born in 1749, from Glasgow, from Greenock to

NY on the Matty in May 1774. [PRO.T47.12]

ROBERTSON, ALEXANDER, in NY, 1781. [NAS.CS16.1.138]

ROBERTSON, DANIEL, born 1757, weaver from Perth, via Leith to
Philadelphia on the Friendship in May 1775 [PRO.T47.12]

ROBERTSON, GEORGE, born 1681, a thief in Edinburgh, indented in
Chester Co., PA, 14 July 1697. [Sgen.29.1.12][NAS.PC2/26]

ROBERTSON, HENRY, laborer from Lothian, via Greenock to
Philadelphia on the Sally in Oct. 1774. [PRO.T47.12]

ROBERTSON, JAMES, a printer and bookseller in Edinburgh, to America
in 1759, a newspaper publisher in Charleston, SC, then a printer in
Boston and NY, to NS in 1783. [NAS.CS236.R12/3]

ROBERTSON, JAMES, born in 1742, a weaver from Paisley, with his wife
Jean and their children James, Robert and Jean, from Greenock to NY
on the Commerce in Feb. 1774. [PRO.T47.12]

ROBERTSON, MARGARET, a gypsy, transported via Greenock to NY 21
Oct.1682. [NAS.HH11]

ROBERTSON, MARGARET indentured servant, to East NJ 1685.
[NJSA.EJD.A225]

ROBERTSON, PATRICK, from Islay, Argyll, in June 1739 bound for NY
and Wood Creek on the Hudson River, by 1763 he was dead but his
cousin John McDonald a carpenter in NY claimed his proportion of
grants on the Argyle Patent, NY, and undertook to settle on it.
[HSBC][NY.Col.MS#72/171]

ROBERTSON, PETER, merchant in Philadelphia, 1740.
[NAS.CS16.1.170]

ROBERTSON, ROBERT, born in Edinburgh on 6 Apr. 1740, a freeman of
NY 7 Feb. 1769, a merchant in NY, died on 6 Nov. 1805, buried in
Trinity Churchyard. [ANY#1.218]

ROBERTSON, ROBERT, a merchant in Perth then in Philadelphia,
husband of Mary Stewart, 1780. [NAS.CS16.1.179]

ROBERTSON, ROBERT, born in 1744, a weaver from Glasgow, via
Greenock to NY on the Matty in May 1774. [PRO.T47.12]

ROBERTSON, WILLIAM, a physician from Burntisland, Fife, to East NJ
in 1685, settled in Monmouth Co. [NJSA.EJD.D209]

ROBERTSON, WILLIAM, a petitioner in NY 1701.[DNY.IV.934]

ROBERTSON, WILLIAM, a planter in Crambiny, NJ, by 1739.
[NAS.S/H][NAS.CS16.1.69]

ROBERTSON, WILLIAM, from Edinburgh, settled in NY by 1750.
[NAS.RD4.176.448]

ROBESON, THOMAS, born in 1735, a farmer from Stirling, with his wife
Mary and their children Mary, Agnes, Alexander, James and Betty,
from Greenock to NY on the Monimia in May 1775. [PRO.T47.12]

ROBINSON, ALEXANDER, born in 1755, a student from Loch Broom,
Wester Ross, from Stornaway to Philadelphia on the Clementina in
July 1775.[PRO.T47.12]

ROBINSON, DONALD, born in 1743, a farmer from Kilenbrie, via
Greenock to NY on the Lilly in Apr. 1775.[PRO.T47.12]

ROBINSON, DONIAN, born in 1738, a farmer from Kilenbrie, via
Greenock to NY on the Lilly in Apr. 1775. [PRO.T47.12]

ROBINSON, GEORGE, born 1681, indented in Chester Co., PA, 1696.
[Sgen.29.1.14]

ROBINSON, JOHN, indented in Chester Co., PA, Sept.1695.
[Sgen.29.1.11]

ROBINSON, JOHN, absconded from James V. Cortlandt in Oct.1774.
[NYGaz-Merc.10.10.1774]

ROBINSON, MARGARET, indentured servant, to East NJ 1684.
[NJSA.EJD.A]

ROBINSON, MARGARET, born 1746, spinner from Paisley from
Greenock to NY on the Commerce in Feb. 1774.
[PRO.T47.12]

ROBINSON, PATRICK, indentured servant, to East NJ 1684.
[NJSA.EJD.A195]

ROBINSON, PATRICK, a lawyer in Philadelphia 1694. [Sgen.29.1.15]

ROBINSON, THOMAS, born 1683, indented in Chester Court, PA, 1696.
[Sgen.29.1.14]

ROBINSON, WILLIAM, a physician from Burntisland, Fife, via Leith to
East NJ in 1684. [Insh#236]; pro 20 July 1693 NJ

ROBINSON, WILLIAM, born in 1750, a smith from Paisley, via
Greenock to NY on the Lilly in Apr. 1775. [PRO.T47.12]

ROBSON, GEORGE, born 1726, tailor from Perthshire, with his wife
Marion Weir, from Greenock to NY on the Monimia in May 1775.
[PRO.T47.12]

ROCHEAD, JAMES, from Edinburgh, a merchant in NY, probate 26
Jan.1740 Monmouth, NJ. [Monmouth Wills, liber C, fo.378]

ROGER, JOHN, a minister from Muckart, Perthshire, to America in 1770,
settled in PA. [UPC#656]

RONALD, WILLIAM, indentured servant, to East NJ 1684.
[NJSA.EJD.A/B403]

ROSE. BETTY, born in 1758, from Inverness, via Stornaway to
Philadelphia on the Clementina in July 1775. [PRO.T47.12]

ROSS, AENEAS, a minister, to PA in 1740. [EMA#53]

ROSS, ALEXANDER, born 1682, to Philadelphia in 1693, indented for
service in Chester Co. 3 Oct.1693. [Sgen.29/1.11]

ROSS, ALEXANDER, born in 1742, a carpenter from Galloway, with Jean
his wife, and their children Isabel, Jean and Margaret, from Stranraer
to NY on the Gale in May 1774. [PRO.T47.12]

ROSS, ALEXANDER, son of John Ross in Cairnbrock, Kirkham,
Galloway, settled in Mount Holly, NJ, by 1770, [NAS.CS16.1.138];
probate 3 June 1780 NJ. [NJSA.Lib.23/196]

ROSS, ANN, born in 1754, from Kilsyth, via Greenock to NY on the
George of Greenock, in May 1774.[PRO.T47.12]

ROSS, CHARLES, born in 1722, deserted from Cap. Wetterstom's Royal
Regiment of North America in 1756. [NYMerc.26.7.1756]

ROSS, DAVID, born in Edinburgh 1744, absconded from the transport ship
Hercules in 1762. [NYGaz-Merc.29.11.1762]

ROSS, DONALD, to America during the French and Indian Wars as a
soldier, settled on the Kingsborough Patent, NY, in 1763, a Loyalist
and soldier of the Royal Regiment of NY from 1776 to 1777, died in

1787. [DF.pp][PRO.AO12.9.53]

ROSS, FINLEY, born in 1740, to America in 1773, settled on the Kingsborough Patent, NY, a Loyalist and soldier of the Royal Regiment of NY from 1776 to 1783, later in Charlottenburg, Ontario, died in 1830. [DF.pp][PRO.AO.12.29.86]

ROSS, GEORGE, from Ross-shire, a minister educated at Edinburgh University, to NJ in 1705, settled in Newcastle and Chester, Del. [AP#308][SCHR#14.147][EMA#53]

ROSS, HUGH, born in 1757, a farmer in Strathspey, from Greenock to NY on the George in May 1774. [PRO.T47.12]

ROSS, JAMES, born in 1744, a farmer from Strathspey, from Greenock to NY on the George in May 1774. [PRO.T47.12]

ROSS, JEAN, from Islay, Argyll, to NY in July 1738 to have settled at Wood Creek on the Hudson River.[HSPC]

ROSS, JEAN, a spinster in NY, probate 15 May 1777 NY.

ROSS, JOHN, born in Tain, Ross and Cromarty, on 29 Jan. 1729, son of Murdoch Ross and Catherine Simson, a merchant in Perth later by 1762 in NY, and Philadelphia in 1763, married Clementina Ross from Aberdeen in Philadelphia on 8 Dec. 1768, died there on 8 Apr. 1800. [ANY#1.400][AP#311][NAS.CS16.1.117]

ROSS, JOHN, born in 1750, a farmer from Strathspey, via Greenock to NY on the George in May 1774. [PRO.T47.12]

ROSS, LUCY, born in 1754, a servant from Caithness, from Leith to Philadelphia on the Friendship in May 1775. [PRO.T47.12]

ROSS, MARY, from Islay, Argyll, to NY in July 1738 to have settled at Wood Creek on the Hudson River.[HSPC]

ROSS, NELLY, born in 1753, a servant from Cullen, Banffshire, from Leith to Philadelphia on the Friendship, in May 1775. [PRO.T47.12]

ROSS, RACHEL, born in 1745, from Paisley, via Greenock to NY on the George of Greenock, in May 1774. [PRO.T47.12]

ROSS, SAMUEL, in Newark, East NJ, 1693. [NJSA.EJD.B368]

ROSS, THOMAS, a tailor, to America in 1773, settled on the Kingsborough Patent, NY, by Sep. 1773, a Loyalist and soldier of the Royal Regiment of NY from 1776 to 1783, later settled in Lancaster, Glengarry, Ontario. [DF.pp][PRO.AO12.64.124]

ROSS, THOMAS, born in Drumvaich, to America in 1773, settled on the Kingsborough Patent, NY, a Loyalist and soldier of the Royal Regiment of NY from 1776 to 1783, later settled in Cornwall, Ontario. [DF.pp][PRO.AO12.29.351]

ROSS, THOMAS BANE, born in Creich, Sutherland, during 1729, a soldier at the Siege of Quebec in 1763, settled on the Kingsborough Patent, NY, a Loyalist and soldier of the Royal Regiment of NY from 1779 to 1783, later settled in Lancaster, Ontario, buried in South Lancaster cemetery on 10 Aug. 1806. [DF.pp]

ROSS, WILLIAM, born in 1734, a painter from Edinburgh, from London to Philadelphia on the Sally in May 1774. [PRO.T47.9/11]

ROSS, WILLIAM, born in 1760, a farmer from Strathspey, from Greenock to NY on the George of Greenock in May 1774. [PRO.T47.12]

ROXBURGH, ROBERT, born in 1757, a laborer from Kippen, from
    Greenock to NY on the Lilly in May 1775. [PRO.T47.12]
ROY, DONALD, born in 1750, a tailor from Glasgow, from Greenock to
    NY on the Monimia in May 1775. [PRO.T47.12]
ROY, JAMES, a shipmaster, son of James Roy in Lanark, married Elizabeth
    Wishart, settled in NY by 1777. [NAS.RD4.773.618]
ROYLE, MARY, to Philadelphia in 1697, indented for service in Chester
    Co. 14 July 1697. [SG29/1.11]
RUDDERFORD, JOHN, born in 1766, from Tongland, Kirkcudbrightshire,
    from Kirkcudbright to NY on the Gale of Whitehaven, in May 1774.
    [PRO.T47.12]
RUDDIMAN, JANET, born in 1755, from Montrose, Angus, from
    Greenock to NY on the Lilly in Apr. 1775. [PRO.T47.12]
RUDIMAN, WILLIAM, born in Turriff on 5 Sep. 1703, a baker from
    Aberdeen, died in NY during Nov. 1769. [APB.4.91]
RUSSELL, GEORGE, born in 1757, a farmer from Avis, from
    Stornaway to Philadelphia on the Clementina in July 1775.
    [PRO.T47.12]
RUSSELL, JOHN, born in 1758, a weaver from Paisley, via Greenock to
    NY on the Commerce in Feb. 1774. [PRO.T47.12]
RUSSELL, PETER, a Covenanter, transported from Leith to East NJ
    aboard the Henry and Francis on 5 Sep. 1685. [RPCS#11.154]
RUSSELL, THOMAS, a Covenanter, transported from Leith to East NJ
    aboard the Henry and Francis on 5 Sep. 1685. [RPCS#11.164]
RUTHERFORD, WALTER, born on 29 Dec. 1723 in Edgerston,
    Roxburghshire, son of Sir John Rutherford and Elizabeth Cairncross,
    to America by 1758, settled in Hunterdon County, NY, married
    Catherine Alexander, father of John, died in NY on 10 Jan. 1804.
    [NAS.RD2.210.911] [BLG#2897]
ST. CLAIR, Major General ARTHUR, born in Thurso, Caithness, on 23
    Mar. 1734, educated at the University of Edinburgh, to America as an
    officer of the 60th [Royal American] Regiment in 1758, married
    Phoebe Bayard in Boston inMay 1760, settled in Bedford, PA, in
    1764, public official, Revolutionary General, died on 31 Aug. 1818 in
    Ohio, buried in Greensburg. [AP#329]
SANDS, ALEXANDER, born in 1758, a chapman in Edinburgh, from
    Leith to Philadelphia on the Friendship in May 1775. [PRO.T47.12]
SANDYLANDS, JAMES, soldier, quit rents in Delaware 1668, 13 June
    1670, died 1692.[NY.Hist.MS.Dutch.XX/XXI, p28] [Sgen.29/1/11]
SAUNDERS, WILLIAM, born 1758, ploughman from Angus, via Leith to
    Philadelphia on the Friendship in May 1775. [PRO.T47.12]
SCHAW, WILLIAM, born 1754, laborer from Paisley, via Greenock to NY
    on the Commerce in Feb. 1774. [PRO.T47.12]
SCOTT, ALEXANDER, indentured servant, to East NJ 1684.
    [NJSA.EJD.A195]
SCOTT, ARCHIBALD, born in 1748, a tailor from Glasgow, from
    Greenock to NY on the Commerce in Feb. 1774. [PRO.T47.12]
SCOTT, CHRISTIAN, a Covenanter, transported from Leith to East NJ on
    the Henry and Francis on 5 Sep.1685. [RPCS#11.166]

SCOTT, EUPHEMIA, daughter of <u>George</u> Scott of Pitlochie, from Leith to East NJ on the <u>Henry and Francis</u> on 5 Sep. 1685, married John Johnston. [Insh#178][NWI.I.423]

SCOTT, GEORGE, of Pitlochie, Fife, from Leith to East NJ on the <u>Henry and Francis</u> on 5 Sep. 1685, died at sea, cnf 1692 Edinburgh. [NAS.CC8.8.79]; pro 26 Feb.1692 Middlesex, NJ.

SCOTT, JAMES, born in Ewis, Dumfries-shire, on 12 Feb. 1764, son of Reverend Richard Scott and Mary Turnbull, a merchant in NY from around 1780, died on 24 Dec. 1826, buried in Prospect Cemetery, Jamaica, Long Island, NY. [ANY#2.186][F#2.234]

SCOTT, JOHN, with 400 acres in St <u>George</u>'s Neck, Delaware, on 5 June 1676.[NY.Hist.MS.Dutch.XX/XXI, 111]

SCOTT, JOHN, son of Sir John Scott of Ancrum, in Duckesburg, Staten Island, NY, in 1701. [NAS.NRAS.0479.29]; a petitioner in NY 1701. [DNY.IV.934]

SCOTT, JOHN, Lieutenant of H.M. Independent Company at Albany, NY, Administrations 30 Mar. 1726 NY

SCOTT, ROBERT, quit rent in Delaware, 1 Oct.1669. [NY..MS.Dutch,XX/XXI, 28]

SCOTT, ROBERT, indented in Chester Court, PA, 14 Dec.1698. [Sgen.29.1.13]

SCOTT, ROBERT, born in Edinburgh 2 Oct. 1745, to VA, an engraver, settled in Philadelphia, died there on 3 Nov. 1823, buried in the Friends burial ground. [AP#312]

SCOTT, THOMAS, an indentured servant from Selkirk, from London to PA in Feb. 1721. [CLRO/AIA]

SCOTT, WILLIAM, jr., born 1749, weaver from Paisley, with his wife Margaret, from Greenock to NY on the <u>Commerce</u> in Feb. 1774. [PRO.T47.12]

SCOTT, WILLIAM, sr., born 1734, weaver from Paisley, with his son John, from Greenock to NY on the <u>Commerce</u>, in Feb. 1774. [PRO.T47.12]

SCOULLAR, JOHN, indentured servant, to East NJ, 1685. [NJSA.EJD.A225]

SCRIMGEOUR, JAMES, indentured servant, to East NJ 1685. [NJSA.EJD.A225]

SCRIMGEOUR, JAMES, born 1745, mariner from Greenock, via Greenock to NY on the <u>George</u> in May 1774.[PRO.T47.12]

SEATON, JAMES, indentured servant, to East NJ 1684. [NJSA.EJD.A]

SELKIRK, JAMES, born in 1752, a tailor from Gatehouse, Kirkcudbrightshire, from Stranraer to NY on the <u>Gale of Whitehaven</u> in May 1774. [PRO.T47.12]

SEMPLE, JOHN, a merchant in NY before 1776, a Loyalist who returned to Scotland in 1783. [PCCol#5.543]

SEMPILL, WILLIAM, a merchant from NY trading in Delaware 1676; was appointed as a Justice in Delaware in 1679. [NY.Hist.MS.Dutch.XX/XXI,102, 313]

SENZEOUR, CICELLA, indentured servant, to East NJ 1685. [NJSA.EJD.A225]

SENZEOUR, JOHN, indentured servant, to East NJ 1685.
    [NJSA.EJD.A225]

SETON, DAVID, drummer on HMS Preston, pro 14 Apr. 1778 NY

SETON, JOHN, born 1733, enlisted in the PA Regiment on 23 May
    1759.[Pa.Archives#5/1/299]

SETON, MARGARET, born 1753, servant from Aberdeen, via Leith to
    Philadelphia on the Friendship, in May 1775. [PRO.T47.12]

SHANTERS, MARGARET, married James Rorison in Castle Douglas,
    Kirkcudbrightshire, on 23 Dec. 1756, settled in PA before
    1776.[CF#6.451]

SHARP, GEORGE, indentured servant, to East NJ 1684. [NJSA.EJD.E330]

SHARP, Mr JOHN, who had been educated at King's College, Aberdeen, to
    Virginia during 1699, a chaplain to HM garrison in NY 1702-1714,
    graduated Doctor of Theology from King's College, Aberdeen, in Jan.
    1714. [FA#442][EMA#54][KCA#99]

SHAW, ALEXANDER, born in 1755, a servant from Daimie, via
    Stornaway to Philadelphia on the Clementina in July 1775.
    [PRO.T47.12]

SHAW, CATHERINE, from Islay, Argyll, in June 1739 aboard the
    Happy Return, bound for NY and Wood Creek on the Hudson River,
    by 1763 she was married and living with her child in NY and was
    granted 150 acres on the Argyle Patent, NY. [HSBC]
    [NY.Col.MS#72/170]

SHAW, DAVID, dead by 1763 when his widow then living in Tappan was
    granted 150 acres on the Argyle Patent, NY. [NY.Col.MS#72/170]

SHAW, DAVID, son of Reverend Lachlan Shaw and Helen Stuart in Elgin,
    Morayshire, to NY on the Lovely Jane in 1759, a merchant
    in NY, married Polly Dey on 24 Nov. 1761, father of Lachlan,
    William, Janet and Maria, died in NY on 1 Oct. 1767, buried in
    Hackensack graveyard. [ANY#1.84]

SHAW, DONALD, with his wife Merrin McInish, from Islay, Argyll,
    aboard the Happy Return to NY in July 1738 to have settled at Wood
    Creek on the Hudson River, by 1763 he was dead but his son and
    daughter were allocated 200 acres on the Argyle Patent,
    NY.[HSPC][NY.Col.MS#72/170]

SHAW, GUSTAVUS, from Islay, Argyll, in June 1739 aboard the
    Happy Return bound for NY and Wood Creek on the Hudson River,
    by 1763 he was dead and his nephew Neil Shaw, a ropemaker in NY,
    claimed the right to a grant on the Argyle Patent, NY, on behalf of
    the heirs. [HSBC][NY.Col.MS#72/171]

SHAW, JANE, indentured servant, to East NJ 1684. [NJSA.EJD.A]

SHAW, JOHN, and his wife Mary McNeil, with sons Neil and Duncan,
    from Islay, Argyll, aboard the Happy Return in June 1739 bound for
    NY and Wood Creek on the Hudson River, dead by 1763 when Neil
    and two other children were granted 200 acres on Argyle Patent,
    NY.[HSBC][NY.Col.MS#72/170]

SHAW, JOHN, with his wife Merran or Sarah Brown, with their children
    Donald, Mary from Islay, Argyll, aboard the Happy Return in Nov.
    1740 bound for NY and Wood Creek on the Hudson River, daughter

Margaret born on the voyage, in 1763 his widow and two sons, Daniel and Neil, and two daughters, Mary and Christian Brown, were granted 250 acres on the Argyle Patent, NY, petitioned Governor William Tryon on 12 Aug. 1771.
[HSBC][NY.Col.MS#72/170; 97/73]

SHAW, JOHN, born in 1751, a smith from Galloway, from Stranraer to NY on the Gale of Whitehaven in May 1774. [PRO.T47.12]

SHAW, JOHN, born in 1761, from Fordardich, via Stornaway to Philadelphia on the Clementina in July 1775. [PRO.T47.12]

SHAW, NEIL, from Islay, Argyll, on the Happy Return in June 1739 bound for NY and Wood Creek on the Hudson River. [HSBC]

SHAW, NEIL, with Florence McLachlin his wife, from Islay, Argyll, aboard the Happy Return in June 1739 bound for NY and Wood Creek on the Hudson River. [HSBC]

SHAW, THOMAS, married Ann, widow of Thomas Hancock, in the Dutch Reformed Church in NY on 20 Apr. 1692. [DRC.Reg.]

SHEARER, THOMAS, indentured servant, to East NJ 1685. [NJSA.EJD.A225]

SHEDDAN, JAMES, 5'5", a laborer, 'strong, well made', enlisted in the PA Regiment in York, PA, on 9 May 1758. [Pa.Arch#5/1/133]

SHEDDEN, WILLIAM RALSTON, of Roughwood, born on 23 Apr. 1747 in Beith, Ayrshire, son of John Shedden and Jean Ralston, to America in 1770, a merchant in VA, Bermuda, and NY, father of Jane, died there on 13 Nov. 1798.
[AJ#2661][NAS.GD1.67/1][HAF#1.275][NAS.S/H]
[NAS.CS17.1.7,265] [Probate July 1852 PCC]

SHILESTON, THOMAS, a Covenanter from Hillend, Dunspurn, was transported from Leith to East NJ on the Henry and Francis on 5 Sep. 1685. [RPCS#11.155]

SHIRAR, JOSEPH, born in 1744, a weaver from Paisley, with Janet his wife and their son Archibald, from Greenock to NY on the Commerce in Feb. 1774. [PRO.T47.12]

SHIRMLAW, WILLIAM, born in 1761, from Glasgow, from Leith to Philadelphia on the Friendship in May 1775. [PRO.T47.12]

SHIRREFF, CHARLES, a former Lieutenant of the 45th Regiment who was granted land in NY in 1773. [PCCol#5.597]

SIBBALD, JOHN, a merchant in Philadelphia around 1772, son of David Sibbald, a skipper in Kirkcaldy, Fife, and his wife Janet Hoggan. [NAS.B41.7.8/187]

SILVER, ARCHIBALD, married Christian Cheyne in Matocopine, West Jersey, 16.... [NJSA.EJD.A226/D]

SIMM, HUGH, born 1737, from Paisley, via Glasgow to Philadelphia on the Peggy, arrived there on 7 Aug. 1768, librarian at the College of NJ and later a schoolteacher in Freehold, NJ, at Flatten Barrack Street, NY, and in Albany, a Loyalist and Quartermaster of the Loyal American Regiment during the Revolution, returned to Paisley, died in 1810. [Hugh Simm pp, Princeton University]
[PRO.AO12.100.189]

SIM, JOHN, born in 1758, a weaver from Paisley, via Greenock to NY on the Commerce in Feb. 1774. [PRO.T47.12]

SIM, P., in NY around 1765. [EUL:Laing MS/II/82]

SIMPSON, ADAM, indentured servant, to East NJ 1685. [NJSA.EJD.A225]

SIMPSON, ARTHUR, indentured servant, to East NJ 1684.
  [NJSA.EJD.A266]

SIMPSON, DAVID, minister educated at the University of St Andrews in
  1650, husband of Jean Thomson and father of David, a Covenanter
  transported from Leith to East NJ on the Henry and Francis on 5 Sep.
  1685, died in NJ before Aug. 1697. [F#4.66]

SIMSON, DUGALD, a minister educated at Glasgow University in 1682,
  to America in 1685, settled in Brookhaven, married Jean Hutchison,
  died in Scotland 1704. [F#7.665][NJSA.EJD.A225]

SIMPSON, JAMES, indentured servant, to East NJ 1684. [NJSA.EJD.A]

SIMPSON, JEAN, born in 1755, a servant from Dunbar, East Lothian,
  from Leith to Philadelphia on the Friendship in May 1775.
  [PRO.T47.12]

SIMPSON, JOHN, in NY, died during Nov. 1784, cnf 26 May 1785
  Edinburgh. [NAS.CC8.8.126]

SIMPSON, MAGNUS, indented in Chester Co., PA, 3 Oct.1693.
  [Sgen.29.1.11]

SIMPSON, MARGARET, indentured servant, to East NJ 1684.
  [NJSA.EJD.A196]

SIMPSON, MARGARET, born 1752, a servant from Dunfermline, Fife,
  from Leith to Philadelphia on the Friendship, in May 1775.
  [PRO.T47.12]

SIMPSON, MARGARET, born in 1757, a spinner from Crawforddykes,
  via Greenock to Philadelphia on the Sally in Oct. 1774.
  [PRO.T47.12]

SIMPSON, PATRICK, indentured servant, to East NJ 1685.
  [NJSA.EJD.A225]

SIMPSON, WILLIAM, born in 1744, a laborer from Lochwinnoch, ,
  from Greenock to NY on the Lilly in Apr. 1775. [PRO.T47.12]

SINCLAIR, ALEXANDER, born in 1748, a laborer who deserted from the
  1st Battalion of the Royal American Regiment in 1772.
  [NY.Gaz.&Wkly.Merc., 12.10.1772]

SINCLAIR, CHARLES, former Ensign of the 78th [Fraser's Highlanders] a
  land grant in NY during 1773. [PCCol#5.597]

SINCLAIR, DUNCAN, born 1765, servant from Inverness, via
  Stornaway to Philadelphia on the Clementina in July 1775.
  [PRO.T47.12]

SINCLAIR, JOHN, former soldier, then a publican in NY, Loyalist in 1776.
  [PRO.AO12.101.50]

SINCLAIR, JOHN, born in 1730, a tailor from Inverness, via
  Stornaway to Philadelphia on the Clementina in July 1775.
  [PRO.T47.12]

SINCLAIR, JOHN, born in 1760, a servant from Inverness, from
  Stornaway to Philadelphia on the Clementina in July 1775.
  [PRO.T47.12]

SINCLAIR, ROBERT, born in Kirkwall, Orkney Islands, in 1660, a

mariner who settled in NY during 1680. [PRO.HCA#81, Phillips
v.Mauritz, 1692]; married Maryken Duycking from NY, in the Dutch
Reformed Church in NY on 15 Aug. 1683. [DRC.Reg.]; took the
Oath of Association in NY on 26 May 1696. [PRO.C213.OR470]; in
NY 1699, [SPAWI.1699/628]; probate 8 Oct. 1704 NY. [Liber 7,
fo.196]

SINCLAIR, ROBERT, indented in Chester Co., PA, 5 August 1697.
[Sgen.29.1.13]

SINCLAIR, ROBERT, born in 1685, a minister who to America by 1709,
settled in Newcastle, Del. [SCHR#14.148][SPG#2.11]

SINCLAIR, ROBERT, a merchant in Albany, NY, grand-nephew of Joseph
and Thomas Rankin sons of Thomas Rankine a merchant in
Greenock, 1766.[NAS.RS81.8.135/136/227]

SINCLAIR, Captain ROBERT, a merchant in NY, husband of Janet
Stevens, before 1777. [NAS.CS16.1.171]

SINCLAIR, ROBERT, settled in NY before 1772. NAS.RD4.219.95]

SINCLAIR, WILLIAM, quit rent in Del., 1671.
[NY.Hist.MS.Dutch.XX/XXI,28]

SINCLAIR, WILLIAM, born 1686, indented in Chester Co., PA, 14 July
1697. [Sgen.29.1.12]

SKENE, DAVID, former soldier, land grant in NY 1765, Loyalist.
[PRO.AO13.83.420]

SKENE, JOHN, educated at Marischal College, Aberdeen, in 1663, later
Governor of East NJ. [KCA#2.229]

SKINNER, WILLIAM, born in 1687, a schoolmaster and minister, to
America in 1718, settled in Philadelphia and in NJ, died in Perth
Amboy, NJ, during 1758. [EMA#55][SCHR#14.145]

SITLINGTON, JAMES, a Covenanter from Dunspurn, from Leith to East
NJ on the Henry and Francis in 1685. [RPCS.11.155/291]

SLATER, GEORGE, born 1685, indented in Burlington Co., NJ, 21 July
1697. [Sgen,29,1,14][Burlington Court Book, p.198]

SLATER, JAMES, born in 1734, a chapman from Glasgow, from
Greenock to NY aboard the Commerce in Feb. 1774. [PRO.T47.12]

SLATER, JOHN, born 1685, indented in Chester Co., PA, 14 July 1697.
[Sgen.29.1.12]

SLOAN, JOHN, born in 1735, a weaver from Inch, Wigtownshire, with
Eliza McCubbin his wife and their children Grizel, Alexander, John
and Jean from Stranraer to NY on the Jackie of Glasgow in May
1775. [PRO.T47.12]

SMALL, ROBERT, born in 1759, a barber from Perth, from Leith to
Philadelphia on the Friendship in May 1775. [PRO.T47.12]

SMALL, THOMAS, a smith from Glasgow, via Greenock to NY
on the Christy in May 1775. [PRO.T47.12]

SMART, DAVID, a founder from Strathmiglo, Fife, settled in NY before
1775. [NAS.S/H]

SMEALL, Mrs FRANCES, daughter of William Smith and Mary Nimnah
in Linlithgow, West Lothian, settled in NY before 1783.
[NAS.RD5.33.98]

SMELLIE, THOMAS, born in 1757, a weaver from Paisley, via Greenock to NY on the <u>Commerce</u> in Feb. 1774. [PRO.T47.12]

SMITH, ALEXANDER, born in 1723, a laborer, enlisted in Captain John Shannon's Company of the PA Regiment on 19 July 1746. [PaArch#5/1/11]

SMITH, DUNCAN, from Islay, Argyll, aboard the <u>Happy Return</u> bound for NY in July 1738 to have settled at Wood Creek on the Hudson River. [HSPC]

SMITH, FRANCES, daughter of William Smith and Mary Nimnah in Linlithgow, West Lothian, married .... Smela, parents of Mary, to NY before 1783. [NAS.RD5.33.98]

SMITH, GILBERT, born in Argyll during 1730, enlisted in Captain John Haslet's Company of the PA Regiment on 9 May 1758. [Pa.Arch#5/1/149]

SMITH, ISOBEL, born in 1749, from Crawforddykes, via Greenock to NY on the <u>George</u> of Greenock in May 1774. [PRO.T47.12]

SMITH, JAMES, to East NJ in 1684. [NJSA.EJD.A266]

SMITH, JAMES, born in 1714, schoolmaster at Urquhart or Glen Moriston, Inverness-shire, from Mull, Argyll, to NY on the Moore of Greenock in July 1774. [AJ#1387]

SMITH, JANET, born in 1742, from Kirkcudbright, via Kirkcudbright to NY on the <u>Adventure</u> in May 1774. [PRO.T47.12]

SMITH, JEAN, born in 1754, a servant from Dunfermline, Fife, via Leith to Philadelphia on the <u>Friendship</u> in May 1775. [PRO.T47.12]

SMITH, JEAN, born in 1757, a spinner from Paisley, via Greenock to NY on the <u>Commerce</u> in Feb. 1774. [PRO.T47.12]

SMITH, JOHN, ' a Scotchman', in Raritan and Woodbridge, East NJ, in Dec. 1669. [NJA#21]

SMITH, JOHN, a Covenanter from Kirkintilloch, Dunbartonshire, who was transported from Leith to East NJ aboard the <u>Henry and Francis</u> on 5 Sep. 1685. [RPCS#11.167]

SMITH, JOHN, died in PA, pro.1689 PCC

SMITH, JOHN, born in 1735, a mariner, enlisted in the PA Regiment in Philadelphia on 2 May 1758. [Pa.Arch.#5/1/152]

SMITH, JOHN, soldier of the 42nd Regiment, married Hannah Murray, a widow, in NY on 27 Dec. 1758. [PCR]

SMITH, LEWIS, born in 1751, a silvesmith from Aberdeen, from Leith to Philadelphia on the <u>Friendship</u>, in May 1775. [PRO.T47.12]

SMITH, MARGARET, born in Irvine 1736, absconded from Gilbert Shearer on 5 July 1762. [NYGaz-Merc.5.7.1762]

SMITH, MARGARET, born in 1744, a servant from Galson, Isle of Lewis, via Stornaway to Philadelphia on the <u>Friendship</u>, in May 1774. [PRO.T47.12]

SMITH, MARY, indentured servant, to East NJ 1685. [NJSA.EJD.A236]

SMITH, MARY, born in 1750, from Edinburgh, from Greenock to NY on the <u>Lilly</u> in Apr. 1775.[PRO.T47.12]

SMITH, ROBERT, born on 14 Jan. 1722 in Lugton, Dalkeith, Midlothian, son of John Smith and Martha Lawrie, to America in 1748, a builder and architect in Philadelphia, died there on 7 Apr. 1777. ['Scotland and America in the Age of Enlightenment', pp275/6, R. Scher,

Edinburgh, 1990][AP#315]

SMITH, STOFIL,(?), 5'7", a blacksmith, enlisted in the PA Regiment on 4 May 1758 in Bucks County, PA. [Pa.Archives#5/1/358]

SMITH THOMAS, indentured servant, to East NJ 1684. [NJSA.EJD.A984]

SMITH, THOMAS, born in 1730, a laborer who absconded from the 44th Regiment of Foot in 1758. [NY Postboy, 24 Oct. 1758]

SMITH, THOMAS, born in Oct. 1745 in Aberdeenshire, arrived in Philadelphia on 10 Feb. 1769, settled in Bedford, PA, a judge and public official, died on 31 Mar. 1809, buried in Christ Church, Philadelphia. [AP#319]

SMITH, THOMAS, born in 1746, son of James Smith a blacksmith in Edingham, a minister of the Seceder Congregation in Huntington, PA, died on 24 Aug. 1825. [Colvend g/s, Kirkcudbrightshire]

SMITH, THOMAS, born in 1757, a weaver from Glasgow, from Greenock to NY on the Commerce in Feb. 1774. [PRO.T47.12]

SMITH, WILLIAM, born in Aberdeenshire on 7 Sep. 1727, educated at the University of Aberdeen around 1747, to America in 1751, first Provost of the University of PA, married Rebecca Moore, died on 14 May 1803 near the Falls of Schuylkill, and was buried in Philadelphia.[AP#323][EMA#56]

SMITH, WILLIAM, born in Dumfries during 1717, died in NY during 1768.[Matthew's American Armory& Blue Book, London, 1903]

SOUTAR, ANGUS, born in 1758, a spinner from Paisley, via Greenock to NY on the Commerce in Feb. 1774. [PRO.T47.12]

SOUTAR, CHARLES, born in 1743, a weaver from Paisley, via Greenock to NY on the Commerce in Feb. 1774. [PRO.T47.12]

SOUTAR, JAMES, born in 1739, a weaver from Paisley, via Greenock to NY on the Commerce in Feb. 1774. [PRO.T47.12]

SOUTAR, JAMES, born in 1759, a weaver from Paisley, via Greenock to NY on the Commerce in Feb. 1774. [PRO.T47.12]

SPENCE, GEORGE, son of George Spence a maltman in Dundee, settled at Albany Fort, North America, by 1741. [NAS.RS35.16.117]

SPENS, GEORGE, from Glasgow, in Philadelphia during 1778. [NAS.NRAS.0396/TD37.16]

SPENCE, JAMES, born in 1749, a cartwright from Paisley, via Greenock to NY on the Commerce in Feb. 1774. [PRO.47.12]; absconded from Abraham Schenk in New Rochelle Aug.1774. [NY Gaz-Merc.22.8.1774]

SPENS, JOCK, from Glasgow, in Philadelphia during 1778. [NAS.NRAS#0396/TD37.16]

SPENCE, JOHN, born in 1745, a weaver from Paisley, with Margaret his wife, from Greenock to NY on the Commerce in Feb. 1774. [PRO.T47.12]

SPENCE, MARGARET, daughter of James Spence in Queensferry, West Lothian, and widow of John Vernor of Dalvick, Admin. 11 Aug. 1689 NJ.[NJSA.EJD. Liber B, fo.475-522]

SPENCE, ROBERT, a merchant in NY, 1781. [NAS.CS16.1.184]

SPROAT, HUGH, born in 1747, a farmer from Kirkcudbright, from Kirkcudbright to NY on the Adventure May 1774. [PRO.T47.12]

SPROAT, ("Sprat"), JOHN, from Wigtown, married Maria de Peyster, widow of Paul Schrick, in the Dutch Reformed Church in NY on 26 Aug. 1687. [DRC.Reg.]

SPROAT, JOHN, born in 1751, a laborer from Milne of Borgue, Kirkcudbrightshire, from Kirkcudbright to NY on the Adventure of Liverpool May 1774. [PRO.T47.12]

SPROAT, THOMAS, born in 1738, a joiner from Kirkcudbright, via Kirkcudbright to NY on the Adventure in May 1774 [PRO.T47.12]

SPROUT, WILLIAM, a Covenanter from Clontarch, was transported from Leith to East NJ aboard the Henry and Francis on 5 Sep. 1685. [RPCS#10.612]

SQUIRE, GEORGE, born in 1745, a mason from Aberdeen, from Greenock to NY on the George in May 1774. [PRO.T47.12]

STARK, THOMAS, possibly from Paisley, settled in New Perth north of Albany, NY, in 1774. [Hugh Simm papers, Princeton Univ.]

STEDMAN, ALEXANDER, born in Kinross during 1703, Jacobite refugee in 1746, settled in Philadelphia, a lawyer and judge in PA, a Loyalist in 1776, died in Swansea, Wales, in 1794. [AP#332][PRO.AO12.100.313]

STEDMAN, CHARLES, born in Kinross during 1713, Jacobite refugee in 1746, settled in Philadelphia, a Loyalist in 1776, died in London. [AP#333][PRO.AO12.42.266]

STEDMAN, CHRISTIAN, widow of Hugh Steel, a shipmaster from Bo'ness, West Lothian, after in Philadelphia, 1763. [NAS.CS16.1.115]

STEEL, ALEXANDER, born in 1748, a laborer from Glasgow, from Greenock to NY on the Lilly in May 1775. [PRO.T47.12]

STEEL, HUGH, from Bo'ness, West Lothian, a shipmaster in Philadelphia who died in 1757, cnf 13 Feb. 1759 Edinburgh. [NAS.CC8.8.118][NAS.S/H]

STEEL, MARY, indentured servant, to East NJ 1684. [NJSA.EJD.A]

STEEL, PETER, absconded from David Thompson a shipbuilder in Philadelphia on 31 Aug.1766. [NYGaz-Merc.25.8.1766]

STEEL, MARY, born in 1757, a spinner from Paisley, via Greenock to NY on the Commerce in Feb. 1774. [PRO.T47.12]

STEEL, ROSS, born in 1754, a servant from Heriot, Midlothian, from Leith to Philadelphia on the Friendship in May 1775. [PRO.T47.12]

STEEL, WILLIAM, born in 1744, a laborer from Glasgow, from Greenock to NY on the Matty in May 1774. [PRO.T47.12]

STEENSON, ANN, born in 1756, a servant from Dysart, Fife, from Leith to NY on the Friendship in May 1775. [PRO.T47.12]

STELLER, of Scotter, JOHN, indented in Chester Court. PA, 14 July 1697. [Sgen.29.1.13]

STEUART, JOHN, a minister, to NY in 1770. [EMA#57]

STEVENS, AGNES, from Leith to East NJ on the Henry and Francis in 1685. [NWI.I.423]

STEVENS, DAVID, born 1756, servant from Inverness, via Stornaway to Philadelphia on the Clementina in July 1775. [PRO.T47.12]

STEVENS, ..., possibly from Paisley, , settled in New Perth north of

Albany, NY, in 1774. [Hugh Simms papers, Princeton University]

STEVENSON, HAY, born in the Borders, later a merchant in NY from 1783, married Jessie Graham on 29 July 1790, father of John Graham Stevenson, died on 24 Sep. 1799. [ANY#2.189]

STEVENSON, JANET, born in 1755, a servant from Aberdeen, from Leith to Philadelphia on the <u>Friendship</u> in May 1775. [PRO.T47.12]

STEVENSON, ROBERT, a shipmaster in NY, son of William Stevenson a wright in Irvine, Ayrshire, 1774. [NAS.CS16.1.75]

STEWART, AGNES, indentured servant, to East NJ 1684. [NJSA.EJD.A255]

STEWART, ALEXANDER, to East NJ 1684. [NJSA.EJD.A187]

STEWART, ALEXANDER, to Philadelphia in 1697, indented for service in Chester Co. 5 Aug.1697. [Sgen#29/1.11]

STEWART, ALEXANDER, a minister, to NY in 1703. [EMA#57]

STEWART, ARCHIBALD, surgeon, via London to NY 1699. [DP#175][NAS.GD406]

STEWART, CATHERINE, born in 1756, a spinner from Paisley, via Greenock to NY on the <u>Commerce</u> in Feb. 1774. [PRO.T47.12]

STEWART, DAVID, Woodbridge, Middlesex County, NJ, probate 9 June 1733 NJ. [NJSA.EJD.B/419]

STEWART, ISABEL, indentured servant, to East NJ 1684. [NJSA.EJD.A255]

STEWART, JAMES, a Covenanter who was transported from Leith to East NJ on the <u>Henry and Francis</u> in 1685. [RPCS#11.329]

STEWART, JAMES, from Islay, Argyll, aboard the <u>Happy Return</u> bound for NY in July 1738 to have settled at Wood Creek on the Hudson River.[HSPC]

STEWART, JAMES, a minister, to PA in 1760. [UPC#655]

STEWART, JAMES, born in 1743, a farmer from Strathspey, with Mary,George, Henry, and Gilbert, his children, from Greenock to NY on the <u>George</u> of Greenock in May 1774. [PRO.T47.12]

STEWART, JAMES, born in 1752, a farmer from Strathspey, from Greenock to NY on the <u>George</u> in May 1774. [PRO.T47.12]

STEWART, JAMES, born in 1752, a clerk or book-keeper from Edinburgh, via London to Philadelphia on the <u>Two Friends</u> in Oct. 1774.[PRO.T47.9/11]

STEWART, JAMES, born in 1754, a farmer from Blair Atholl, Perthshire, from Greenock to NY on the <u>Monimia</u> in May 1775. [PRO.T47.12]

STEWART, JEAN, born in 1753, from Greenock to NY on the <u>Lilly</u> in Apr. 1775. [PRO.T47.12]

STEWART, JOHN, indentured servant, to East NJ 1684. [NJSA.EJD.A187]

STEWART, JOHN, born in 1739, a farmer from Strathspey, from Greenock to NY on the <u>George</u> in May 1774. [PRO.T47.12]

STEWART, JOHN, born on 23 Dec. 1743 son of Angus Stewart and Christine McFearson in Dundee, a wright from Dundee, via Greenock to Philadelphia on the <u>Magdalene</u> in Aug. 1774. [PRO.T47.12]

STEWART, JOHN eldest son of Alexander Stewart, tenant in Foss,

Perthshire, settled Albany, NY, by 1786. [NAS.RD2.241/2.776]

STEWART, ROBERT, a petitioner in NY 1701.[DNY.IV.934]

STEWART, ROBERT, possibly from Paisley, settled in Brunswick, NJ, by 1768. [Hugh Simm papers, Princeton University]

STEWART, Mrs ..., born in 1736, from Glasgow, from Greenock to NY on the <u>Lilly</u> in May 1775. [PRO.T47.12]

STEWART, ROBERT, born in 1756, a smith from Glasgow, from Greenock to Philadelphia on the <u>Sally</u> in Oct. 1774. [PRO.T47.12]

STEWART, ROBERT, born in 1757, a laborer from Paisley, from Greenock to NY on the <u>Commerce</u> in Feb. 1774. [PRO.T47.12]

STEWART, WILLIAM, born in 1752, a wright from Galloway, from Stranraer to NY on the <u>Gale of Whitehaven</u> in May 1774. [PRO.T47.12] possibly settled Cambridge, Albany Co., NY, Loyalist in 1776. [PRO.AO12.26.334]

STIRLING, WILLIAM, born in 1746, a weaver from Glasgow, with John and Mary his children, from Greenock to NY on the <u>Matty</u> in May 1774.[PRO.T47.12]

STOBO, ..., a former Captain of the 15th Regiment, who settled at Seignory Aux Loutres,Lake Champlain, and at Otter Creek, before 1775. [PCCol#5.147]

STOCKTON, RICHARD, a counsellor at law in NJ who was admitted as a Burgess of Edinburgh on 4 Mar. 1767. [EBR]

STODDART, LAWRENCE, born in 1750, a laborer from Greenock, via Greenock to Philadelphia on the <u>Magdalene</u> in Aug. 1774. [PRO.T47.12]

STRACHAN, ALEXANDER, agent for four Independent Companies in NY on 11 Sep. 1712. [CTP.vol.CLI]

STRACHAN, JOHN, born in 1758, a weaver from Paisley, , from Greenock to NY on the <u>Commerce</u> in Feb. 1774. [PRO.T47.12]

STRANG, CHRISTOPHER, a Covenanter from Kilbride, was transported from Leith to East NJ on the <u>Henry and Francis</u> on 5 Sep. 1685. [RPCS#11.154]

STRATTON, EFFIE, indentured servant, to East NJ 1684. [NJSA.EJD.A196]

STUART, JAMES, former soldier, settled in NY, Loyalist in 1776. [PRO.AO12.30.294]

STUART, JOHN, soldier of the Albany Garrison, killed there by Indians 1671. [CMA#13/333]

STUART, JOHN, in Albany, NY, July 1676. [CMA#92]

STUART, JOHN, born in 1747, a laborer from Leswalt, Wigtown, with Jean McWhinnie and their children Mary and Margaret, from Stranraer to NY on the <u>Jackie</u> on 31 May 1775. [PRO.T.47.12]

STUART, MARGARET, indentured servant, to East NJ 1684. [NJSA.EJD.A195]

STUART, WILLIAM, a minister, to PA in 1747. [EMA#57]

STURRAS, MARGARET, indentured servant, to East NJ in 1684. [NJSA.EJD.A187]

SUMMERS, BARTHOLEMEW, born 1749, a butcher from Elgin, via Greenock to NY on the <u>George</u> in May 1774. [PRO.T47.12]

SUMMERS, JANET, born in 1743, from Glasgow, from Greenock to NY on the Lilly, in May 1775. [PRO.T47.12]

SUMMERS, MARGARET, born 1748, from Paisley, via Greenock to NY on the Lilly, in May 1775.   [PRO.T47.12]

SUMMERS, ROBERT, born in 1747, a joiner from Elgin, via Greenock to NY on the George in May 1774. [PRO.T47.12]

SUSTER, MARGARET, born in 1756, a spinner from Paisley, via Greenock to NY on the Commerce Feb. 1774. [PRO.T47.12]

SUTHERLAND, CATHERINE, born in 1736, a servant from Stornaway, Isle of Lewis, from Stornaway to NY on the Peace and Plenty in Nov. 1774.[PRO.T47.12]

SUTHERLAND, ELISBIE, wife of .... Gillies, and her children James, Alexander, Duncan, Margaret and Elizabeth Gillies, from Islay, Argyll, aboard the Happy Return to NewYork in July 1738 to have settled at Wood Creek on the Hudson River, in 1763 she and four surviving children were granted 400 acres on the Argyle Patent, NY. [HSPC][NY.Col.MS#72/170]

SUTHERLAND, GEORGE, born in 1746, a farmer from Neilston, via Greenock to Philadelphia on the Sally in Oct. 1774. [PRO.T47.12]

SUTHERLAND, JOHN, born 1753, servant from Duffus, Moray, via Stornaway to Philadelphia on the Clementina in July 1775. [PRO.T47.12]

SUTHERLAND, KATHERINE, born in 1747, a servant from Stornaway, Isle of Lewis, from Stornaway to Philadelphia on the Friendship in May 1774.[PRO.T47.12]

SUTHERLAND, WILLIAM, a sergeant of the 77th Regiment of Foot from 1756 to 1764, discharged in NY, received a land grant near Fort Ticonderoga, Crown Point, Charlotte County, NY, a Loyalist in 1776.[PRO.AO13.15.487/491]

SUTTON, ANDREW, born 1753, a gentleman, via London to NY on the Earl Dunmore in Feb. 1774. [PRO.T47.9/11]

SWAN, JOHN, Covenanter, from Leith to East NJ in 1685.[RPCS#11.329]

SWAN, ROBERT, born in 1753 a laborer from Kilmalcolm, via Greenock to Philadelphia on the Sally in Oct. 1774. [PRO.T47.12]

SWINTON, JOHN, from Teviotdale, Roxburghshire, a Quaker, was transported from Leith to East NJ on the Henry and Francis on 5 Sep. 1685. [RPCS#11.154]

SYMINGTON, JANET, from Leith to East NJ on the Henry and Francis in 1685. [NWI.I.423]

TAGGART, JOHN, a Covenanter from Roaderheuk, Annandale, Dumfries-shire, was transported from Leith to East NJ aboard the Henry and Francis on 5 Sep. 1685. [RPCS#11.155]

TAIT, MAGNUS indentured servant, to East NJ 1685. [NJSA.EJD.A225]

TANNIS, AGNES, a Covenanter, transported from Leith to East NJ aboard the Henry and Francis on 5 Sep. 1685. [RPCS#11.154]

TANYHILL, JOHN, born in 1755, a farmer from Glasgow, from Greenock to NY on the Commerce in Feb. 1774. [PRO.T47.12]

TANYHILL, ROBERT, born in 1749, a farmer from Glasgow, from

Greenock to NY on the Commerce Feb. 1774. [PRO.T47.12]

TAYLOR, ANNE, born in 1756, a servant from Findhorn, Morayshire, via Stornaway to Philadelphia on the Clementina, in July 1775. [PRO.T47.12]

TAYLOR, DANIEL, born in 1721, 'lately from the Highlands of Scotland', an indentured servant who absconded from John O'Brian, Eastchester,Westchester County, NY, on 1739. [NY.Gaz., 29.10.1739]

TAYLOR, DUNCAN, with his wife Mary, and their daughter Mary, from Islay, Argyll, aboard the Happy Return bound for NY in July 1738 to have settled at Wood Creek on the Hudson River, in 1763 he, his wife and eight children were granted 500 acres on the Argyle Patent, NY.[HSPC][NY.Col.MS#72/170]

TAYLOR, EDWARD, indentured servant, to East NJ before 1692. [NJSA.EJD.D]

TAYLOR, JOHN, born in 1749, a bricklayer from Argyll, from Greenock to Philadelphia on the Magdalene in Aug. 1774. [PRO.T47.12]

TAYLOR, THOMAS, born 1686, indented in Chester Court, PA, 14 July 1697. [Sgen.29.1.12]

TELFAIR, Reverend DAVID, a Burgher minister in Doune, to Philadelphia in 1766, died there in Apr. 1789. [GM#XII.603.230]

TENNANT, WILLIAM, indentured servant, to East NJ 1684. [NJSA.EJD.A266]

TENNANT, WILLIAM, born in 1736, a cabinetmaker, enlisted in the PA Regiment in Philadelphia on 29 Apr. 1758. [Pa.Arch#5/1/153]

TELLER, WILLIAM, sr, a merchant in NY, pro. 23 May 1701 NY

TEMPLETON, WILLIAM, born in 1747, a weaver from Paisley, with Margaret his wife, from Greenock to NY on the Commerce in Feb. 1774. [PRO.T47.12]

THANE, DANIEL, born in 1721 son of Robert Thain and Jean Robertson in St Nicholas parish, Aberdeen, educated at Aberdeen and at Princeton by 1748, a minister in Virginia, NY and in Delaware, settled at Connecticut Farm, NJ, died in 1764. [AP#338][F#7.666]

THOMAS, ROBERT, born in 1748, a tailor from Paisley, via Greenock to NY on the Lilly in Apr. 1775. [PRO.T47.12]

THOMSON, Dr ADAM, a physician educated at Edinburgh University, to PA by 1744, settled in Upper Marlborough, Prince George's County, Maryland, then in NY, died there 18 Sep. 1767. [AP#339][NY.Merc.9.1767][SA#183][NAS.CS16.1.75/148]

THOMSON, ALEXANDER, indentured servant, to East NJ 1685. [NJSA.EJD.A225]

THOMSON, ALEXANDER, born during 1722, a farmer in Corkerhill, Paisley, with his family to America in 1771, settled on Conecocheague Creek, Chambersburg, PA, died on 26 Feb. 1800, buried at Rocky Spring, Chambersburg. [PMHB#8/313]

THOMSON, ALEXANDER, born in 1727, a farmer from Breadalbane, Perthshire, with his wife Janet Forrest and children William, Katherine, Betty and Henry, from Greenock to NY on the Commerce in June 1775.[PRO.T47.12]

THOMSON, ALEXANDER, born in 1745, a wright from Stirling, from
Greenock to NY on the Monimia in May 1775. [PRO.T47.12]

THOMSON, ALEXANDER, born in 1752, a wright from Stirling, from
Greenock to NY on the Lilly in Apr. 1775. [PRO.T47.12]

THOMSON, ALLEN, from Islay, Argyll, aboard the Happy Return bound
for NY in July 1738 to have settled at Wood Creek on the Hudson
River.[HSPC]

THOMSON, ANDREW, took the Oath of Association in NY on 26 May
1696. [PRO.C213.OR470]

THOMSON, ANDREW, a merchant in Edinburgh then in NY, 1769.
[NAS.CS16.1.134]

THOMSON, ANNE, from Perthshire, a servant guilty of infanticide,
transported from Greenock to NJ in Nov. 1764.
[NAS.B59.26.11.639]

THOMSON, BARBARA, indented in Chester Court, PA, 14 Dec.1698.
[Sgen.29.1.13]

THOMSON, DANIEL, born in 1761, from Forfar, Angus, from Leith to
Philadelphia on the Friendship in May 1775. [PRO.T47.12]

THOMSON, DUGALD, with his wife Margaret McDuffie, and their
children Archibald, Duncan, and Christie, also his brother's daughter,
from Islay, Argyll, in June 1739 aboard the Happy Return bound for
NY and Wood Creek on the Hudson River, granted 300 acres on the
Argyle Patent, NY, in 1763. [HSBC][NY.Col.MS#72/170]

THOMPSON, ELISBIE, of Dunardie, from Islay, Argyll, aboard the
Happy Return bound for NY in July 1738 to have settled at Wood
Creek on the Hudson River.[HSPC]

THOMSON, GEORGE, born in 1734, a farmer from Breadalbane,
Perthshire, with his wife Janet Wilson and son Peter, from Greenock
to NY on the Commerce in June 1775. [PRO.T47.12]

THOMSON, ISABEL, born in 1735, from Burghead, Morayshire, with
John, Isobel, William and George her children, via Stornaway to
Philadelphia on the Clementina in July 1775. [PRO.T47.12]

THOMSON, JANET, indentured servant, to East NJ 1685.
[NJSA.EJD.A225]

THOMSON, JOHN, a tenant farmer in Yester Mains, East Lothian, settled
in NY by 1772. [NAS.CS16.1.148]

THOMSON, JOHN, born in 1742, from Burghead, Morayshire, from
Stornaway to Philadelphia on the Clementina in July 1775.
[PRO.T47.12]

THOMSON, JOHN, a merchant in NY, 1782. [NAS.CS17.1.1]

THOMSON, MARGERY, indentured servant, to East NJ 1685.
[NJSA.EJD.A225]

THOMSON, MARY, from Islay, Argyll, in June 1739 aboard the Happy
Return bound for NY and Wood Creek on the Hudson River, by
1763 she had settled in PA and her cousin Duncan Reid of NY.
[HSBC]; claimed her proportion of grant on the Argyle Patent, NY,
with the intention of settling. [NY.Col.MS#72/171]

THOMSON, PATRICK, a merchant in Edinburgh then in NY, 1768.
[NAS.CS16.1.133/134]

THOMSON, ROGER, from Islay, Argyll, aboard the Happy Return in
Nov. 1740 bound for NY and Wood Creek on the Hudson River, he
died in the Provincial Service by 1763 his widow and children were
living in Amboy, NJ. [HSBC][NY.Col.MS#72/170]

THOMSON, WILLIAM, a Covenanter who was transported from Leith to
East NJ in 1685. [RPCS#11.131][NJSA.EJD.A225]

THOMPSON, Mr...., was drowned in the North River, NY City, in June
1765.[NY Weekly Postboy, 6.6.1765]

THORBURN, JOHN, born 1756 in Penicuik, Midlothian, carpenter in
Morristown, NJ, 1775, Loyalist. [PRO.AO12.17.119]

THORNTON, JAMES, born in 1765, from Paisley, via Greenock to NY on
the Commerce in Feb. 1774. [PRO.T47.12]

TODD, GEORGE, merchant in Philadelphia 1782. [NAS.CS17.1.1/318]

TOD, WILLIAM, a coachbuilder from Edinburgh, and his children
Alexander and Helen, settled in Philadelphia before 1775.
[NAS.RD4.718.858][NAS.CS17.1.1/318]

TOLMIE, DONALD, born 1757, servant from Downie Castle, via
Stornaway to Philadelphia on the Clementina in July 1775.
[PRO.T47.12]

TOLMIE, NORMAND, born in Skye, Inverness-shire, a merchant skipper
and ship's chandler in NY from 1756 to 1776, a Loyalist soldier. died
in NY 1788. [ANY#1.70][PRO.AO12.22.389]

TORBURN, ANDREW, born in 1767, from Glen Luce, via Stranraer to NY
on the Gale in May 1774. [PRO.T47.12]

TORRY, GEORGE, from Islay, Argyll, aboard the Happy Return in June
1739 bound for NY and Wood Creek on the Hudson River, by 1763
he was dead but his child then living in NY was granted 150 acres on
the Argyle Patent, NY. [HSBC][NY.Col.MS#72/170]

TORRY, JAMES, with his wife Florence McKay, and their daughters Mary
and Catherine, from Islay, Argyll, aboard the Happy Return in June
1739 bound for NY and Wood Creek on the Hudson River, in 1763
his two sons and two daughters were granted 200 acres on the Argyle
Patent, NY. [HSBC][NY.Col.MS#72/170]

TORRY, JOHN, by 1763 he had married and was living in NY when he
was granted 200 acres on the Argyle Patent, NY.
[NY.Col.MS#72/170]

TOSH, WILLIAM, indentured servant, to East NJ 1685. [NJSA.EJD.A225]

TOSHACH, DAVID, of Monivaird, Perthshire, from Leith to East New
Jersey in 1684. [Insh#236][NJSA.EJD.A223/431; B1/4]

TRENT, JAMES, son of William Trent and Mary Burge in Inverness,
Captain of HMS Charles, died in PA, pro. April 1698 PCC

TRENT, MAURICE, son of William Trent and Mary Burge in Inverness, a
mariner in Philadelphia 1681, married Mary, daughter of James
Sandeland, died 1730.[NJSA.1.11.88][Sgen.29.1.11]

TRENT, WILLIAM, born in Inverness, to PA 1682, settled in NJ, settled in
Philadelphia, died 1714. [NJSA.11.88/89]

TROUP, ROBERT, settled in Morris County, NY, died on 28 Feb.
1769.[SM#31.111]

TURNBULL, GEORGE, born in Perthshire, an Ensign in General

Marjorybanks' Scots Regiment, discharged on 18 Apr. 1756, an officer of the 60thRegiment from 1756 to 1772, then Lieutenant Colonel of the NY Volunteers, settled in NY during 1788, died in NY, 13 Oct. 1810. [ANY#1.191] NAS.B59.38.6.263]

TURNBULL, JAMES, born in 1755, a laborer from Glasgow, from Greenock to Philadelphia on the Sally, Oct. 1774. [PRO.T47.12]

TURNBULL, WILLIAM, a Covenanter, transported from Leith to East NJ on the Henry and Francis 5 Sep. 1685. [RPCS#11.154]

TURPNEY, JOHN, a Covenanter who was transported from Leith to East NJ on the Henry and Francis, 5 Sep. 1685. [RPCS#11.154]

TYNNETT, WILLIAM, indentured servant, to East NJ 1684. [NJSA.EJD.B159]

URE, ANDREW, absconded from Robert Aitken, bookseller opposite London Coffee House, Front Street, Philadelphia, on October 30, 1774.[NYGaz-Merc.7.11.1774]

URIE, JOHN, a Covenanter, transported from Leith to East NJ on the Henry and Francis, 5 Sep. 1685. [RPCS#11.154]

URIE, PATRICK, a Covenanter who was transported from Leith to East NJ on the Henry and Francis, 5 Sep. 1685. [RPCS#11.154]

URQUHART, ANDREW, born in 1755, a servant from Duffus, Morayshire, from Stornaway to Philadelphia on the Clementina in July 1775. [PRO.T47.12]

URQUHART, ANN, born 1758, a servant from Ross-shire, via Leith to Philadelphia on the Friendship in May 1775. [PRO.T47.12]

URQUHART, WILLIAM, a minister who to America in 1702, settled on Long Island, NY, as rector of Jamaica parish, Queens County, died in 1709, probate 23 Sep. 1710 NY. [EMA#61] [SNQ#1.59][SPAWI#1712/1168][NY Wills liber 7, fo.181]

URQUHART, WILLIAM, to America in 1773, settled on the Kingsborough Patent, NY, a Loyalist and soldier of the Royal Regiment of NY from 1776 to 1783, later settled River aux Raison, Ontario. [DF.pp][PRO.AO12.31.95]

URQUHART, WILLIAM, a merchant in Tain, Ross-shire, then in NY, 1782. [NAS.CS17.1.1]

VERNOR, JOHN, and wife, from Leith to East NJ on the Henry and Francis in 1685. [NWI.I.423]

VIOLENT, DAVID, a lawyer from Edinburgh, from Leith to East NJ in 1684, settled in Amboy, NJ, by 1699. [Insh#242][NAS.RD3.91.605]; a petitioner in NY 1701. [DNY.IV.934]; a merchant in NY, probate 15 July 1710 NY.

WABER, ROBERT, indentured servant, to East NJ 1684. [NJSA.EJD.A196]

WAID, RICHARD, born in Philadelphia 20 July 1768, son of ....Waid and Susan Waid, died on 28 Oct. 1787. [Howff g/s, Dundee]

WAIT, HUGH, born in 1748, a farmer from Neilston from Greenock to NY or GA on the Christy in May 1775. [PRO.T47.12]

WALE, JAMES, mate of the St Peter of New York, died in Apr. 1692, cnf 18 June 1692 Edinburgh. [NAS.CC8.8.79]

WALKER, CATHERINE, from New Luce, Wigtownshire, via Stranraer to NY aboard the <u>Jackie</u> on 31 May 1775. [PRO.T47.12]

WALKER, DAVID, born 1757, a piper from Breadalbane, Perthshire, via Greenock to NY on the <u>Commerce</u> in June 1775. [PRO.T47.12]

WALKER, DONALD, born 1762, a tailor from Breadalbane, via Greenock to NY on the <u>Commerce</u> in June 1775. [PRO.T47.12]

WALKER, ELIZA, born in 1757, a servant from Breadalbane, Perthshire, from Greenock to NY on the <u>Commerce,</u> in June 1775. [PRO.T47.12]

WALKER, EMANUEL, only son of Alexander Walker of Craigbate a merchant in Port Glasgow, in NY during 1779. [NAS.CS16.1.174; CS17.1.1.409]

WALKER, ISABEL, indentured servant, to East NJ in 1684. [NJSA.EJD.A187]

WALKER, JAMES, born 1724, a blacksmith, from London to Philadelphia with his wife Ann, on the <u>Bellar</u> in Mar. 1774. [PRO.T47.9/11]

WALKER, JANET, indentured servant, to East NJ 1684. [NJSA.EJD.A195]

WALKER, JOHN, born in 1750, a shoemaker from Paisley via Greenock to NY on the <u>Lilly</u> in Apr.1775. [PRO.T47.12]

WALKER, JOHN, born in 1753, a weaver from Glasgow, from Greenock to NY on the <u>Matty</u> in May 1774. [PRO.T47.12]

WALKER, JOSEPH, born on 3 Mar. 1706 in Dunnottar, Kincardineshire, son of George Walker, an indentured servant who from London to PA in July 1728. [CLRO/AIA]

WALKER, JOSEPH, born in 1744, a blacksmith, with his wife Mary, via London to Philadelphia on the <u>Bellar</u> in Mar. 1774. [PRO.T47.9/11]

WALKER, PATRICK, a Covenanter who was transported from Leith to East NJ on the <u>Henry and Francis</u> on 5 Sep. 1685. [RPCS#11.155]

WALLACE, ALEXANDER, born in Perthshire during 1699, married Agnes Campbell [1702-1772], father of Jean [1731-1811], to America in 1734, settled in York County, PA, died in 1767. [Sgen#32.2.60]

WALLACE, ALEXANDER, in NY, 1781. [NAS.GD35.64]

WALLACE, HUGH, in NY 1781. [NAS.GD35.64]

WALLACE, JOHN, born on 7 Jan. 1718, son of Reverend John Wallace and Christine Murray in Drumelzier, Peebles, settled in Burlington, NJ. [F#1.269]

WALLACE, JOHN, born in 1749, a weaver from Paisley, via Greenock to NY on the <u>Commerce</u> in Feb. 1774. [PRO.T47.12]

WALLACE, THOMAS, a mariner in NY, probably from Aberdeenshire, probate 3 June 1777 NY.

WALLACE, WILLIAM, born in 1739, a weaver from Paisley,via Greenock to NY on the <u>Lilly</u> in Apr. 1775. [PRO.T47.12]

WALSTON, WILLIAM, in Bristol, PA, 1782. [NAS.CS17.1.1.114]

WARDEN, THOMAS, in NY 1699. [SPAWI.1699/738]

WARDROBE, JOHN, born in 1744, a tailor from Glasgow, via Greenock to NY on the <u>Commerce</u> in Feb. 1774. [PRO.T47.12]

WARRAND, JAMES, born in 1750, a farmer from Strathspey, from Greenock to NY on the <u>George</u> in May 1774. [PRO.T47.12]

WATSON, ALEXANDER, born in 1718, a laborer, enlisted in the PA

Regiment in Philadelphia on 7 May 1758. [Pa.Arch.#5/1/153]

WATSON, ALEXANDER, born in 1739, a farmer from Strathspey, via Greenock to NY on the George in May 1774. [PRO.T47.12]

WATSON, JAMES, born in 1744, a farmer from Stirling, viaGreenock to NY on the Matty in May 1775. [PRO.T47.12]

WATSON, JAMES, born in 1750, a servant from Duffus, Morayshire, from Stornaway to Philadelphia on the Clementina in July 1775. [PRO.T47.12]

WATSON, JOHN, born in 1753, a servant from Duffus, Morayshire, from Stornaway to Philadelphia on the Clementina, , in July 1775. [PRO.T47.12]

WATSON, JOHN, born in 1756, a servant from Bayble, Isle of Lewis, from Stornaway to Philadelphia on the Friendship, in May 1774. [PRO.T47.12]

WATSON, JOHN, born in Dalranick, Inverness-shire, during 1738, a laborer who deserted from the 55th Regiment of Foot in America during 1759.[NY. Merc., 12.3.1759]

WATSON, PETER, from Selkirk, from Leith to East NJ in 1683, settled in New Perth, father of Richard. [Insh#247]

WATSON, PETER, educated at Edinburgh and St Andrews Universities, a schoolmaster in NY 1764. [NYMerc.20.8.1764]

WATSON, SAMUEL, a petitioner in NY 1701.[DNY.IV.934]

WATT, JOHN, transported from Leith to East NJ aboard the Henry and Francis on 5 Sep. 1685. [RPCS.11.167]

WATT, ROBERT, son of John Watt of Rosehill, a merchant from Edinburgh, settled in NY before 1717. [REB#213]

WATTS, THOMAS, born 1753, a baker from Ballantrae, Ayrshire, from Greenock to Philadelphia on the Sally in Oct. 1774. [PRO.T47.12]

WAUGH, THOMAS, factor for James Henderson, late of Jedburgh, Roxburghshire, then resident in NY, surgeon to the Royal Artillery, 1778. [NAS.GD53.198]

WEBSTER, JOHN, indentured servant. to East NJ 1684. [NJSA.EJD.A]

WEBSTER, PHILIP, son of William Webster in Birse, Aberdeenshire, to NY in 1729, died by 1749. [APB#3.151]

WEBSTER ROBERT, indentured servant, to East NJ 1684. [NJSA.EJD.A184]

WELCH, MARGARET, indentured servant, to East NJ 1685. [NJSA.EJD.A226]

WELSH, WILLIAM, gentleman in Newcastle County, Delaware, pro 7 Mar. 1687 Newcastle County, Del.

WEMYSS, ALEXANDER, husband of Mary ..., settled in NY, died in 1782. [NAS.RD3.254.772]

WHITE, HUGH, a merchant from Glasgow then in Crown Point, 1778. [NAS.CS16.1.174]

WHITE, JAMES, a Covenanter from Douglas, Lanarkshire, was transported from Leith to NY in 1684. [RPCS#8.516]

WHITE, JOHN. a merchant in Philadelphia, 1768. [NAS.CS16.1.133]

[PRO.C213.OR470]; a petitioner in NY 1701. [DNY.IV.934]

WHITE, ROBERT, born in 1758, a weaver from Glasgow, via Greenock to NY on the <u>Commerce</u> in Feb. 1774. [PRO.T47.12]

WHITEBURN, JOHN, indentured servant, to East NJ 1684. [NJSA.EJD.A196]

WHITELAW, ELIZABETH, a Covenanter who was transported from Leith to East NJ aboard the <u>Henry and Francis</u> on 5 Sep. 1685. [RPCS#11.154]

WHITELAW, JAMES, born in 1749, a farmer from Glasgow, from Greenock to NY on the <u>Matty</u> in May 1774. [PRO.T47.12]

WHYTE, ELIZABETH, born 1754, servant from Arnot Mill, via Leith to Philadelphia on the <u>Friendship</u> in May 1775. [PRO.T47.12]

WHYTE, JOHN, transported from Leith to East NJ aboard the Henry and Francis on 5 Sep. 1685. [NAS.HH11#379]

WIDROW, JEAN, from Islay, Argyll, aboard the <u>Happy Return</u> in Nov. 1740 bound for NY and Wood Creek on the Hudson River, by 1763 she was married and living with her family of seven children in the Highlands of NY when she was granted 200 acres on the Argyle Patent, NY. [HSBC][NY.Col.MS#72/170]

WILKIE, JOHN, indentured servant, to East NJ 1685. [NJSA.EJD.A225]

WILLIAMSON, JOHN, born 1681, indented in Chester Co., PA, 14 July 1697. [Sgen.29.1.12]

WILLIAMSON, PETER, son of James Williamson in Kirnley, Aberdeenshire, in PA before 1759. [NAS.CS16.1.105]

WILLIAMSON, ROBERT, a petitioner in NY 1701. [DNY.IV.934]

WILLOX, GEORGE, a merchant in East NJ 1684, a witness in NY on 31 May 1687. [NJSA.EJD.A266][NAS.RD4.67.97]

WILSON, ALEXANDER, indentured servant, to East NJ 1685. [NJSA.EJD.A225]

WILSON, ALEXANDER, born in 1750, a mariner from Greenock, to NY on the <u>George</u> in May 1774. [PRO.T47.12]

WILSON, ALEXANDER, born in 1758, a weaver from Paisley, via Greenock to NY on the <u>Commerce</u> in Feb. 1774. [PRO.T47.12]

WILSON, ANDREW, born in 1750, a tailor from Aberdeen, from Greenock to NY on the <u>George</u> in May 1774. [PRO.T47.12]

WILSON, EBENEZER, a petitioner in NY 1701. [DNY.IV.934]

WILSON, GEORGE, born in 1755, a laborer from Paisley, via Greenock to NY on the <u>Commerce</u> in Feb. 1774.[PRO.T47.12]

WILSON, GEORGE, born in 1751, a farmer from Peebles, with his wife born in 1756, and daughter Mary born in 1781, to NY on the Draper of New York on 6 June 1801. [PRO.HO#102.18]

WILSON, HUGH, born 1685, indented in Chester Co., PA, 14 July 1697. [Sgen.29.1.12]

WILSON, JAMES, born in 1755, a laborer from Paisley via Greenock to NY on the <u>Commerce</u> in Feb. 1774.[PRO.T47.12]

WILSON, JAMES, born in Ceres, Fife, on 14 Sep. 1742, educated at the Universities of St Andrews, Glasgow and Edinburgh, to America in 1765, a teacher in NY and by 1766 in Philadelphia, admitted to the PA Bar in 1767, settled in Carlisle, PA, signatory to the Declaration

Independence, Associate Justice of the Supreme Court from 1789 to
1798, died in Edenton, NC, in 1798, buried in Christ Church,
Philadelphia. [AP#365]

WILSON, JOHN, born in 1742, a weaver from Paisley with his sons
William and James from Greenock to NY on the Commerce in Feb.
1774. [PRO.T47.12]

WILSON, JOSEPH, born in 1755, a fruiterer from Glasgow, from
Greenock to NY on the Commerce in Feb. 1774. [PRO.T47.12]

WILSON, MARGARET, a spinner from Sutherland, with three children,
from Greenock to Philadelphia on the Sally in Oct. 1774.
[PRO.T47.12]

WILSON, ROBERT, in Philadelphia, 1771. [NAS.CS16.1.146]

WILSON, THOMAS, born in Edinburgh around 1758, via Greenock to
America, naturalised in NY on 16 Nov. 1818. [Court of Common
Pleas Records]

WILSON, THOMAS, in PA, 1773. [NAS.CS16.1.154]

WILSON, WILLIAM, a Covenanter from Galloway, was transported from
Leith to East NJ aboard the Henry and Francis, on 5 Sep. 1685.
[RPCS#11.154]

WILSON, WILLIAM, born in 1744, a weaver from Paisley, from Greenock
to NY on the Commerce in Feb. 1774. [PRO.T47.12]

WISHART, ELIZABETH, daughter of George Wishart in Bo'ness, West
Lothian, wife of James Roy, to NY before 1777.
[NAS.S/H][NAS.RD4.773.618]

WITHERSPOON, Reverend JOHN, born in Yester, East Lothian, on 5
Feb. 1722 son of Reverend James Witherspoon, educated at
Edinburgh University in 1739, settled in Princeton, NJ, in Aug. 1768,
signatory to the Declaration of Independence, died 15 Nov.
1794.[AP#370][F#7.666][NAS.CS16.1.165/175]

WITHERSPOON, ROBERT, a minister educated at Glasgow University,
in 1713, settled in Appoquinimy, PA, died in May 1718. [F#7.666]

WOTHERSPOON, GRIZZELL, a Covenanter who was transported from
Leith to East NJ aboard the Henry and Francis on 5 Sep. 1685.
[RPCS#11.155]

WRIGHT, ANDREW, born in 1754, a laborer from Glasgow, from
Greenock to Philadelphia on the Sally in Oct.1774.[PRO.T47.12]

WRIGHT, GEORGE, in NY, 1783. [NAS.CS17.1.2]

WRIGHT, ROBERT, born in 1749, a tinker from Edinburgh, from
Greenock to Philadelphia on the Sally in Oct. 1774.[PRO.T47.12]

WRIGHT, WILLIAM, born in 1707, a postillion from Glasgow, as an
indentured servant from London to PA or Maryland in May
1725.[CLRO/AIA]

WRIGHT, WILLIAM, born in 1751, a tinker from Edinburgh, from
Greenock to Philadelphia on the Sally in Oct. 1774.[PRO.T47.12]

WYLLIE, THOMAS, born 1735, weaver from Dalry, from Greenock to
Philadelphia on the Magdalene in Aug. 1774. [PRO.T47.12]

YEAMAN, JAMES, born in 1759, a barber from Dundee, from Leith to
Philadelphia on the Friendship in May 1775. [PRO.T47.12]

YOUNG, ALEXANDER, soldier in the French and Indian Wars, settled

Skenesborough, Charlotte Co.NY, Loyalist in 1776.
[PRO.AO12.27.87]

YOUNG, ALEXANDER, born in 1749, a wright from Glasgow, from
Greenock to NY on the Matty in May 1774.[PRO.T47.12]

YOUNG, ANDREW, born in 1755, a tailor from Glasgow, from Greenock
to Philadelphia on the Sally in Oct. 1774.[PRO.T47.12]

YOUNG, ANDREW, born in 1735, a farmer from Stirling, with his wife
Mary, and their children James, Katherine, John and William, from
Greenock to NY on the Monimia in May 1775. [PRO.T47.12]

YOUNG, CHARLES, took the Oath of Association in NY on 26 May
1696.[PRO.C213.OR470]

YOUNG, Mrs ELIZABETH, born in 1751, wife of James Young, who
recently on arrival from Scotland set out from Philadelphia for
Tinicum township to reach her husband, sought in Nov. 1773.
[Pa.Chron:15.11.1773]

YOUNG, ELIZABETH, born in 1755, a servant from Edinburgh, from
Leith to Philadelphia on the Friendship in May 1775. [PRO.T47.12]

YOUNG, GEORGE, a Covenanter from Teviotdale, transported from Leith
to East NJ in 1685. [RPCS.8.114/130/136/329]

YOUNG, JAMES, born in 1751, a laborer from Glasgow, from Greenock
to NY on the Commerce, in Feb. 1774. [PRO.T47.12]

YOUNG, JOHN, born 1685, a servant indentured by James Trent in
Burlington, NJ, on 21 July 1697. [Sgen.29.1.11]

YOUNG, ROBERT, a Covenanter from Goodsburn, Avondale,
Lanarkshire, who was transported from Leith to East NJ aboard the
Henry and Francis on 5 Sep. 1685. [RPCS#11.154]

YOUNG, WILLIAM, a cooper in Paisley, later in Christianbridge,
Philadelphia, 1773. [NAS.CS16.1.154]

YUILL, ALEXANDER, born in 1747, a wright from Glasgow, from
Greenock to NY on the Commerce in Feb. 1774. [PRO.T47.12]